E

as a

Emily Dickinson as a Second Language

Demystifying the Poetry

GREG MATTINGLY

Foreword by Cindy Dickinson

McFarland & Company, Inc., Publishers
Jefferson, North Carolina

ISBN (print) 978-1-4766-6655-6 ∞
ISBN (ebook) 978-1-4766-3195-0

Library of Congress cataloguing data are available

British Library cataloguing data are available

Printed in the United States of America

McFarland & Company, Inc., Publishers
Box 611, Jefferson, North Carolina 28640
www.mcfarlandpub.com

To the pilgrims
who visit the Emily Dickinson Museum
in Amherst, Massachusetts,
every year in search of Emily

Acknowledgments

When I began this book, I worked first with Leslie Clark, a friend and local editor, who made several valuable contributions, including this advice: "If you're going to introduce something, introduce it!" I hope that I have complied. My fellow Emily Dickinson museum guide, Terry Allen, likewise offered valuable observations. I thought that I would not show the manuscript to so exacting a critic as my friend Margaret Freeman, fearing that it might not merit even a lukewarm assessment. She ran across a misplaced copy by chance, and her enthusiastic support gave a great boost to my confidence. My heartfelt thanks goes out to Cristanne Miller, who helped me navigate certain potentially fatal shoals of copyright issues. Some very fine photographs among the illustrations in this book are the work of two Dickinson museum stalwarts, Mike Medeiros and Jeff Morgan.

Table of Contents

Foreword by Cindy Dickinson

> "If I read a book and it makes my whole body so cold no fire can warm me I know that is poetry. If I feel physically as if the top of my head were taken off, I know that is poetry. These are the only way I know it. Is there any other way?"—Emily Dickinson (L342a)

To Emily Dickinson, poetry was visceral. Words were alive. She was on intimate terms with the sources of their vitality—their etymologies, their meanings, their sounds—and she mined those sources to create some of the most powerful poetry ever written.

Dickinson's poetry affects today's readers in similar ways. Her intriguing images, bold statements, and challenging puzzles can take the tops of our heads off—a pleasurable sensation for many readers, a bewildering one for others. Her compressed syntax, difficult diction, and obscure allusions beckon some readers but leave others baffled.

To all Dickinson readers, Greg Mattingly's book offers new ways of "knowing" her poetry. Mattingly has created a travel guide to the greatest obstacles we face in reading her verse: our distance from the English language as it was written and spoken in nineteenth-century New England, our unfamiliarity with much of Dickinson's vast reading, our struggles with the mechanics of her poems. In this guide, Mattingly leads us to a deeper understanding of and appreciation for Dickinson's poetry and genius.

Hold on to the top of your head.

> A word is dead
> When it is said,
> Some say.
> I say it just
> Begins to live
> That day.
> —J1212/F278/M702

Cindy Dickinson is the director of education at Hancock Shaker Village in western Massachusetts. For nineteen years she worked in education and public programming at the Emily Dickinson Museum in Amherst, Massachusetts. She is not related to the poet.

Preface

This book is written for the general reader as an introduction to the poetry of Emily Dickinson. It relies on established scholarship which is cited in the text and in endnotes. It was conceived with two distinct though not dissimilar audiences in mind. The first is comprised of those who have an interest in the poetry and want to cultivate a deeper appreciation of it. The second is comprised of those non-native speakers of American English who have already developed a love of, or a keen interest in, the poetry.

Except when otherwise noted, quotations from Emily Dickinson's letters are taken from *The Letters of Emily Dickinson,* edited by Thomas H. Johnson, Associate Editor, and Theodora Ward, Cambridge, Mass.: The Belknap Press of Harvard University Press, 1958 (three volumes). Letters from which the quotations are taken are identified by their Johnson-assigned number in the format Lnnnn (where n is a numeral from 0 to 9). The reader may find that some poems in this book are at variance with some of those in his or her possession. The poems presented in this book are taken from *The Poems of Emily Dickinson: Including Variant Readings Critically Compared with All Known Manuscripts,* edited by Thomas H. Johnson, from Little, Brown, and Company, 1955 (three volumes). A second collection of the complete poems, *The Poems of Emily Dickinson: Variorum Edition* edited by Ralph W. Franklin, from the Belknap Press of Harvard University Press, 1998, is also widely available. These editions contain all known Dickinson poems and retain her original word choices and her non-standard punctuation. Generally, the poem is essentially the same in both editions, but not always. Dickinson often included alternate word choices in her manuscripts, and sometimes wrote out more than one version of a poem. In some such instances each editor has selected differently in his single volume "readers edition," which include just one version of each poem. The most recent book, similarly containing all the poems, worthy of special note is *Emily Dickinson's Poems: As She Preserved Them* by Cristanne Miller, also from The Belknap Press of Harvard University Press, 2016. This edition presents the poems as Dickinson arranged them in groups, as explained later in this book. Both Johnson and Franklin assigned a number to each poem to indicate their estimation of chronological order, and in this respect the editors usually differ. Miller, like Dickinson, does not assign numbers to the poems. For each poem in this book, I provide the chronological numbers for both the Johnson and Franklin editions, along with page number in the Miller edition in the format Jnnnn/Fnnnn/Mpppp. With rare exception, Dickinson did not title her poems. Without a Johnson or Franklin number, or a Miller page number, they are commonly identified by the first line alone. I have used first lines in place of titles throughout the book. Some of Dickinson's sometimes unorthodox spelling will also be preserved in these pages. Some poems will be discussed more than once. This will happen when different aspects of a poem are better treated in separate chapters. Because of the multiplicity of ways to read and interpret the poems, approaching them in different ways helps to focus attention, and locate meaning. This book combines three main strategies to accomplish this.

First, examine the language practices that were available to Dickinson in her time and place. Her vocabulary included words and meanings not generally recognized today. Identifying such usages can bring a previously obscure or indeterminate poem to life. For example, consider the word *candid* in the poem "Pink - small - and punctual -":

Pink - small - and punctual -
Aromatic - low -
Covert - in April -
Candid - in May -

Dear to the Moss -
Known by the Knoll -
Next to the Robin
In every Human Soul -

Bold little Beauty -
Bedecked with thee -
Nature forswears
Antiquity -

—J1332/F1357/M587

This poem was signed "Arbutus" and describes the trailing arbutus, or Mayflower, which appears punctually in early spring, and changes from pink to white as the season progresses. Emily Dickinson's dictionary (An 1844 printing of the 1841 edition of Webster's *American Dictionary of the English Language*) defines the word *Candid* thus:

CAN'DID, a

1. White. - [But in this sense rarely used.]

2. Fair; open; frank; ingenuous; free from undue bias; disposed to think and judge according to truth and justice, or without partiality or prejudice; applied to persons.

3. Fair; just; impartial; applied to things; as, a candid view, or construction.

Understanding what meaning and connotations words held in nineteenth-century America often illuminate the poet's work in startling ways. Using the word "candid" to mean white may have been rare, but Dickinson does so in this poem, conveying along with the literal color, a sense of virtue, as conveyed in definitions 2 and 3 above, as well.

Second, identify distinctly personal, biographical, and local references, along with historical context, including the American Civil War and the religious phenomenon in America and elsewhere known as the Second Great Awakening. This will add great emotional weight and profound implication to certain words. Without awareness of the context of the following poem for example, the impact, and even the meaning could easily be lost:

If any sink, assure that this, now standing -
Failed like Themselves - and conscious that it rose -
Grew by the Fact, and not the Understanding
How Weakness passed - or Force - arose -

Tell that the Worst, is easy in a Moment -
Dread, but the Whizzing, before the Ball -
When the Ball enters, enters Silence -
Dying - annuls the power to kill -

—J358/F616/M303

Emily Dickinson wrote this poem in 1862, when the American Civil War had already taken a toll from among the young men of her community, and accounts of the bloody battles were in all the newspapers. The *Balls* are Minie (pronounced min-AY) Balls, the most common ammunition used by soldiers on both sides of the conflict.

Third, consider her vocabulary and literary tropes in the context of the entire body of her work, including material from her letters. I show how she uses certain words and images in a consistent way. An example of how this approach can shed light on a word arose in a discussion of the poem below that took place in Amherst in 2013. A person present found this poem depressing. To her, the word *mines* suggested a feeling of darkness and cold, which mines admittedly are. Because the poem also contains the word *Dungeons,* it's easy to see how someone might hear the word *mines* as suggesting a dank hole in the ground. Here is the poem.

Talk with prudence to a Beggar
Of "Potosi," and the mines!
Reverently, to the Hungry
Of your viands, and your wines!

Cautious, hint to any Captive
You have passed enfranchised feet!
Anecdotes of air in Dungeons
Have sometimes proved deadly sweet!
—J119/F118/M74

But consider other mines in Dickinson's poetry. What do you find in these first two verses of one poem?

One of the ones that Midas touched
Who failed to touch us all
Was that confiding Prodigal
The reeling Oriole -

So drunk he disavows it
With badinage divine -
So dazzling we mistake him
For an alighting Mine -
—J1466/F1488/M617

Midas, whose touch turned any object to gold! *Dazzling!* It should be clear here that the poet uses the word *Mine* to suggest the brilliance of gold. Even without knowing that *Potosi* is a city in Bolivia associated with rich silver mines, knowing that Dickinson associates mines with wealth would encourage a like reading in *Talk with prudence to a Beggar.* Furthermore, consider the third stanza from the poem "Your Riches - taught me - Poverty -":

Of Mines, I little know - myself -
But just the names, of Gems -
The Colors of the Commonest -
And scarce of Diadems
—J299/F418/M165

Gems! Diadems! For Dickinson, it becomes clear from these additional examples of *mines* in her poems, the word is meant to convey a sense of riches. Seeing this, the reader would read the poem "Talk with prudence to a Beggar" very differently than did the discussion participant noted above. The poet advises us not to speak carelessly before a poor beggar of riches that he will never enjoy himself.

It is important to understand that before the Johnson edition (1955) all Dickinson poetry then in print was edited; unorthodox spelling, punctuation, and capitalization were changed. Moreover, Dickinson's "slant rhymes," were often altered. For example, at the hands of her early posthumous editors, the third verse of the famous poem "Because I could not stop for Death" (J712/F479/M239) was re-written. Dickinson wrote this.

> We passed the School, where Children strove
> At Recess, in the Ring -
> We passed the Fields of Gazing Grain -
> We passed the Setting Sun -

It became this.

> We passed the school where children played
> Their lessons scarcely done
> We passed the fields of grazing grain
> We passed the setting sun

These earlier, heavily edited collections of poems are in the public domain, free of copyright restrictions, and in wide circulation. If you are in possession of any such volume, what you see in it will differ from the poems in this book.

I will refer to a particularly valuable resource throughout this book, The Emily Dickinson Lexicon (EDL), at http://edl.byu.edu/index.php.[1] The EDL gives definitions of words in Dickinson's poems that are often very helpful, and I will provide those definitions from this source. The *Emily Dickinson Lexicon* is a dictionary of alphabetized entries for all of the words in Emily Dickinson's collected poems (Johnson 1955 and Franklin 1998 editions). The scope of the Dickinson lexicon is comprehensive. A team of lexicographers and reviewers has examined almost 100,000 individual word occurrences to create approximately 9,275 entries. The website is sponsored and maintained by Brigham Young University. You do not need to access the EDL to use this book at all, but you will know where the definitions that you find here come from, and you may want to take advantage of this resource for your own study. A brief tutorial on the EDL is in Appendix B, and further instruction on its use and resources are given on the EDL website.

I will often refer to "the speaker" of the poem, or "the narrator." Common in much poetry commentary and analysis, it acknowledges that the poet is not necessarily expressing her own thoughts or recounting experience from her own life. As Baudelaire wrote: "The poet enjoys the incomparable privilege of being, at will, both himself and other people. Like a wandering soul seeking a body, he can enter, whenever he wishes, into anyone's personality. He takes as his own all the professions, rejoicings and miseries that circumstance brings to him." Emily Dickinson acknowledged as much in a letter to a friend. "When I state myself, as the Representative of the Verse - it does not mean - me -but a supposed person" (L268).

If English is not your first language, don't be discouraged about reading Emily Dickinson in English! Cristanne Miller points out that Dickinson's "cryptically elusive poems baffle even sophisticated readers."[2] You needn't understand every word in the poem to appreciate the images, thoughts, and sheer music that come through to you. As Margaret H. Freeman has advised, "you have to experience a poem first in order to begin to understand it." One of Dickinson's first editors, Mabel Loomis Todd, also said it well: "Yet there is a strange cadence of hidden music underlying her verse, which is like an orchid growing among the ordinary flowers of the field." To better hear what Todd heard, to better understand what Freeman said, read these chapters sequentially. Each one holds keys that unlock doors to the next—keys that I have collected through years of study and formal discussions of the poetry with others who love it.

Introduction

I first encountered Emily Dickinson almost thirty years ago, in the nineteen-eighties. It took only one poem to "get me." In "I taste a liquor never brewed" (J214/F207/M135) the poet describes herself as "inebriate of air," intoxicated by endless days of summer. One thing that struck me in the poem was her description of the summer sky as "molten blue," an unusual combination of words, as molten material is usually orange or red, or even white. I turned the words over in my mind for days, as one savors a mouthful of fine wine. I didn't need wine though, as I felt a bit intoxicated just from reading the poem (This poem is discussed in Chapter 2). As I read more poems, looking for more such gems, I printed out my favorites and put them in a notebook to learn by heart. I began to feel that I had to know who this person was, who could write such things, and so began reading biographies and the poet's wonderful letters. Eventually, it felt as though I couldn't get enough of her. Even so, I was often completely puzzled by parts of what I read. I was eventually to learn that I was not, and am not, alone in this regard. In fact, I find myself in very good company.

In August of 2008, I drove ninety minutes west from my home at the time near Boston, Massachusetts, to Amherst Massachusetts, the birthplace and home of Emily Dickinson and the site that year of the annual meeting of the Emily Dickinson International Society (EDIS), of which I had recently become a member. EDIS is primarily an organization of academic scholars, but any Dickinson enthusiast can join. I found myself surrounded by scores of people just as keen on Dickinson as me, many of whom have taught or written about her for many years. When speaker Paul Ryan described the poems as "experiential," and then as "thrill rides," I thought to myself, "I'm home!"

Since 2010, I've been guiding tours at the Emily Dickinson Museum in Amherst, in "The Homestead," where the poet was born, worked, and died, and in "The Evergreens," the home of her brother, Austin, where she spent many treasured hours. Visitors come from all over the world to immerse themselves in the surroundings, including three acres of the family gardens and grounds, extensive collections of family furnishings, personal objects and works of art, where this gifted and most original artist wrote the extraordinary poems that draw them there.

Dickinson enthusiasts fortunate enough to live near Amherst, as I now do, find themselves blessed with abundant and rich resources. The Emily Dickinson Collection at Amherst College documents the creative work and personal life of the poet, spanning her lifetime. The collection includes original manuscript poems and letters, research indices, and material from or about Dickinson's friends and family, including correspondence, photographs, objects, and scrapbooks. The nearby Jones Library, Special Collections, contains nearly 8,000 items including original manuscript poems and letters, Dickinson editions and translations, family correspondence, scholarly articles and books, and related documents on the poet's life and work. The world's best-known Dickinson scholars visit and several of them live and work in the area. I am able to participate in discussions of Dickinson's poems almost every week, often with one or more of these scholars present. Having access to these resources, and being able to discuss Dickinson's life and work with other devotees, has enriched my appreciation of the poetry immeasurably. The more I learn about her, the richer the harvest from the poems. I have not forgotten, however, my difficulty through many years wrestling with those poems in solitude.

I was inspired to write this book after meeting someone struggling to know Dickinson better, and who did not enjoy the blessings of which I tell. I was guiding a group of educators from Asia through the Emily Dickinson Museum. They were interested in everything I could show and relate to them, had many questions, and it was evident that they were "soaking it all in" eagerly. After the formal tour was over and I was leaving the museum, one of the members of the group stopped me politely and asked if he might ask a few questions. We stood there on the lawn outside "The Homestead," and talked for a while. He spoke earnestly and with a hint of urgency in his voice. Eventually he told how, where he lived, he had no good library to resort to, no knowledgeable sources to consult, and even very limited internet access, to help him know and appreciate Emily Dickinson's poetry, which he had been teaching for seven years already. I felt humbled by this dedicated, hard-working man, striving to become a better educator, with such scant resources at his disposal. I am writing this book for him and for the many others striving toward Dickinson. I remember his first question.

"What is 'tis?" he asked.

I explained that this is an example of a contraction in English grammar and that it means "it is." As an example, *'Tis not that Dying hurts us so* translates as "It is not that dying hurts us so." "'Tis" is no longer in common use today, and my spell checker doesn't even recognize it. I'm sorry that I didn't think to mention that to my visitor, and that "'tis" is just one example of this kind of contraction in the English language. Something like the following table would probably help him:

Contraction	*Meaning*	*Example*
'twere	It were	As 'twere a bright bouquet
'twill	It will	I said "'Twill keep"
'twould	It would	'twould crumble with the weight
'twas	That was	It just reminded me, 'twas all *(This is another meaning for 'twas besides "It was")*

My encounter with this man was a catalyst. From years listening to questions in poetry discussion groups and noting where readers come to an impasse, from answering questions from curious and often ardent visitors at The Emily Dickinson Museum, I've come to realize that, in fact, Emily Dickinson is a second language to all of us, and we all could use some help to a fuller appreciation of her work. That is the purpose of this book. Even her most dedicated readers will find themselves wondering if, perhaps, they're missing something in a poem. They find multiple meanings, seemingly contradictory words placed together, and language that, though once familiar to all, may be unfamiliar to us in modern times. In spite of these difficulties, she has continued to captivate readers all over the world. Our dilemma as readers is well expressed, I think, in the reaction of an early critic, written shortly after the first volume of her poems was issued, four and one-half years after her death.

> Madder rhymes one has seldom seen - scornful disregard of poetic technique could hardly go further - and yet there is about the book a fascination, a power, a vision that enthralls you, and draws you back to it again and again. Not to have published it would have been a serious loss to the world. I have read this book twice through already. I foresee that I shall read it scores of times more. It enthralls me and will not let me go [Louise Chandler Moulton, *Boston Sunday Herald*, November 23, 1890].

Modern readers are less perplexed by the violations of nineteenth-century conventions to which Moulton objected, but the passage of time has placed new obstacles in our paths, as our very language has changed and historical context has been obscured. But if you are reading this, then you have perhaps felt something of what Moulton wrote, the fascination, the power, the enthrallment. You have also felt perplexed and puzzled. Dickinson's unusual syntax (the order of words and phrases in a sentence), novel and startling ways of using vocabulary, and perhaps most challenging, what she leaves unsaid, pose difficulties to all of her readers. Dickinson has a voice which, as you read this book, will become more recognizable and more familiar to you. As it does, the poems will yield ever more riches, as perplexity and puzzlement give way to awe.

ONE

Words to Lift Your Hat To

> "We used to think, Joseph, when I was an unsifted girl and you so scholarly that words were cheap & weak. Now I don't know of anything so mighty. There are those to which I lift my hat when I see them sitting princelike among their peers on the page. Sometimes I write one, and look at his outlines till he glows as no sapphire."—Letter to Joseph B. Lyman, undated[1]

In the introduction to this book, we considered the contraction "'tis," meaning "it is," noting that it is seldom heard in conversation today. In fact, it was seldom heard in Dickinson's day either, having become, even then, more of a literary device than a spoken word. You can, however, find "'tis" in a modern English dictionary and read its definition there. That is not quite so for some other words, for while you may find them in *your* dictionary, they will be defined differently there than they were in hers. Further, the poet uses words in ways that are not defined—as she is using them—in any dictionary. In this chapter we will uncover definitions and applications of words that have been obscured or lost to us today, and we will show how that can clarify a poem and even reveal unsuspected richness and depth of meaning. Moreover, Emily Dickinson created her own words, as other poets, including Shakespeare, had before her. These "coined words," as they are often called, can puzzle the unsuspecting reader. Dickinson's coined words are identified and explained here. Once they are recognized for what they are, your own intimate communication with the poet has begun. Speaking of Shakespeare, the expression "unsifted girl" in the letter noted above is an allusion to Shakespeare's Hamlet, Act I, Scene 3:

> OPHELIA
> He hath, my lord, of late made many tenders
> Of his affection to me
> POLONIUS
> Affection! Pooh, you speak like a green girl,
> Unsifted in such perilous circumstance.

Emily Dickinson drew from many sources to create her world of words. We will find examples of all of these cases in the following pages.

Forgotten Words and Meanings from 19th-Century America

Emily Dickinson's dictionary contained 82,971 entries. As suggested in our preface, a modern reader would be here and there surprised at some of the definitions found in it, even for words familiar to us today. For example, when we speak of something as being "adequate," we usually mean that it's good enough for the job, or that it's okay if nothing better is available, and in modern dictionaries "barely suitable" is among the definitions that it now carries. Not so in Emily Dickinson's dictionary, where the full definition given is "Equal; proportionate; correspondent to; fully sufficient."[2] "Fully sufficient" and "barely suitable" are nearly opposite meanings! The word has become weaker. Many a modern reader must have puzzled over the final stanza of Dickinson's "Remorse - is Memory - awake," for instance.

Remorse is cureless - the Disease
Not even God - can heal -
For 'tis His institution - and
The Adequate of Hell -
—J744/F781/M383

The stronger definition of this adjective, "equal," fits well here and leaves little question of how to read the stanza.

Nor was Dickinson's vocabulary limited to English as spoken in America. English authors, including the Brownings, the Brontë sisters, George Eliot, and of course, Shakespeare, were among her very favorite writers. She absorbed and selected words from these sources and others, too. That's why it's important to examine the language practices that were available to her when she was writing.

It seems only right to begin with one of Dickinson's better-known poems, "There is no Frigate like a Book." It is surely among the most frequently anthologized of them all. In the very first line we find a word which, while still in use today, has evolved from what it described in the nineteenth century.

There is no Frigate like a Book
To take us Lands away -
Nor any Coursers like a Page

Of prancing Poetry -
This Traverse may the poorest take
Without oppress of Toll -
How frugal is the Chariot
That bears the Human soul.
—J1263/F1286/M569

In the 18th and 19th centuries, a *frigate* was a medium sized, square-rigged warship. Dickinson did not choose a sailboat or a dinghy. This is not an outing on a lake; this is a serisous mission. How times have changed! In today's modern navies, a frigate is larger than a destroyer (but smaller than a cruiser). Definitions below, again, are from Emily Dickinson's own dictionary

FRIG′ATE
A ship of war, of a size larger than a sloop or brig, and less than a ship of the line; usually having two decks and carrying from thirty to forty four guns. But ships mounting a less number than thirty guns are sometimes called frigates; as are ships carrying a larger number.

The poet extends the metaphor interestingly. There is no Frigate … *Nor any Coursers*. There are no means on land or sea to compare with a book for transport.

COURS′ER
1. A swift horse; a runner; a war horse; a word used chiefly in poetry
2. One who hunts; one who pursues the sport of coursing hares.

Consider finally the word *Traverse*. This word was used as a noun, adjective, adverb, preposition, or transitive or intransitive verb. (A transitive verb is one which takes a direct object, an intransitive verb does not.) Here are the first four definitions for the transitive verb:

TRAV′ERSE, v.t.
1. To cross; to lay in a cross direction.
2. To cross by way of opposition; to thwart; to obstruct.
3. To wander over; to cross in traveling; as, to traverse the habitable globe.
4. To pass over and view; to survey carefully.

Note that the accent is on the first syllable. Modern speakers will, especially when applying the verb form, commonly place the accent on the last syllable. Accenting the first syllable, however, preserves the meter of the verse. As a *Book* takes the poet "lands away," she traverses the globe, crossing seas and continents. But perhaps there is more here in this little word than that. Defined as a noun we have:

TRAV′ERSE, n.
1. Any thing laid or built across. "There is a traverse placed in the loft where she sitteth."

> 2. Something that thwarts, crosses or obstructs; a cross accident. "He is satisfied he should have succeeded, had it not been for unlucky traverses not in his power."

Note again the accent on the first syllable in the noun form as well.

In the early half of the nineteenth century, a traveler in Massachusetts might find herself blocked by a pike (a long shaft) spanning the width of the road, barring the way. These "pike roads" were owned and operated by private enterprises that had been granted that right by the state legislature. The traveler would have to pay a *toll* (a fee) in order to proceed, whereupon the operator would turn the pike, allowing the traveler to pass. Such roads were therefore referred to as "turnpikes," or "toll roads." One may travel via a book without the oppression of a toll!

The traveler would have been on horseback, or in a horse-drawn carriage. Dickinson wrote this poem, or fragment, in pencil on a scrap of paper.

> The sun in reining to the West
> Makes not as much of sound
> As Cart of man in road below
> Adroitly turning round
> That Whiffletree of Amethyst
> —J1636/F1656/M652

There are three words here that deserve our attention; one because it will be unfamiliar to most readers, the other two for their nineteenth-century connotations. The first is *rein.* This word is still in common use wherever people handle horses. Used in its verb form in the poem, it may also function as a noun.

> REIN, n
> The strap of a bridle … by which the rider of a horse restrains and governs him.

By using the verb form, the poet compares the movement of the setting sun to that of the horse and cart below.

> REIN, v.t.
> To govern by a bridle

As the online Emily Dickinson Lexicon (EDL) interprets it, the sun seems to "fly across the sky as if pulled by Apollo's horse-drawn chariot in Greco-Roman mythology," a more evocative effect than had she written "The sun in setting in the West."

The one antiquated word in the poem is *whiffletree* (or, whippletree).

> WHIFFLETREE,
> The bar to which the traces of a carriage are fastened for draught

"Draught" in this definition is more often spelled "draft" today, and that is how it's pronounced. Modern editions of Webster's dictionary define the word "draught," or "draft" as "The act of drawing or pulling." In the nineteenth century the definition was much the same, with a close association with beasts of burden.

DRAUGHT, v.t.
1. The act of drawing or pulling, as of a vehicle or a load.

The illustration below shows a triple whiffletree arrangement. The three draught animals thus driven would have been horses or oxen.

The third word of interest in this poem is *amethyst,* but for a different reason. Both now and centuries ago, it named a certain gemstone, a subspecies of quartz, of a violet blue color. It is thought to have had special significance for Dickinson. Amethyst makes the twelfth foundation of the wall of the city of New Jerusalem, as described in Chapter 21 of the Bible's Book of Revelation (King James Version). There is evidence that Dickinson was especially drawn to this particular book, referring to Chapter 21 as "the gem chapter."[3] Used as an adjective *amethyst* refers to the violet or purple color of the stone. The whiffletree that the "man" is turning around is certainly not made of amethyst, nor would it likely to be purple or violet-colored. Here, while bringing to mind the purples of a sunset, the word also acts poetically, without literal translation into the physical world. "Seeing the world through rose-colored glasses" is an expression in common

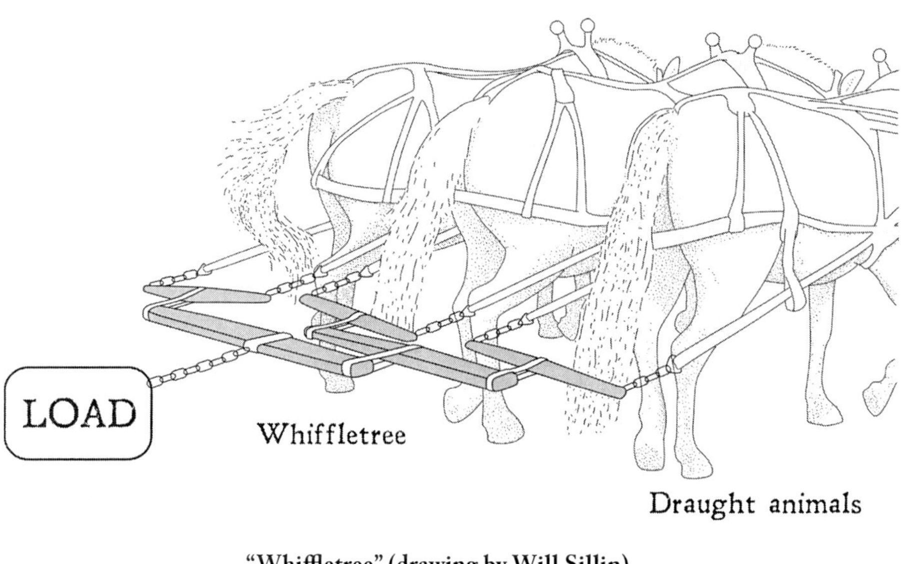

"Whiffletree" (drawing by Will Sillin).

use today. It means looking at the world in a way colored by naïve optimism or nostalgia while ignoring its more sordid aspects. In this poem, *amethyst* lends to the sunset a nostalgia and a sweet feeling of longing. Dickinson used the word *amethyst* in six poems: "The Daisy follows soft the Sun" (J106/F161/M89), "As Watchers hang upon the East" (J121/F120/M75), "I held a Jewel in my fingers" (J245/F261/M128), "I'll tell you how the Sun rose" (J318/F204/M119), and "Sunset that screens, reveals" (J1609/F1644/M649) are the other five. The reader may find it enlightening to see how she uses *amethyst* elsewhere.

In the poems considered so far, and in many that will follow, Dickinson capitalized words internal to the line, and placed dashes between words and at ends of lines. In so doing, she was neither eccentric nor unorthodox. Rather she was following what was then common practice in handwriting, although seldom found in print. *Parker's Aid to English Composition,* a textbook in use at Amherst Academy when ED attended classes there,[4] states the following concerning dashes.

> The proper use of the dash is to express a sudden stop, or a change of subject; but, by modern writers, it is employed as a substitute for almost all the other marks.; being used sometimes for a comma, semicolon, colon, or period; sometimes for a question or an exclamation crotchets and brackets to enclose a parenthesis.

And, concerning capitalization, the same volume says, "Any words, when remarkably emphatical [sic], or when they are the principal subject of the composition, may begin with capitals."[5]

Additionally, the book that she undoubtedly studied later, at Mount Holyoke Female Seminary, William Harvey Wells' *Grammar of the English Language,* approved these same practices. Situating oneself in Emily Dickinson's time and place demystifies many a seemingly arcane feature of her work.

The Language of Home

Dickinson made much use of domestic imagery in her poems. She has been credited by critics for taking images from what was, in nineteenth-century New England, considered the properly limited female sphere, and using them with new power. She chose the humblest subjects that she saw around her—bees, crickets, birds, and leaves in the wind. This much others were doing, too, and had done before her; but, as Gerda Lerner[6] has observed, Dickinson created a feminine universe, with metaphors that derive from the domestic life of women. She employs her homely images in the most ambitious way to address the great questions of humankind—death, God, the human condition, and immortality. In so doing, she claimed for herself the authority to take on topics from which women were largely proscribed in a still quite patriarchal society. Lerner writes, "she opened the path to the future and won the immortality she so boldly claimed by speaking as a free soul, a free mind, and a woman. In this sense, Dickinson appears as the perfection and culmination of centuries of women's struggles for self-definition."[7] Note how, in a deceptively light-hearted poem, Dickinson uses the images of a flower, a girdle and a bee, along with a coy tone, to question a fundamental power relationship between men and women.

Did the Harebell loose her girdle
To the lover Bee
Would the Bee the Harebell *hallow*
Much as formerly?

Did the "Paradise" - persuaded -
Yield her moat of pearl -
Would the Eden be an Eden,
Or the Earl - an Earl?
— J213/F134/M527

Perhaps a suitor has told the speaker of this poem that it is *Paradise* to be with her. She has placed it in quotation marks, indicating that she has heard it from someone or somewhere else. Here, Paradise is a metaphor for herself. The Book of Revelation tells of the gates of pearl surrounding God's kingdom. The suitor stands outside her defensive *moat of pearl*. The bee and the flower (*Harebell*) are familiar metaphors for the sexual relationship between men and women. In Emily Dickinson's time and place, the roles assigned to the sexes were still fairly fixed. Man's was the sphere of reason and work in the world. Woman's role was that of feeling and caring for the home. In marriage, women were expected to be pious, pure, and submissive.[8] Such expectations were supported, in this church-centered community, by no lesser authority than the Bible:

> Wives, submit yourselves unto your own husbands, as unto the Lord. For the husband is the head of the wife, even as Christ is the head of the church: and he is the saviour of the body. Therefore as the church is subject unto Christ, so *let* the wives *be* to their own husbands in every thing [Ephesians 5:22–24].

Emily Dickinson not only challenges this arrangement, but by so doing she claims authority to operate in the male sphere, to question the fundamental tenets of a patriarchal society. This is a very subversive poem posing as a coy flower in a metaphorical girdle. Note: Where the editor gives a word or phrase in italics, that word or phrase is not italicized in Dickinson's manuscript, it is underlined.

In the following poem, she employs homely unravelling balls of yarn and seams of fabric to describe a mental trouble.

I felt a Cleaving in my Mind -
As if my Brain had split -
I tried to match it - Seam by Seam -
But could not make them fit.

The thought behind, I strove to join
Unto the thought before -
But Sequence ravelled out of Sound
Like Balls - upon a Floor.
—J937/F867/M423

Yarn comes into the home in a long, loosely wound coil that somebody would have to hold while the other one made the ball. The balls were not machine rolled, and they unrolled very easily (*ravelled* is Dickinson's spelling of "raveled"). Related to yarn is an item called a distaff. While still in use today, distaffs have been largely replaced with mechanized equipment. Here is the definition from Emily Dickinson's Webster's dictionary.

DISTAFF, n
The staff of a spinning-wheel, to which a bunch of flax or tow is tied, and from which the thread is drawn

However, there is another form of distaff which is not defined in her Webster's. Spinning *by hand,* without a spinning wheel, the distaff is a simple staff, held under the arm while holding a spindle in the other. Fiber is drawn from the distaff onto the spindle as yarn. This way of spinning predates the spinning wheel.

In the following poem, the word *distaff* appears in a meditation on the afterlife and those departed, whom the poet imagines living in a *Seraphic May.* The distaff hangs idle now, unused, a mute reminder of the departed "bird" that once spun fiber from it.

SE-RAPH′IC, or SE-RAPH′IC-AL, a.
1. Pertaining to a seraph; angelic; sublime; as, seraphic purity; seraphic fervor.

Here are the first two stanzas of the poem:

There is a morn by men unseen -
Whose maids upon remoter green
Keep their Seraphic May -
And all day long, with dance and game,
And gambol I may never name -
Employ their holiday.

"Spindle and distaff" (drawing by Will Sillin).

Here to light measure, move the feet
Which walk no more the village street -
Nor by the wood are found -
Here are the birds that sought the sun
When last year's distaff idle hung
And summer's brows were bound.
—J24/F13/M36

According to some Christian teachings, the time will come when God establishes his kingdom on earth and the righteous are raised to new life. This time is also called the New Day. The *Morn by men unseen* is the dawn of this New Day; it is the afterlife. In referring to the *remoter green* there, the poet again adds a touch of her home. As was the case with almost all the towns in her part of the United States, there was a *green,* a parcel of land set aside for public use, featuring lawn, trees, and perhaps shrubs and flowers. A contemporary of the Dickinson family, Mary Adele Allen, wrote a slim volume describing life in Amherst. To best convey the flavor of life in her home town, she chose for a title, *Around a Village Green.*

And how are the brows of summer bound? The word "bound" has many definitions—"limited to an area by a boundary," for example, or it can mean "destined," or "about to go," as in "she's bound for glory." It can also mean fastened or encircled by a band, as of fabric, or perhaps gold, as in the first stanza of "Two Crowns," by the Canadian poet, Norah M. Holland (1876–1925):

> The young King rode through the City street,
> So gallant, gay and bold;
> There were roses strewn 'neath his horse's feet,
> His brows were bound with gold,
> And his heart was glad for his people's cheers
> Along his pathway rolled.

Being able to picture how a distaff and spindle are used is simply vital to recognizing the image in the second stanza of a six-stanza poem describing a sunset, as the scarlet of the sun's rays is hand-spun onto the spindle of a church steeple.

> How the old Mountains drip with Sunset
> How the Hemlocks burn -
> How the Dun Brake is draped in Cinder
> By the Wizard Sun -
>
> How the old Steeples hand the Scarlet
> Till the Ball is full -
> Have I the lip of the Flamingo
> That I dare to tell?
>
> —J291/F327/M156

HAND, v.t.

1. To give or transmit with the hand.
2. To lead, guide and lift with the hand; to conduct.
3. To manage; as, I hand my oar.

There were no Flamingoes in Emily Dickinson's part of the world, but she evidently learned of them and learned of their reputation as noisy, chattering birds. "*Have I the lip of the Flamingo?*" she demands. No, she will not try to describe how the spindle-like steeple seems to wrap itself in the scarlet sunset, how the hemlock trees seem to be on fire at this magic moment. Ah, but she just did, didn't she! This is a fine Dickinson literary device. She pretends that she's not up to the task of painting so glorious a picture, and then she makes us see it vividly for ourselves.

Dickinson also drew from life in the farming community in which she lived, as in this early poem. The Dickinson homestead included a great barn and an 11-acre hayfield.

I cautious, scanned my little life -
I winnowed what would fade
From what w'd last till Heads like mine *["w'd" is a contraction of "would"]*
Should be a-dreaming laid.

I put the latter in a Barn -
The former, blew away.
I went one winter morning
And lo - my priceless Hay

Was not upon the "Scaffold" -
Was not upon the "Beam" -
And from a thriving Farmer -
A Cynic, I became.

Whether a Thief did it -
Whether it was the wind -
Whether Deity's guiltless -
My business is, to find!

So I begin to ransack!
How is it Hearts, with Thee?
Art thou within the little Barn
Love provided Thee?

—J178/F175/M102

Two more words, still in our common vocabulary are *scaffold* and *beam.* In the farming area where Emily Dickinson lived, though, these two words had specific applications.

SCAFFOLD, n.
1. Drying rack for fodder; wooden frame for storing hay in a barn.
2. Gallows; gibbet; pillory; platform for executing someone by hanging.
3. Framework; support; platform.

The first definition above does not appear in modern dictionaries that I have consulted. In New England, the smaller barns often had a raised platform at one end for storing hay or grain, or over the cow stalls. It was called a *scaffold*, and was usually pronounced *scaffle.* It is seldom understood in this way today. *Beam* probably refers to the regional term, "high-beams," or "great-beams," which was a platform right under the sloping sides of the roof of the barn used for storing hay. These terms are common in the neighboring Worcester County, Massachusetts, and in the upper Connecticut Valley.[9] Dickinson places these words in quotes to indicate familiar colloquial terms heard among her neighbors. This is a poem involving careful husbandry, cast in the familiar terms of the farm.

In one of Emily Dickinson's best-known poems, which she herself once referred to as "my snake,"[10] there is a reference to a thermometer which has been missed by more than one reader. In the Dickinson's farming community it would not have been missed, as the thermometer was an important tool of daily recourse. A nineteenth-century agricultural report explains:

> Every man should keep a thermometer in his stable. The heat of the stable should rarely rise above sixty degrees. […] A thermometer in the stable is as indispensable as a thermometer in your cellar where you keep your vegetables. […] It shouldn't be a casual thing to look at a thermometer occasionally, but you should make a regular record of the reading of the thermometer at least three times a day."[11]

The following is a good example of a widely anthologized poem that often is printed in versions changed by early editors, and Dickinson herself left three copies of it, which differ in small ways from one another. The version presented below is thought to be the latest that Dickinson left us.[12]

A narrow Fellow in the Grass
Occasionally rides -
You may have met Him - Did you not
His notice sudden is -

The Grass divides as with a Comb -
A spotted shaft is seen -
And then it closes at your feet
And opens further on -

He likes a Boggy Acre
A Floor too cool for Corn -
Yet when a Boy, and Barefoot
I more than once at Noon
Have passed I thought a Whip lash
Unbraiding in the Sun
When stooping to secure it
It wrinkled and was gone -

Several of Nature's People
I know, and they know me -
I feel for them a transport
Of cordiality -

But never met this Fellow
Attended, or alone
Without a tighter breathing
And Zero at the Bone -

—J986/F1096/M489

The last line, *And zero at the Bone,* has generated volumes of comment and analysis. To many, it suggests emptiness, or an existential loss, as when, in a moment of primal fear, one loses one's very identity. And, for many such readers, it does have a powerful effect. This book is written with non-native speakers of American English in mind, but rest assured, Dickinson poses knotty challenges for her American readers, too. How? This line offers one good example. The word *zero* is in all of our English dictionaries. Older and more modern editions will give the definition as the numeral zero, a cipher, and also as "nothing," "naught," etc. Read with such meanings in mind, "zero at the bone" may well inspire similar interpretations to that described above, or of having nothing—being stripped bare of defenses. However, "zero" may also refer to a point on the thermometer.

> ZE´RO, n
> Cipher; nothing. The point of a thermometer from which it is graduated. Zero, in the thermometers of Celsius and Reaumur, is at the point at which water congeals. The zero of Fahrenheit's thermometer is fixed at the point at which the mercury stands when immersed in a mixture of snow and common salt...

When her husband was away one winter, Emily Norcross Dickinson, the poet's mother, wrote to her husband, "The weather still continues mild, not like winter at all. I think old zero has lost very much of his self-respect."[13] One does not hear the word *zero* used in this way today, but apparently it was in common use once, perhaps even a cliché. Years later, her teenaged daughter Emily wrote, "It seems as if old winter had forgotten himself."[14] (Perhaps more was passed from mother to daughter than recipes!) Read in this sense, "zero at the bone" evokes the feeling of cold—the chill that can come with a feeling of dread, in contrast with the *transport* that she feels toward others of Nature's People. "Transport" appears 30 times in the poems, 29 of them conveying strong emotion or being emotionally carried away.[15]

We conclude this section on the language of home with a poem that presents multiple challenges to interpretation. What, for example, is a *Screw of Flesh?* What does *witnessed of the Gauze* mean? The poem includes both biblical and mythological allusion, recognizable words with unsuspected meanings, and unnamed referents.

> A single Screw of Flesh
> Is all that pins the Soul
> That stands for Deity, to Mine,
> Upon my side the Vail -
>
> Once witnessed of the Gauze -
> Its name is put away
> As far from mine, as if no plight
> Had printed yesterday,
>
> In tender - solemn Alphabet,
> My eyes just turned to see,
> When it was smuggled by my sight
> Into Eternity -
>
> More Hands - to hold - These are but Two -
> One more new-mailed Nerve

Just granted, for the Peril's sake -
Some striding - Giant - Love -

So greater than the Gods can show,
They slink before the Clay,
That not for all their Heaven can boast
Will let its Keepsake - go

—J263/F293/M138

The first word of interest is *Screw*. Today, as a noun, it would identify a piece of fastening hardware. In the nineteenth-century, however, it could also mean a small packet. One could purchase a small amount of tea, tobacco, sweets, or other commodity in loose form. The merchant would measure it out onto a square of paper, fold the paper over and twist the ends to seal the contents. One could thus buy a screw of salt, for example. This definition does not appear in Dickinson's Webster's, nor does it appear in all modern dictionaries. The online mirriam-webster.com dictionary gives this one:

4 *chiefly British* : a small packet (as of tobacco)

The Oxford English Dictionary (1836) offers this:

II 3. A small portion (of a commodity) wrapped up in a twist or cornet of paper; esp. a penny packet of tobacco.

Here is a use from Charles Dickens: "The little screw of tea with which yonder hard worked mother of a family is trudging home along the miry lane that leads to her thatched cottage is twice as dear as that which figures on the squire's breakfast table."[16]

But what would a *Screw of flesh* be? William Schurr identifies three persons in the first stanza, restating the stanza this way: "The single screw of flesh pins the soul that stands for deity to my soul."[17] He goes on to say, "The poem memorializes a small person intimately connecting her and the 'Thee' of the other fascicles,[18] taken out of this world before its time." The body of the departed is draped with, or wrapped in, funeral *Gauze* (Not customarily practiced in America, Emily would have learned of the practice through her reading). *The soul that stands for Deity* is *put away* after being *witnessed of* this gauze. As the body is lowered into the grave—*smuggled out of my sight*—she turns back to look, only to see the letters on the headstone, a *tender—solemn Alphabet.* Now, in the afterlife, among all the other departed, he or she will have *More Hands to hold*—the poet here on earth could offer *but two. Mail* is a kind of armor used in past centuries, and will be explained more fully later in this book. *New-mailed Nerve* is the poet's expression for the way she will have to protect herself from succumbing to the pain of separation. She has her *Keepsake* to help her, Schurr continues: "In Vergil's Aeneid, Dido appeals to Aeneas for just such a keepsake, a child of theirs to play in their courtyard and remind her of him when he is gone."

This earthly love is so great that the Gods *slink before the Clay.* The clay is us mortals. The mortal flesh as clay was very familiar to ED from her Bible. "Behold, I *am* according to thy wish in God's stead: I also am formed out of the clay" (Job 33:6, KJV). And, from her dictionary:

> CLAY, n.
> 3. In Scripture, clay is used to express frailty, liableness to decay and destruction. They that dwell in houses of clay. — Job iv.

The soul of the departed person is now separated from the speaker of the poem figuratively by a *Vail.* We cannot see beyond this vail. This is a word with weighty cultural and religious connotations, to which we will return later in a later chapter.

Victorian Flower Language

In August of 1870, Emily Dickinson received a distinguished visitor. Col. Thomas Wentworth Higginson, prominent man of letters, public speaker and social reformer, had been in correspondence with her since 1862, and was about to meet her for the first time. Later, in a letter to his wife, he left us one of the few descriptions of a personal meeting with the poet: "A step like a pattering child's in entry & in glided a plain little woman with two smooth bands of reddish hair…. She came to me with two day lilies which she put in a sort of childlike way in my hand & said 'These are my introduction'"

Early in the nineteenth century, there developed in Europe a novel method of communication by way of flowers. Individual varieties of flowers were assigned specific symbolic meanings, and in Victorian times, when overt expressions of emotion were so often constrained, one could express oneself indirectly by sending or presenting the appropriate flower. Dictionaries were published containing alphabetical lists of flowers with their associated meanings and were wildly popular. The practice soon spread to England and the United States during the reign of Queen Victoria. In such dictionaries, the day lily was associated with "coquetry." (The dictionaries did not uniformly agree with one another however.) While it's hard for this particular writer to imagine that Emily Dickinson was sending a coquette's subliminal flirtation to the august Col. Higginson, the use of

Victorian Flower Language seems evident in some of her poems. Always keeping in mind that "sometimes a cigar is just a cigar,"[19] knowing the significance of a flower in a Dickinson poem can prove illuminating.

Essential Oils - are wrung -
The Attar from the Rose
Be not expressed by Suns - alone -
It is the gift of Screws -

The General Rose - decay -
But this - in Lady's Drawer
Make Summer - When the Lady lie
In Ceaseless Rosemary -
—J675/F772/M358

Our focus in this poem is the *Rosemary,* a flowering herb. Before we reach it, however we encounter first a *Rose.* "Essential Oil" is the term for the liquid obtained by forcefully pressing a plant. In the nineteenth century, the mechanics of the press involved the turning of screws. If we so press a rose, for example, we get the *attar,* the concentrated "essence" of the rose with its *essential* characteristic fragrance. In the coldness of winter, this essence *makes Summer*—remains to remind us of summer. The fragrance in a lady's drawer brings her back to us in memory after she is gone. In ancient times, it was believed that rosemary aided the memory and was good for the brain in general. In Shakespeare's time, it was also associated with the faculty of memory: "There's rosemary, that's for remembrance. Pray you, love, remember!" (Hamlet, Act 4 Scene 5).

Moreover, in some parts of England, rosemary would be placed into the coffin with the body of the deceased, and mourners at a funeral would toss sprigs of rosemary into the grave.[20] Shakespeare again: "Dry up your tears, and stick your Rosemary on this fair corse" (Romeo and Juliet, Act 4 Scene 5).

CORSE, n.
A corpse; the dead body of a human being; a poetical word.

The practice continued through Victorian times. The *rosemary* in this poem suggests both the literal plant as used at a funeral, together with the connotation of memory, and by extension, immortality, in the sense that memory may continue after a mortal life expires. Just as the fragrance continues in the lady's drawer, so poetry remains after the poet is gone. This poem offers a fine example of what readers mean when they speak of "layers of meaning" in Dickinson. The word *express* can mean physically pressing out, but it can also mean putting thought and feeling into words. Emily Dickinson knew that great art comes through hard work, self-sacrifice, and discipline. "Power is only Pain -/Stranded, thro' Discipline,/Till Weights - will hang -" she advises in "I can wade Grief" (J252/F312/M149). The *General Rose*, the rose growing out in the sunshine with all the other roses, cannot produce attar. For that, the rose must undergo the fierce pressure of screws. Or, less poetically, "No pain, no gain."

EX-PRESS′, v.t.
1. To press or squeeze out; to force out by pressure; as, to express the juice of grapes or of apples.
2. To utter; to declare in words; to speak.

Understanding the "screws" that one must endure in order to produce true poetry, Dickinson divined it in the poets whom she admired. We know from her letters that she admired certain other writers, and wrote poems in their honor. "I think I was enchanted" (J593/F627/M308), for example, is thought to be in honor of Elizabeth Barrett Browning, whom Dickinson held in highest esteem. As noted above, she also admired the Brontë sisters, all three of whom wrote under pseudonyms. Charlotte Brontë, from Haworth, England, where she is buried, wrote under the pseudonym Currer Bell. In this tribute to Charlotte Brontë, the *Asphodel* is not chosen arbitrarily, but speaks in the language of flowers.

All overgrown by cunning moss,
All interspersed with weed,
The little cage of "Currer Bell"
In quiet "Haworth" laid.

Gathered from many wanderings -
Gethsemane can tell
Thro' what transporting anguish
She reached the Asphodel!

Soft fall the sounds of Eden
Upon her puzzled ear -
Oh what an afternoon for Heaven,
When "Bronte" entered there!
—J148/F146/M86

The great Charlotte Brontë has passed, and her American admirer composes this poem, including an *Asphodel*, which said in the language of flowers, "*My regrets follow you to the grave.*" In the garden of *Gethsemane*, according to the gospel of Luke, Christ anguished hours before his crucifixion. Gethsemane appears in three other poems ("I should have been too glad, I see" (J313/F283/M346), "One Crucifixion is recorded - only" (J553/F670/M317), and "Spurn the Temerity" (J1432/F1485/M720) besides this one, as a symbol for human travail and suffering. Here we see again the theme expressed in "Essential Oils - are wrung." Brontë is presumed to have had to pass through her own garden of pain—must have had to endure the "screws" of life's trials—before she could produce her art.

The rose, of course, has long been associated with love and passion. In the language of flowers, it was the red rose specifically, while a burgundy colored rose meant "unconscious beauty." Roses in several other shades all had their different meanings. In the next poem, Emily Dickinson sets the rose and the mistletoe together. Victorians prized the mistletoe highly. It was a traditional part of Christmas celebrations, when it hung in hallways and on doors along with wreaths of evergreen and holly. One might wear a sprig of mistletoe in a buttonhole of a dress or a coat. The custom of kissing under the mistletoe gave it another pleasant association. In the language of flowers, the mistletoe meant "I surmount all obstacles." This meaning probably derives from this plant's ability to remain fresh and green while all surrounding vegetation shows no life. In ancient times, it was thought to have magical properties. The Druids worshipped it. So, there were strange and mysterious aspects of the mistletoe along with the lighthearted and festive ones. It was forbidden for use in churches because of the old pagan associations.

> If she had been the Mistletoe
> And I had been the Rose -
> How gay upon your table
> My velvet life to close -
> Since I am of the Druid,
> And she is of the dew -
> I'll deck Tradition's buttonhole -
> And send the Rose to you.
>
> —J44/F60/M48

The poet implies that she is the mistletoe and someone else is the rose, and speculates on what would happen if their roles were reversed. She associates herself with the magic, mystery, and power of the mistletoe, and someone else with the gifts of love and passion. In her late twenties she sent this early poem to a family friend, Mr. Samuel Bowles, who was married.

When encountering a flower in a Dickinson poem, remember that it might imply more than just a flower. For example, read "Did the Harebell loose her girdle" again, knowing that in the language of flowers, the Harebell is *Grief; Retirement; Submission.*

Coining Her Own Words

As noted previously, Emily Dickinson's poems include words that you will not find in any dictionary. Generally, her made-up words, or "coinings," are compounds of words or parts of words that do exist. Recognizing these invented words clears away some puzzlement and replaces it with a feeling of familiarity with the poet. It's as if you and she now share a private language. A very small number of her coinings are unlike any of her others, and they are worth knowing for the sheer delight of them. In only one poem, Brita Lindberg-Seyersted finds,[21] did she make up an entirely new word—*Optizan*—"presumably one skilled in the science of optics," as Lindberg-Seyersted interprets it. To that interpretation the Emily Dickinson Lexicon (EDL) adds, "seer; visionary; scientist; wise man; person of discernment."

> So glad we are - a Stranger'd deem
> 'Twas sorry, that we were -
> For where the Holiday should be
> There publishes a Tear -
> Nor how Ourselves be justified -
> Since Grief and Joy are done
> So similar - An Optizan
> Could not decide between -
> —J329/F608/M278

There is a somewhat novel use of the word *Holiday* here as well. The prosaic definition is "A day set apart for commemorating some important event in history; a festival intended to celebrate some event deemed auspicious to the welfare of a nation; particularly an anniversary festival, devoted to religious solemnities; as, Christmas holydays." On a holiday, people will celebrate and likely feel some measure of joy, happiness or elation, as well as freedom. Dickinson will extend her use of the word to include those connotations of happiness and joy (see for example "The Sun - just touched the Morning" (J232/F246/M117), and "Unto my Books - so good to turn" (J604/F512/M250) as she does in line three of the preceding poem. Recasting it into prose, we have: "We are so glad, a stranger would deem that we are sorrowful, because where the happiness should show on our face, a tear appears. Nor do we know how we ourselves might prove otherwise. Grief and Joy are expressed so similarly, an Optizan couldn't tell them apart."

An invented compound word that is also unique among Dickinson's coinings is *By-Thyme.* Even considered apart, it seems to conjure up a time just gone by, but leaving a lingering stimulus, like the spicy scent of thyme still in the air. You are left at the end of this delirious revel of a poem as if you had just been through its escapades yourself and are now remembering it all in a happy reverie.

> We - Bee and I - live by the quaffing -
> 'Tisn't all Hock - with us -

Life has its *Ale* -
But it's many a lay of the Dim Burgundy -
We chant - for cheer - when the Wines - fail -

Do we "get drunk"?
Ask the jolly Clovers!
Do we "beat" our "Wife"?
I - never wed -
Bee - pledges his - in minute flagons -
Dainty - as the trees -on her deft Head -

While runs the Rhine -
He and I - revel -
First - at the vat - and latest at the Vine -
Noon - our last Cup -
"Found dead" - "of Nectar" -
By a humming Coroner -
In a By-Thyme!

—J230/F244/M116

Both the bee and the speaker of this poem live by *quaffing,* which is to drink—especially something alcoholic—with gusto. The word has a flavor of hearty abandon, as heard in this from Milton:

> They eat, they drink, and in communion sweet
> Quaff immortality and joy[22]

The Bee quaffs nectar. What is the speaker of the poem quaffing? Well, whatever it is, it isn't all *Hock*—an old name for German white wine that was allowed to age, sold in Britain, and highly esteemed. The poet names the Rhine River in Germany where some of the finest white wines in the world are produced. The name Hock here carries almost sublime connotations. Nevertheless, sometimes we must make due with *Ale,* a reliable friend, but not exactly the nectar of the Gods. And in such circumstance, what do we do? We chant a *lay*—a song—of the blessed vineyards of Burgundy, only *Dim* in our imagination, to cheer us when the vintage fails.

Drunkenness was a problem in Amherst as it was elsewhere in America and as it continues today. Emily Dickinson would have known of instances such as the ones in lines 6 and 8 from town gossip (We will encounter one such episode in Chapter 6). The speaker of the poem seems free of any such failures. She refers us to the *clovers,* which yield to the bee their *nectars,* for confirmation. The bee *pledges*—toasts, drinks to the health of—in very small *flagons*—a vessel with a narrow mouth, used for storing and carrying liquors. The *trees* on her deft—neat; handsome; spruce—head some see as the bee's antennae, others as the golden pile that gives the bee his fuzzy look.

The poet and the bee will drink and revel together as long as the

Rhine River and the wine keep flowing. "Found Dead of Drink," was a familiar heading in newspaper reports. The poet imagines a similar fate befalling her and her bee companion, intoxicated on nature's bounty. The official who investigates suspicious, violent, or sudden deaths is the *coroner*. Our coroner in this poem is another *humming* bee. It happens in a *By-Thyme*, a humorous compound made up of two words seldom if ever heard together in speech. Thyme is a homonym for time. Reading that way, we hear a pun. "By," can mean near or close, but it can also mean past, as in "a time gone by." Thyme itself is a fragrant herb, associated in Victorian Flower Language with activity, strength and courage. Read this way, the poet and the bee have expired in a nearby bed of fragrant thyme. Further, there is yet another suggestion of the word "by-law," a local ordinance passed to regulate the behavior of the citizenry. Emily Dickinson would have been familiar with bylaws prohibiting public drunkenness and limiting or even prohibiting sale of alcoholic beverages.

Dickinson coined her own nouns often by adding the suffix "-less" or "-ness" to other parts of speech. Some, such as "escapeless," "stopless," and "graspless" you can find in some dictionaries. Indeed, "stopless" appears in Dickinson's own dictionary, albeit with the notation "not in use," and it is also in the OED. Others, such as "wakelessness" and "overtakelessness," you probably will not find in any dictionary. In this poem, the poet invites you to find meaning in *overtakelessness.*

> The overtakelessness of those
> Who have accomplished Death
> Majestic is to me beyond
> The majesties of Earth
>
> The soul her "Not at Home"
> Inscribes upon the flesh -
> And takes her fair aerial gait
> Beyond the Writ of touch
>
> —J1691/F894/M533

The dead cannot be overtaken. This, to the poet, seems more *Majestic* than anything on Earth. The dead are more aloof to our approach than any earthly, majestic sovereign. *"Not at Home,"* is a phrase from a feature of the Victorian-era custom of paying visits, or social calls on households within one's own social sphere. In the days before telephones, the etiquette involved was quite ritualized. The visitor or her servant would present a calling card at the door, which would be brought in to the mistress of the household. If she was not prepared to have the visitor in, she would write "Not at Home" on the caller's card and send it back. This act signaled that the visit was not welcome, at least not at present. In using this phrase, the poet ascribes to *Death* a courtly civility. This personification of death may remind the reader of one of Dickinson's "Because I could not stop for Death" (J712/F479//M239), in which Death is a presented as a courteous gentleman caller (We discuss this poem further in Chapters 6 and 8). The soul takes her *fair aerial* gate to heaven, now beyond the power of human touch to summon back. A *writ,* as the word is used here, is a written order from a proper authority to the Sherriff or a subordinate in his office. A writ may contain a summons, but the subjects of this poem are beyond summoning back to our *touch.*

Besides adding a suffix to an existing word, Dickinson coined words by compounding parts of two different existing words. What is *Gianture?* One of the many pleasures of reading Dickinson is seeing Gianture and Optizans in the imagination.

Size circumscribes - it has no room
For petty furniture -
The Giant tolerates no Gnat
For Ease of Gianture -

Repudiates it, all the more -
Because intrinsic size
Ignores the possibility
Of Calumnies - or Flies.
—J641/F707/M344

Gianture is created from "giant" and, perhaps, "nature" or "stature," giving us a new word suggesting "the nature of a giant," or "the stature of a giant," or perhaps both. What would a giant's nature be like? It would probably not so much as notice a *Gnat.* A giant's stature would be too great even to acknowledge the existence of *petty furniture.* Furniture had a slightly more general meaning than it does in modern usage:

FUR′NI-TURE, n.

1. Goods, vessels, utensils and other appendages necessary or convenient for housekeeping; whatever is added to the interior of a house or apartment, for use or convenience.
2. Appendages; that which is added for use or ornament; as, the earth with all its furniture.
3. Equipage; ornaments; decorations; in a very general sense

The Giant will therefore limit his contacts and his company:

CIR-CUM-SCRIBE′, v.t

To enclose within a certain limit; to limit, bound, confine.

GI′ANT, n

1. A man of extraordinary bulk and stature.
2. A person of extraordinary strength or powers, bodily or intellectual.

Note the close relationship between circumscribe and circumference. The giant's circumscribing sets boundaries on his experience, excluding gnats and flies, which lie outside of his circumference. Circumference is an especially important word in Dickinson's vocabulary, which we explore in Chapter 3. Finally, the word *intrinsic* must not be overlooked:

> IN-TRIN′SIC, or IN-TRIN′SIC-AL, a.
> 1. Inward; internal; hence, true; genuine; real; essential; inherent; not apparent or accidental; as, the intrinsic value of gold or silver; the intrinsic merit of an action; the intrinsic worth or goodness of a person.

Dickinson seems to have regarded giants favorably. For other examples, see "I think I was enchanted" (J593/F627/M308), and "Who Giants know, with lesser Men" (J796/F848/M390).

In another poem, a lovely new word is coined by combining "diminish" with "minuet."

> Oh what a Grace is this,
> What Majesties of Peace,
> That having breathed
> The fine - ensuing Right
> Without Diminuet Proceed!
> —J1615/F1669/M734

The Emily Dickinson Lexicon (EDL) offers this fine definition of *diminuet*:

> DIMINUET, n.
> Decrescendo; decline; diminution; diminuendo; reduction; gradual decrease in volume; [fig.] relenting; growing quieter; yielding to death; [word play on "minuet"] ceasing to dance; giving up the majestic movement of life.

The speaker has experienced a blessing, perhaps life itself, for which she is very grateful, and rejoices that she still abides in the blessing without weakening or failing. She *proceeds* without diminishing in the least. Dickinson has given us a very uplifting expression of gratitude, so much so that we feel for ourselves her state of grace. Consider how much would have been lost had she substituted some more prosaic expression, from or related to the definitions above, for example, "Without gradual decrease to proceed."

As we see in later chapters, the Reformed Protestantism[23] that prevailed in Amherst when Emily Dickinson was alive influenced her vocabulary and imagery greatly. A foretaste of the power of this vocabulary is found in *The Morning after Woe.* In that poem and one other—"He touched me, so I live to know" (J506/F349/M184)—she used a noun, "crucifix," to form her own adjective, *crucifixal.*

The Morning after Woe -
'Tis frequently the Way -
Surpasses all that rose before -
For utter Jubilee -

As Nature did not care -
And piled her Blossoms on -
And further to parade a Joy
Her Victim stared upon -

The Birds declaim their Tunes -
Pronouncing every word
Like Hammers - Did they know they fell
Like Litanies of Lead -

On here and there - a creature -
They'd modify the Glee
To fit some Crucifixal Clef -
Some key of Calvary -

—J364/F398/M212

A *Woe* has befallen the speaker on the previous day, or she is remembering such a time. The next day is particularly bright, and the world outside seems to be celebrating in *jubilee* (a joyous public festival). The *Birds* are singing their *Tunes* as usual, but if they only knew that their songs—*their Litanies*—fell on the listener's ears like *Hammers*, like *Lead*, they'd change their tunes a little to ones more appropriate to her condition of suffering.

LIT′A-NY, n.
A solemn form of supplication, used in public worship. Supplications for the appeasing of God's wrath, were by the Greek church termed litanies, by the Latin, rogations

A fine piano player, Emily Dickinson knew the G and base clefs and the keys of written music. She imagines a kind of music more appropriate to a crucifixion. *Calvary*, where Jesus was crucified, is a powerful symbol of suffering. It also carries with it the promise of grace.

In some other printings of this poem, the word *upon* is spelled *Opon,* which is how it actually appears on her manuscript. In other printings, as in those in this book, it is amended to *upon*. She did so in many poems, but not in her letters, so it had to be intentional. One explanation is that she simply liked the way the big, open "O" looked on the page. Her manuscripts often exhibit an interest in the appearance of the letters on the page, as the quote that opened this chapter indicates. Even more to the point, expressing her unwillingness to follow advice from a correspondent to whom she had submitted poems for comment, she wrote, "You say I confess the little mistake, and omit the large - Because I see Orthography."[24] Elsewhere, Dickinson pairs a Latin root, "omni" meaning "all," with the suffix "-fold," which can mean "a specific number of instances," or "having a stated number of parts," as in the sentence "Your hard work will repay you tenfold." In the final poem for this chapter, Dickinson personifies a mountain, and gives him an *observation omnifold.*

> The Mountain sat upon the Plain
> In his tremendous Chair -
> His observation omnifold,
> His inquest, everywhere -
>
> The Seasons played around his knees
> Like Children round a sire -
> Grandfather of the Days is He
> Of Dawn, the Ancestor -
>
> —J975/F970//M449

The mighty mountain sees all, in all places and in every direction. In two words, *observation omnifold,* the poet has said much, and in a poetic setting that conveys a sense of majesty.

In this chapter, we've seen how Dickinson coins words by adding suffixes such as -ness and -less to existing words. She also creates compound words from parts of existing words. Examples of unique coinings such as Optizan and By-Thyme are actually rare in Dickinson. When you come across an unfamiliar word in the poems, then, and don't find it in a dictionary, consider that it might be just such a construction as one of these. In joining her in finding meaning, you become a participant in the poem, rather than just a passive reader.

Two

New England

I went to Heaven -
'Twas a small Town -
—J374/F577/M263

The name "New England" identifies six states in the Northeast part of the United States. Emily Dickinson's Amherst, Massachusetts, is there, in a fertile part of that state known as the Connecticut River Valley. When visitors come to The Emily Dickinson Museum in Amherst from other parts of the country and the world, they often marvel at thick stands of lush green trees and meadows in the summer and at the resplendent, vividly colored foliage in the autumn. Indeed, even lifelong New England residents seem surprised by autumn's splendor again each year, blinking in wonder and exclaiming to one another how bright such-and-such a place is right now. During Dickinson's lifetime, much of the land that is now grown over had been cleared of trees for pasture, tillage, and buildings. Wooded areas shared the landscape with prosperous farms. Resident Ora White Hitchcock tried to capture it all in a watercolor, dated 1833.

Pictures of an Agricultural Community

Much of Emily Dickinson's poetry evokes the atmosphere of her rural village and the natural world around her. Familiarizing yourself with some of the features of her world helps to situate you there and to see through her eyes, leading to a fuller experience of many of the poems. She casts in words the very spells that the light, colors, and animals do in nature. We will consider several examples. The landscape painted by Ora White Hitchcock, Emily Dickinson paints in words.

"Amherst 1833" by Ora White Hitchcock (courtesy Amherst College).

I'm sorry for the Dead - Today -
It's such congenial times
Old Neighbors have at fences -
It's time o' year for Hay.
And Broad - Sunburned Acquaintance
Discourse between the Toil -
And laugh, a homely species
That makes the Fences smile -

It seems so straight to lie away
From all of the noise of Fields -
The Busy Carts - the fragrant Cocks -
The Mower's Metre - Steals -

A Trouble lest they're homesick -
Those Farmers - and their Wives -
Set separate from the Farming -
And all the Neighbors' lives -

A Wonder if the Sepulchre
Don't feel a lonesome way -
When Men - and Boys - and Carts - and June,
Go down the Fields to "Hay" -

—J529/F582/M266

In June, New England farmers would mow their hayfields, gather the hay into hay*cocks* to protect it from dew or possible showers, and then carry it to the barn in carts. It was very hard work, perhaps the most strenuous time of year for a farmer. The word *toil* in line 6 would have carried that association with it in this context. The laughter of the neighbors is a *homely species*. What does she mean? The word *homely* is a mild pejorative in modern use, and, in his 1841 dictionary, Mr. Webster seems to have thought so too.

HOME´LY, a. [from home.]
1. Of plain features; not handsome; as, a homely face. It expresses less than ugly. Let time, which makes you homely, make you wise.
2. Plain; like that which is made for common domestic use; rude; coarse; not fine or elegant; as, a homely garment; a homely house; homely fare.

Here, however, is a twentieth century definition from Webster's New Universal Unabridged Dictionary, Third Edition:

HOME´LY a.
1. originally, (a) of the home; domestic; (b) familiar; intimate; (c) fond of home
2. (a) characteristic of, or suitable for, home life; simple; plain; every day; as, homely virtues; (b) crude; unpolished.
3. Not attractive; plain; ugly

It is perhaps the earlier, more charitable meaning of the word that the poet applies to her neighbors. The Emily Dickinson Lexicon (EDL) concurs:

HOMELY (HOMELIER, HOMELIEST), adj.
Humble; simple; common; modest; ordinary; everyday.

The word *species*, mostly used in a zoological context today, and which calls Charles Darwin to mind, had several definitions, from science to coinage; the third of these was:

SPE-CIES, n
3. Sort; kind; in a loose sense; as, a species of low cunning in the world; a species of generosity; a species of cloth.

A certain kind of laugh is heard, then, of the sort heard every day, humble, simple, common. Also heard is the sound of the *mower*. By mid–nineteenth century, mechanized means of cutting the hay had come into use; the hand-wielded scythe was being replaced by the mechanical mower. The man operating the mower could also be called the mower. The poet hears the regular sound of the mower at work, suggesting the rhythm heard in a metrical poem, its *metre*. It's spelled "meter" today. Mr. Webster had something to say about that!

ME´TRE, n. [See METER.]
ME´TER, n.

Measure; verse; arrangement of poetical feet, or of long and short syllables in verse. Hexameter is a meter of six feet. This word is most improperly written metre. How very absurd to write the simple word in this manner, but in all its numerous compounds, meter, as in diameter, hexameter, thermometer, &c.

Well, Emily Dickinson seems to have preferred the French spelling! *Sepulchre* is also the French spelling of the English *sepulcher*:

SEP´UL-CHER, n.
A grave; a tomb; the place in which the dead body of a human being is interred, or a place destined for that purpose.

For another poem evoking rural life in mid-century America, see "'Twas just this time, last year, I died" (J445/F344/M181).

Feeling the Cycles of the Seasons

Besides portraying a part of rural life, "I'm sorry for the Dead - Today -" conveys a seasonal feeling—that of summer, when the hay is mown and gathered. Each of the four seasons in New England brings with it pronounced change in climate, landscape, flora and fauna. One of the first signs of spring was the arrival of the robin, returning from his winter range in the south (with the warmer weather of recent years, the robins have begun to remain through the winter in some areas), as were the appearance of the daffodil, and the bees. When you read of the *first Robin* in the next poem, you are to realize that spring has arrived, the natural world is waking from its winter slumber, and more temperate weather is felt once more.

I dreaded that first Robin, so,
But He is mastered, now,
I'm some accustomed to Him grown,
He hurts a little, though -

I thought if I could only live
Till that first Shout got by -
Not all Pianos in the Woods
Had power to mangle me -

I dared not meet the Daffodils -
For fear their Yellow Gown
Would pierce me with a fashion
So foreign to my own -

I wished the Grass would hurry -
So - when 'twas time to see -
He'd be too tall, the tallest one
Could stretch - to look at me -

"A Spring Robin at the Dickinson Homestead" (photograph by Michael C. Medeiros).

I could not bear the Bees should come,
I wished they'd stay away
In those dim countries where they go,
What word had they, for me?

They're here, though; not a creature failed -
No Blossom stayed away
In gentle deference to me -
The Queen of Calvary -

Each one salutes me, as he goes,
And I, my childish Plumes,
Lift, in bereaved acknowledgment
Of their unthinking Drums -
—J348/F347/M183

Several of Dickinson's poems welcome the arrival of spring ("Dear March - Come in -" J1320/F1320/M577), and others express a disinclination toward winter ("Distrustful of the Gentian -" J20/F26/M34), yet this poem seems to take the opposite view. Why, Dickinson doesn't tell us, so we readers are left to supply our own possible reason. When we do so, the poem becomes about us, about you. When the anniversary of the death of someone we once held dear approaches, whatever the season, it can bring that sorrowful loss sharply back to us. This may also happen after a lost love, or other painful experience. I am reminded of an old jazz song title, "Spring can really hang you up the most." Spring brings new awakenings, the robin's song, and the bright yellow daffodils. All become unbearable reminders of our loss. A similar theme is present in "The Morning after Woe" (Chapter 1).

A final note on the *Pianos*. Emily Dickinson played the piano from an early age, reportedly beautifully. A friend described her as "often at the piano, playing weird and beautiful melodies, all from her own inspiration."[1] The image of "pianos in the woods" has seemed to some readers a strange, surrealistic one, but surely the poet refers here to the music of the birds, insects, and breezes coming from the woods, not actual pianos out among the trees!

Spring leads into summer, and the poet creates an everlasting summer in words. As noted in the introduction, Dickinson's poems have been called "experiential." That is to say, the engaged reader often experiences in mind and body something of what is being related in the poem. David Porter expressed it well: "The poem ceases to become an external object of contemplation and becomes in fact experience, recreating within the reader a semblance of the experience itself, and not merely an inert reference to it."[2]

Here, then, is summer. Take this poem into your life. Learn it by heart and speak it as if it were your own. See if you don't feel a little intoxicated at some point!

> I taste a liquor never brewed -
> From Tankards scooped in Pearl -
> Not all the vats upon the Rhine
> Yield such an alcohol!
>
> Inebriate of air - am I -
> And debauchee of dew -
> Reeling, through endless summer days -
> From inns of Molten Blue -
>
> When "Landlords" turn the drunken Bee
> Out of the Foxglove's door, -
> When Butterflies - renounce their "drams"-
> I shall but drink the more!
>
> Till Seraphs swing their snowy Hats -
> And saints - to windows run -
> To see the little Tippler
> Leaning against the Sun -
>
> —J214/F207/M135

Landlords were innkeepers. *Inns* provided lodging and included taverns, where alcohol was served. Such establishments were not always the most reputable in town, and were frowned upon by the more conservative members of a community. Amherst, with its occasionally rowdy college students, was no exception, and ED's father, Edward Dickinson, was a leading force in the town's temperance movement, dedicated to restricting or prohibiting the sale of alcohol. This did not prevent the Dickinsons from keeping a wine cellar, and ED herself wrote to a favorite cousin, "When will you come to see us, and taste the currant wine?"[3] This apparent double standard arises from definite class-based sentiments that characterized much of the temperance movement. Upstanding citizens like the Dickinsons could be trusted to partake of "ardent spirits" responsibly, but not the lower classes. ED reverses the positions by having saints and angels looking approvingly at her in her drunken state, albeit drunk on the intoxicating air and *endless summer days*, not alcohol. The informal *thro* in the second stanza rather than "through" helps to lend the a more ballad-like light-heartedness to the poem. When intoxicated, you may act outside of social norms, and people will stare at you, but this *Tippler* is transforming heaven; the *Seraphs* are swinging their *snowy hats* in greeting rather than regarding her disapprovingly. The poem has a boastful tone—as drunkards often will. Drunkards were often pictured as leaning against lampposts to support themselves, but this tippler has a heavenly *Sun* for the purpose. She's out-drinking the butterflies and the bees, outdoing her drinking companion from "We - Bee and I" (Chapter 1). Dickinson chooses the *foxglove* for the poem, knowing that it is a favorite flower of the honeybee.

SER´APH, n
An angel of the highest order.

TANK´ARD, n.
A large vessel for liquors, or a drinking vessel, with a cover

The liquor that our *Tippler* tastes is perhaps the perfume of summer' wildflowers—*Tankards scooped in Pearl.* There is another, altogether different, but popular reading of this poem. Could it be a hummingbird?

The next poem moves us from high summer to a later time of year.

A period of unseasonably warm, balmy weather can occur in the autumn in New England, as well as in some other parts of the Northern United States, sometimes called "Indian Summer,"[4] a term of uncertain origin. Usually a killing frost has already occurred, and cold winter temperatures are felt in the air, when the weather takes a somewhat surprising turn. Summer seems to have changed her mind about leaving and to have decided to return. But New Englanders know the respite won't last, which brings a sweet regret to the sensitive soul. Thomas De Quincey, writing in 1878, offered this florid description:

> [...] it was itself attached by its place in the succession of annual phenomena to the *departing year.* [...] for august grandeur, self-sustained, it substituted a frailty of loveliness ; and for the riot and torrent rapture of joy in the fullness of possession, exchanged the moonlight hauntings of a visionary and saddened remembrance [...] The Indian Summer of Canada, and I believe universally of the Northern United States, is in November, at which season, and in *some climates*, a brief echo of summer uniformly occurs [...] it was regarded as a dependency, a season that looked back to something that had departed, a faint memorial (like the light of setting suns) recalling an archetype of splendors that were hurrying to oblivion.

Surely, Emily Dickinson could not have been unmoved at such times. Although she does not specify Indian Summer by name, one feels it in this poem.

> These are the days when Birds come back -
> A very few - a Bird or two -
> To take a backward look.
>
> These are the days when skies resume
> The old - old sophistries of June -
> A blue and gold mistake.
>
> Oh fraud that cannot cheat the Bee -
> Almost thy plausibility
> Induces my belief.
>
> Till ranks of seeds their witness bear -
> And softly thro' the altered air
> Hurries a timid leaf.
>
> Oh Sacrament of summer days,
> Oh Last Communion in the Haze -
> Permit a child to join.
>
> Thy sacred emblems to partake -
> Thy consecrated bread to take
> And thine immortal wine!
>
> —J130/F122/M81

The birds return, seemingly to look "back to something that had departed." Autumn presents its blue skies and golden sunlight, as a *sophist* presents a mistaken argument that is sound in appearance only. What *sophistries of June* are the autumn skies resuming? Is it perhaps the illusion that summer is returning, or that it will last? The bees are not fooled, nor is the speaker, despite *plausible* appearances. Even so, in the final two stanzas, the spell of the season triumphs over reason; the speaker is taken in after all, taking on the persona of a naïve and trusting child, and asking to take part in the *sacrament*. In Emily Dickinson's Protestant church, two sacraments, baptism and communion (or, The Lord's Supper), were recognized. The latter serves as the metaphor here, the communion being with nature. There may be an even more subtle implication, however. In the sacrament of communion, church members are following Jesus' instruction: "And he took bread, and gave thanks, and brake *it*, and gave unto them, saying, 'This is my body which is given for you: this do in remembrance of me'" (Luke 11:19). As the communion of the church is an act of remembrance of departed Jesus Christ, so the *Last Communion in the Haze*, a *Sacrament of summer days,* is an act of remembrance of departed summer days. Finally, in referring to herself as a *child* in the next-to-last stanza, Dickinson recalls the Bible again: "And Jesus called a little child unto him, and set him in the midst of them, And said, Verily I say unto you, Except ye be converted, and become as little children, ye shall not enter into the kingdom of heaven" (Matthew 18:2–3).

In a number of poems, Dickinson expresses a deep-felt, yet sweet regret as summer slips into autumn. In the first two verses of one such, shown below, she likens it to the feeling that a reader of an enchanting book experiences, when she realizes that she is coming closer to the end of the book. She would like it not to end. Pages in books are also sometimes called *leaves*. The *backward leaves* in line four refer to the pages toward a book's end, as well as suggesting the changing leaves on the trees of autumn.

Summer begins to have the look
Peruser of enchanting Book
Reluctantly but sure perceives
A gain upon the backward leaves

Autumn begins to be inferred
By millinery of the cloud
Or deeper color in the shawl
That wraps the everlasting hill
—J1682/F1693/M664

The poet likens the colorful autumn sky to millinery—head-dresses, hats or bonnets, laces, ribbons, and the like. The first stanza is not grammatically correct. Something seems to be missing. We will examine that aspect of this poem later in this book.

Reluctance to relinquish the bounty of summer for the privations of winter is expressed more directly in another poem. The crops, now near harvest time, tell of Autumn in a farming community.

I suppose the time will come
Aid it in the coming
When the Bird will crowd the Tree
And the Bee be booming.

I suppose the time will come
Hinder it a little
When the Corn in Silk will dress
And in Chintz the Apple

I believe the Day will be
When the Jay will giggle
At his new white House the Earth
That, too, halt a little -
—J1381/F1389/M591

The *time* referred to in the first verse is, of course, summer, when the birds are thick among the branches of the trees, and the bees are active in the meadows and gardens. *Aid it in the coming*, the poet prays, that it may arrive sooner rather than later. Instead of "buzzing," as we would usually express it, the poet hears the bees *booming,* as the bee himself must.

Later in the New England summer, the stalks of corn growing on the farms produce *silk*-like threads, for the purpose of pollination. The apples are brightly colored like *chintz*, a multi-colored cotton cloth. These are signs that autumn is nearly upon us. The poet prays, *Hinder it a little.*

More deeply, this poem can be read as a meditation on the passage of time. There is evidence to support such a reading. In 1850, when she was nineteen years old, Emily Dickinson received a written invitation to a candy-pulling party, a popular nineteenth-century entertainment among young people. The invitation was from a student at Amherst College, and there is sound, though not absolutely conclusive, evidence that there was a romantic attachment between the two.[5] Their relationship was thwarted, reportedly by Mr. Dickinson, Emily's father. She kept the invitation for the rest of her life, and twenty-five years after receiving it, she took it from where it had been resting, and wrote this poem about the passing of time on the reverse side.[6]

Another sign of seasonal change in New England is the sound of the crickets chirping in the darkening day and on into the night. We find the cricket in this delightful poem and in others that we will explore later:

'Twas later when the summer went
Than when the Cricket came -
And yet we knew that gentle Clock
Meant nought but Going Home -

'T was sooner when the Cricket went
Than when the Winter came
Yet that pathetic Pendulum
Keeps esoteric Time
—J1276/F1312/M574

Esoteric is held here to mean "Private; interior; confidential; fathomless; incomprehensible" (EDL). Other poems addressing the passing of summer into autumn are "Further in Summer than the Birds" (J1068/F895/M534), discussed in Chapter 4, and "The murmuring of the Bees, has ceased" (J1115/F1142/M540).

We've lingered between summer and autumn long enough. Perhaps we, too, are reluctant to let the birds and flowers go. Move ahead we must, however, with a poem about the cooler season, autumn.

Besides the Autumn poets sing
A few prosaic days
A little this side of the snow
And that side of the Haze -

A few incisive Mornings -
A few Ascetic Eves -
Gone - Mr. Bryant's "Golden Rod" -
And Mr. Thomson's "sheaves."

Still, is the bustle in the Brook -
Sealed are the spicy valves -
Mesmeric fingers softly touch
The Eyes of many Elves -

Perhaps a squirrel may remain -
My sentiments to share -
Grant me, Oh Lord, a sunny mind -
Thy windy will to bear!

—J131/F123/M82

Besides can mean "located by the side of a person or thing." Here it means "over and above, or distinct from." One might say, for example, "I can't take a vacation this year, I can't afford it. *Besides*, I want to finish this project." Certain poets, here identified as *the Autumn poets,* sing the praises of autumn in their poems, but besides them, there are a *few days* that also "sing" its praises. These days come before *the snows* of winter, and after the *hazy* days of summer. The lack of activity in nature indicates that it is late autumn, and winter will soon arrive. This is perhaps why they are *prosaic,* rather than poetical. Two "autumn poets" are named, with reference to a poem by each of them. *Mr. Bryant's "Golden Rod"* refers to William Cullen Bryant's "The Death of the Flowers." Mr. Thomson's "sheaves" is from James Thompson's "Autumn" (See Appendix A). These were familiar poems, from two well-known poets, at a period when poetry was much more widely enjoyed in America than it is today. Nature is closing down in preparation for winter. The spring torrents in *the brook* are *still* now.

Emily Dickinson was a master gardener and studied botany in school. Botanical terms appear in several poems, as in this one. The *valve*s are parts of certain flowering plants through which pollen is released. They are no longer active this late in the season. *Mesmeric,* a quasi-scientific term, can mean attracting and holding interest, as if by a spell. It is derived from the name of Franz Mesmer (1734–1815) who developed a practice which he called "Animal Magnetism," whereby he would induce patients into a deep sleep, and which has evolved into what we now call hypnosis. The *fingers* of the practitioner were especially prominent in Mesmerism. Here is a description from a medical journal of 1848: "Laying the hand upon the forehead or any other part, placing the points of the fingers on the eyes, or the tip of the nose, or the points of the fingers upon the points of his fingers, all are powerful in deepening and producing sleep."[7]

Nature's *Elves* are being prepared by a mysterious force, as if by a spell, for the long sleep of winter. With contrastingly wry humor, the poet speculates on the possible companionship of a squirrel, who will retreat to his den when the weather turns very cold, to share her sentiments. What those sentiments are she does not say, but in the final two lines, she anticipates the cold winds of winter.

The killing frost preceding the Indian Summer, mentioned by Mr. De Quincey above, is another harbinger of winter. In the next poem, the poet refers to it as "The blonde Assassin." In one view, the 18th century clockmaker God set everything in motion, and what he set in motion was natural selection, red in tooth and claw. Reactions to this poem vary widely among readers. Is this poem angry, nihilistic, ironic, resigned, violent?

Apparently with no surprise
To any happy Flower
The Frost beheads it at its play -
In accidental power -
The blonde Assassin passes on -
The Sun proceeds unmoved
To measure off another Day
For an Approving God
—J1624/F1668/M654

The frost is associated with death. It happens *Apparently with no Surprise* because it's the natural course of things. Humans feel that death somehow is unfair—unfair that we must perish, that blossoms must wither and die. The flower—nature itself—recognizes no such unfairness. Nor does *an Approving God,* in a phrase recalling the Bible's book of Genesis, in which God creates the world in a series of days, and "God saw that it was good" each day. This poem has been described as the human response to the Darwinian paradigm. The detached tone contrasts with the violence of the beheading, the assassin, and the accidental power, which in turn combine to mimic the indifference of nature to the survival of individuals.

Dickinson used the word *frost* 43 times in 41 poems. In the following, the association with mortality is quite direct. Yet, in the last stanza, the poem takes a turn. The snow is not pitiless, as one might expect it's *pitying!* End-of-poem surprises are a favorite device of this poet. More are presented in Chapter 9.

'Tis not that Dying hurts us so -
'Tis Living - hurts us more -
But Dying - is a different way -
A Kind behind the Door -

The Southern Custom - of the Bird -
That ere the Frosts are due -
Accepts a better Latitude -
We - are the Birds - that stay.

The Shiverers round Farmers' doors -
For whose reluctant Crumb -
We stipulate - till pitying Snows
Persuade our Feathers Home
—J335/F528/M290

The image of the shivering birds at the farmhouse door is drawn from Emily Dickinson's life in New England's often frigid winters. In 1880 she wrote to an acquaintance:

> The last April that father lived, I mean below, there were several snow storms, and the birds were so frightened and cold they sat by the kitchen door. Father went to the barn in his slippers and came back with a breakfast of grain for each, and hid himself while he scattered it, lest it embarrass them. Ignorant of the name or the fate of their benefactor, their descendants are singing this afternoon.[8]

By the month of April, winter has passed. Snow and freezing weather are unusual by this time. As told in the letter quoted above, the birds have returned from their winter ranges in the warmer southern *latitudes* of the globe, and are doubtless as disconcerted by the weather as are the human villagers. The season is early spring. *The dying*, too, are bound for *a better Latitude.* It is we who must remain and endure without them, and that *hurts us more.* But the metaphorical snows, the winter white toward the end of our own lives, must at last arrive. Taking pity on us, they will persuade us that it is time to go.

The next poem is one that even readers long acquainted with Dickinson have found difficult. Both vocabulary and structure contribute to the challenge. Winter seems to have arrived, and Dickinson expresses a longing for an imagined warmer climate.

Conjecturing a Climate
Of unsuspended Suns -
Adds poignancy to Winter -
The Shivering Fancy turns

To a fictitious Country
To palliate a Cold -
Not obviated of Degree -
Nor eased - of Latitude -
—J562/F551/M281

This poem may qualify as one of the "cryptically elusive poems" mentioned in the introduction to this book. One way to approach such a poem is to try to express it in prose. It's not always helpful, or even possible to do so, but it's worth a try. Beginning with the first word:

CON-JEC′TURE, v.t.
To guess; to judge by guess, or by the probability or the possibility of a fact, or by very slight evidence; to form an opinion at random.

An object may be *suspended* in space. An action may be suspended in time. An *unsuspended Sun* would be one that shines continuously. We might recast the poem this way: "What if there were a climate where the light of the sun is never suspended as it is at night, but shines always?" That thought, in the wintertime, would add a *poignancy* to the season. The imagination of the *shivering* person would *turn* to a make-believe *Country*. It would do so in order to lessen—or abate the *cold*.

PAL′LI-ATE, v.t.
1. To clothe. [Obs.]
2. To cover with excuse; to conceal the enormity of offenses by excuses and apologies; hence, to extenuate; to lessen; to soften by favorable representations; as, to palliate faults, offenses, crimes or vices.
3. To reduce in violence; to mitigate; to lessen or abate; as, to palliate a disease.

The imagined country is not blocked from or prevented from enjoying higher *degree*s of temperature;

OB′VI-ATE, v.t.
Properly, to meet in the way; to oppose; hence, to prevent by interception, or to remove at the beginning or in the outset; hence in present usage, to remove in general, as difficulties or objections; to clear the way of obstacles in reasoning, deliberating or planning.

Nor would it be *eased* away from its temperate latitude on the globe. The word *eased* may be the most challenging to interpret in the poem. It seems to have a special meaning here. Among several definitions is:

EASE, v.t.
....*To ease off* or *ease away*, in seamen's language, is to slacken a rope gradually. *To ease a ship*, is to put the helm hard a-lee, to prevent her pitching, when close hauled.

Even today, to someone acting over-aggressively or hostilely we might say, "Hey, ease off, Mister." Our fictitious country will not be eased off of its latitude to a colder clime. Although Emily Dickinson probably never saw the ocean, she uses nautical terms and metaphors throughout her writing. The interpretation offered here would not be incongruent with the body of her work in any way.

The word poignant can have a softer meaning now than it did when Dickinson used it. Today, we might speak of a poignant piano piece that touches our heart, or we might describe a picture of a mother comforting a tearful child as poignant. However, from ED's Webster's:

POIGN-ANT, a.

1. Sharp; stimulating the organs of taste; as, poignant sauce.—
2. Pointed; keen; bitter; irritating; satirical; as, poignant wit.
3. Severe; piercing; very painful or acute; as, poignant pain or grief.—

Sharp—keen—severe—these words may well convey the poet's meaning and her feeling about winter.

Nevertheless, she did not fail to see the picturesque aspect of a winter scene. In this lovely description of a snowfall, the word "snow" never appears, Yet, we see it by the second line.

It sifts from Leaden Sieves -
It powders all the Wood.
It fills with Alabaster Wool
The Wrinkles of the Road -

It makes an Even Face
Of Mountain, and of Plain -
Unbroken Forehead from the East
Unto the East again -

It reaches to the Fence -
It wraps it Rail by Rail
Till it is lost in Fleeces -
It deals Celestial Vail

To Stump, and Stack - and Stem -
A Summer's empty Room -
Acres of Joints, where Harvests were,
Recordless, but for them -

It Ruffles Wrists of Posts
As Ankles of a Queen -
Then stills its Artisans - like Ghosts -
Denying they have been -

—J311/F291/M248

There are five versions of this poem extant. This is the earliest and the longest. Indeed, ED sent another version of this poem to a correspondent in 1883, referring to it as "the Snow."[9] Is the snow sifting itself from the leaden sieves, or is it being sifted by a hidden force or power? The answer may lie somewhere in later stanzas. *Alabaster* appears in two other poems, "Safe in their Alabaster Chambers" (J216/F124/M83, 122) and "Praise it - 'Tis dead" (J1384/F1406/M595), in both of which it is associated with death. The body of a dead Caucasian person is pale, like alabaster, as is the marble of a mausoleum. And, Dickinson was certainly not the first to liken fallen snow to *wool.* From the Old Testament of the Bible: "He giveth snow like wool; he scattereth the hoarfrost like ashes" (Psalms 47:16).

It should be noted that ED uses the word *wrinkled* in a poetic way that would not be heard in daily conversation. The roads of her time were inlaid with ruts from wagon wheels, and, being unpaved, would have had uneven surfaces even in the best of weather. In describing the roads as "wrinkled," she shows one small example of the originality of word choice that so delights her readers.

In the fourth stanza, the *Vail* of snow-cover has fallen over *stumps* of trees that have been cut, *stacks* of firewood (hopefully, the hay is in the barn by this time), and the *stems* of harvested crops. *Joints* refers to the stems, or stubble, that is left in the fields after the crops are harvested, from a term in botany

> JOINT, n.
> 3. A knot; the union of two parts of a plant; or the space between two joints; an internode; as, the *joint* of a cane, or of a stalk of maiz. [corn]

The field now resembles a room that has been emptied of its furniture, with just a few discarded remnants left behind. We are grateful for the remnants, though, because otherwise the summer's bounty would be *Recordless*—not recorded—we would never have known it had been. The word "Recordless" does not appear in Dickinson's dictionary. In prose, the word would be "unrecorded," but Dickinson coined the word, giving her the three syllables that she required.

And finally, in the last stanza, "it" *stills its artisans like ghosts.* Whose artisans? Does the snow have artisans? During the snowfall, the snow makes a uniform white face of mountain and of plane, wraps fence-posts in celestial fleeces, turns the harvested fields into empty rooms and causes wooden posts to resemble ankles of a queen. The artisans that did this are the snowflakes themselves. "It" now stills the flakes of snow. Again, the question: Is the snow sifting itself from the leaden sieves, or is it being sifted by a hidden force or power?

Some scholars have suggested that ED might have written this poem in response to Ralph Waldo Emerson's "The Snow-Storm" (Appendix A).

With the end of winter, spring returns. Rather than leave our poet there in the cold, why not end the seasonal cycle where it began, with a paean to spring? Enter, then, the Robin, but this time in company with a Cuckoo, a bird not native to America.

> The Robin's my Criterion for Tune -
> Because I grow - where Robins do -
> But, were I Cuckoo born -
> I'd swear by him -
> The ode familiar - rules the Noon -
> The Buttercup's, my Whim for Bloom -
> Because, we're Orchard sprung -
> But, were I Britain born,
> I'd Daisies spurn -
> None but the Nut - October fit -
> Because, through dropping it,
> The Seasons flit - I'm taught -
> Without the Snow's Tableau
> Winter, were lie - to me-
> Because I see - New Englandly -
> The Queen, discerns like me -
> Provincially -
>
> —J285/F256/M126

As has been noted, the returning *Robin* is an early sign of the welcome spring in North America, and the sound of his song lifts the poet's heart. She surmises, though, that were she not a native of New England, but rather a native of some other land, where perhaps the *Cuckoo* is the bird of spring, why then the Cuckoo would be her *Criterion for Tune*—the tune by which she would judge all others. The familiar *ode* (a short poem or song) will always be the one preferred at *Noon* (for ED the choicest of summer hours). Likewise, were she to have a sudden fancy—a *Whim*—for a flower, she would choose *the buttercup,* a very common local wildflower. The Dickinson household owned an *orchard*, and buttercups would have been abundant there, as they are still today on the Dickinson property. Also very common in New England is the *Daisy*, but were she born *in Britain*, she doesn't doubt that she would *spurn* it in favor of a flower native to that country. In the autumn month of *October*, the nuts are ripening and dropping to the ground. For the poet, this seems *fit* to mark the season, as nothing else quite would. And without the *Snow*, it just wouldn't be W*inter*. Even today, a resident of the northern states of America, spending a December in a southern, almost tropical state like Florida will likely remark, "It just doesn't seem like Christmas without snow."

In the last two lines, the poet concludes that the Queen of England—Britain born—would see things the same way, as a native of her particular part of the world. In America, however, the word *provincially* can sometimes have a mildly pejorative flavor. If we judge some persons to be limited in their views by a narrowness born of a life confined to a small place and narrow, limited acquaintance, we might characterize them as provincial. So this is an interesting word in this context—comparing herself (the financially well off Dickinsons were of a socio-economic class sometimes called "the provincial elite" because they lived in rural areas) to a monarch at a time when Queen Victoria of England presided over a global empire. "Oh, you can call me provincial," she seems to say. "Yeah, I'm provincial—like the Queen of an empire!" The message of this poem is universal. We gravitate toward what we're accustomed to. We prefer the places and things with which we've developed an affinity over the course of our lives. Note that the poem has taken us through all four seasons of the year.

The Railroad Comes to Town

During Emily Dickinson's lifetime, railroads were being built and expanded rapidly throughout North America. Her politically active father was instrumental in getting the railroad to come to Amherst in 1853. The line originated in New London, Connecticut, approximately 100 miles to the south of Amherst. In June, shortly after the first locomotives began running, the town celebrated with a march through the streets, augmented by a contingent of enthusiasts who had come up from New London for the occasion. ED records her observations of that event:

> The New London Day passed off grandly - so all the people said - it was pretty hot and dusty, but nobody cared for that. Father was as usual, Chief Marshall of the day, and went marching around the town with New London at his heels like some old Roman General, upon a Triumph Day [...] Carriages flew like sparks, hither, and thither and yon, and they all said t'was fine. I spose ["spose" is a contraction of "suppose."] it was - I sat in Prof Tyler's woods and saw the train move off, and then ran home again for fear someone would see me, or ask me how I did.[10]

In her well known poem about a train, she recorded what she saw from those woods. Note that nowhere in the poem do the words "train" or "locomotive" appear.

> I like to see it lap the Miles -
> And lick the Valleys up -
> And stop to feed itself at Tanks -
> And then - prodigious step
>
> Around a Pile of Mountains -
> And supercilious peer
> In Shanties - by the sides of Roads -
> And then a Quarry pare

To fit it's [*sic*] sides
And crawl between
Complaining all the while
In horrid - hooting stanza -
Then chase itself down Hill -

And neigh like Boanerges -
Then - prompter than a Star
Stop - docile and omnipotent
At its own stable door -
—J585/F383/M204

The engine moves through the landscape of mountains and valleys like an animal, *lapping* and *licking* and *feeding* as it goes, travelling not only around mountains, but also tunneling through them. To do so, it must cut through the rock. Dickinson uses the domestic, household term, *pare,* as one might pare an apple. A place from which stone is cut for use in building or other purposes is called a *Quarry. Boanerges* was a name given to more than one race horse in the nineteenth century and later. The word *lap* serves a dual purpose; race horses run in *laps* around a race track. The locomotive was sometimes referred to as the "iron horse," a term coined by the first Native Americans to behold one. The name Boanerges comes originally from the Bible: "And James the son of Zebedee, and John the brother of James; and he named them Boanerges, which is, The sons of thunder" (Mark 3:17).

The poet gives the engine a haughty, aloof personality as it *peers* into the *shanties* with a *supercilious* air. The shanties were the makeshift dwellings of the men who came to work on the railroads, and of their families. These were largely Irish immigrants, many of whom were escaping a famine that struck Ireland in the 1840's. Edward Dickinson was landlord to some of these workers. Women and girls among these families were often employed as domestic servants by the established and more prosperous residents of the towns. The Dickinsons employed farmhands as well as household help from this community. A number of Irish women worked in the Dickinson Home as maids. "Bridget" was a name that could stand as shorthand for any Irish woman or girl, which is how it is employed in the next poem.

The Spider as an Artist
Has never been employed -
Though his surpassing Merit
Is freely certified

By every Broom and Bridget
Throughout a Christian Land -
Neglected Son of Genius
I take thee by the Hand -
—J1275/F1373/M519

The scene is that of the maid, coming upon a spider web as she goes about her household duties. With her broom she sweeps the web away. The spider is a neglected artist of *surpassing Merit,* but nevertheless is swept away in a trice by the swipe of a broom. Emily's admiration for the spider and her compassion for his common plight can be found again in "The spider holds a Silver Ball" (J605/F513/M251).

THREE

The Private Poet

"My Business is Circumference."—L268, July 1862

The above quotation is among the most often cited from Emily Dickinson's correspondence, yet there is far from unanimous agreement on what, exactly, she meant when she wrote it. In this chapter, we consider words which, for Dickinson, are freighted with private meaning. It's not that she created a coded language for herself, but rather that she appropriated certain words to her own special purposes, purposes that are not always evident to the rest of us. It seems as if she chose words in our standard vocabulary and added her own dimensions to each one. We glean these other dimensions only by examining the words in the context of her entire body of work. For instance, we may find a clue to her meaning in the above quote in another letter, written to Dr. and Mrs. J.G. Holland in which she declares, "My business is to love." Are love and Circumference the same thing, or are they alike in some way? Or, do they both point to something more? Let's begin with the word as commonly used during the poet's lifetime and then move on to discover new and original ways that she used it.

Circumference

The word *Circumference* was in use in Emily Dickinson's lifetime in ways other than mathematically. Ralph Waldo Emerson, in his essay entitled *Nature,* for example, wrote, "A fact is the end, or last issue of spirit. The visible creation is the terminus or the circumference of the invisible world." Whether Dickinson was inspired by Emerson or by some other source, she made this word her own.

CIR-CUM′FER-ENCE, n.

1. The line that bounds a circle; the exterior line of a circular body; the whole exterior surface of a round body; a periphery.
2. The space included in a circle.
3. An orb; a circle; any thing circular or orbicular.

From these definitions, we see that Circumference is a limit, setting a boundary and containing a finite area. Circumference also marks the furthest points out from the center of a circle, the points most remote from that center. When reading a Dickinson Circumference poem (there are seventeen of them) it's helpful to keep these two aspects of the word in mind, as one, or the other, or both may be implied. In the next poem, for instance, *this Circumference* refers to the vastness of time expressed in the first line. Circumference seems to hold all of that vastness within its bounds.

Time feels so vast that were it not
For an Eternity -
I fear me this Circumference
Engross my Finity -

To His exclusion, who prepare
By Processes of Size
For the Stupendous Vision
Of his Diameters -

—J802/F858/M394

The word *Finity* does not appear in ED's Webster's, nor does it appear in standard dictionaries of the English language, but that should not surprise us by now. The online EDL gives "Instance of finiteness or limitation; [fig.] mortal life; short existence" as definition and indeed, the word "finiteness" is what a speaker would use today. *My Finity*, then, we may read as "my finite mortal life." One way to interpret the poem is:

Time feels so vast that if it were not for the fact that *eternity* exists I'm afraid that *this Circumference* would completely *engross* (take up and absorb) this finite life of mine, and it would do so to the *exclusion* of *Eternity* and God. I am preparing, by *processes of size* (expanding my Circumference) for the infinite circumference of eternity, which must be of *stupendous diameters*. *Diameters* evokes the same circle image as circumference does. The sense of circumference as a limit needing expansion is implied.

In this challenging poem, Circumference is a finite boundary between the speaker and eternity, indeed, between *time* itself and eternity. It also contains within it all the vastness of time. Our lives move in time. In eternity, which lies beyond Circumference, there is no time for Dickinson. The distinction between time and eternity is one that will come into focus by repeated encounters with it in other poems later in this book. As she wrote to her dear friend, Susan Gilbert, (Later, her sister-in-law Susan Dickinson): "We were much afflicted yesterday, by the supposed removal of our Cat from time to Eternity."[1]

Her Circumference is expandable toward eternity, but can never encompass it, nor can the speaker know what lies beyond her Circumference. The cure for this condition of not knowing would be faith, which is absent in this poem. Emily Dickinson's personal doubts about immortality, explicitly expressed in so much of her writing, is perhaps manifest here. In this next short poem, we can see that Dickinson associates this threshold, Circumference, with awe.

> Circumference thou Bride of Awe
> Possessing thou shalt be
> Possessed by every hallowed Knight
> That dares to covet thee
> —J1620/F1636/M648

Circumference, situated on the threshold between conscious experience and the unknown, is wedded in the poet's mind to *Awe*. "Thou shalt not covet thy neighbor's wife," God commands.[2] The knight covets Circumference, the *Bride of Awe*. He possesses her and she possesses him, but he has not transcended her to reach Awe. Circumference stands between them. Barton Levy St. Armand has observed,

> "Circumference" is one of Dickinson's most discussed concepts, with Sir Thomas Browne, Elizabeth Barrett Browning, and Ralph Waldo Emerson cited as its immediate progenitors. But anyone who has read Jorge Luis's Borges essay "The Fearful Sphere of Pascal" must realize the difficulty of tracing this topos[3] to any particular source, and a scholar familiar with Romantic literature soon realizes that "circumference" was one of the buzzwords of Dickinson's time, though few used it with such emblematic terseness and density.[4]

Dickinson doesn't write about transcending a limited existence to reach the sublime. Instead, she finds truth and beauty within the limits of experience. We live our lives in finite time and space. Where finite experience meets the infinite sublime is Circumference. Beyond, after death, is unknown. Circumference stands between.

North, South, East and West

"Vinnie would send her love, but she put on a white frock and went to meet tomorrow - a few minutes ago. Mother would send her love - but she is in the 'Eave Spout,' sweeping up a leaf, that blew in, last November. Austin would send his - but he don't live here - now - He married - and went East." So wrote Emily Dickinson to a friend around August 1861.[5] Her brother, Austin, had indeed married five years earlier, but he moved about 300 feet (91 meters) *west* of Emily's house and lived there for the rest of his life. The word "East" in this context cannot refer to a physical direction or geographical location.

Emily Dickinson used the four cardinal points of the compass, North, South, East, and West, to stand for different aspects of life. In this she is perhaps *semi*-private, in that she joins a very old tradition in literature and story-telling that has attached a range of symbolic meaning and emotional significance to each point of the compass. The North is associated with cold, darkness, hardiness, austerity, self-denial, as well as meaning simply a literal direction. The words *arctic* and *polar* can also stand in for the same qualities. She will select where in such a range of associations to locate meaning, according to her need. The south is associated with warmth, passion, sensuality, light, freedom. The East, where the sun rises, is associated with birth, new life. A Dickinson biographer points out that among many Reformed Protestants, "East," or "Eastering," were common coinage for a resurrection after death—in short, going to Heaven.[6] However the East may also be associated with exile and suffering. Adam and Eve were exiled by God from the Garden of Eden eastward. Dickinson also evokes the East of Oriental luxury and gorgeous fabrics in her poems. The West, where the sun sets, may be associated with the end of life, eternity, and the unknown. Scholars have found other ways of interpreting Dickinson's cardinal points beside what's been given here,[7] but on these there does seem to be general agreement.

Ourselves were wed one summer - dear -
Your Vision - was in June -
And when Your little Lifetime failed,
I wearied - too - of mine -

And overtaken in the Dark -
Where You had put me down -
By Some one carrying a Light -
I - too - received the Sign.

'Tis true - Our Futures different lay -
Your Cottage - faced the sun -
While Oceans - and the North must be -
On every side of mine

'Tis true, Your Garden led the Bloom,
For mine - in Frosts - was sown -
And yet, one Summer, we were Queens -
But You - were crowned in June -

—J631/F596/M272

The cold fastness of the North seems to imply privation. This poem, written probably in 1863, is thought by some to honor Elizabeth Barrett Browning, whom ED greatly admired, and who died in June of 1861. In her famous book-length narrative poem, *Aurora Leigh,* Browning's protagonist lives a happy life in sunny Italy, before moving north to England. Dickinson contrasts her own situation, surrounded by *Oceans and the North,* with that of the renowned and gifted Browning, using the North/South symbolism of Browning's *Aurora Leigh.* She does not tell us by whom she was *overtaken in the dark*—the dark associated with the North—but whoever it was brought light, perhaps a new light of poetic inspiration. In a letter to Thomas Wentworth Higginson, she apologized for herself, assigning responsibility for some possible fault to "the North." We don't know what the fault was, because much of the correspondence, especially his letters to her, has been lost, but she imputes a "bleak simplicity" to herself—an austerity—associated with the North: "Dear friend, I trust as you ask - If I exceed permission, excuse the bleak simplicity that knew no tutor but the North."[8]

The "Errand into the Wilderness"[9] of Emily Dickinson's Puritan forebears demanded the utmost in resolution and self-reliance. Dickinsons were among the earliest settlers of the New England colonies, and in the pursuit of religious ends, they endured privation in the harsh northern winters of a new and often hostile land which they called a "howling wilderness." It took strength, courage and fierce determination just to survive. The virtues of self-denial, endurance, simplicity and courage were most valued. These qualities belong to the North, as heard in the next poem.

I think the Hemlock likes to stand
Upon a Marge of Snow -
It suits his own Austerity -
And satisfies an awe

That men, must slake in Wilderness -
And in the Desert - cloy -
An instinct for the Hoar, the Bald -
Lapland's - necessity -

The Hemlock's nature thrives - on cold -
The Gnash of Northern winds
Is sweetest nutriment - to him -
His best Norwegian Wines -

To satin Races - he is nought -
But Children on the Don,
Beneath his Tabernacles, play,
And Dnieper Wrestlers, run.

—J525/F400/M213

The Hemlock seems pleased with his northern clime. He stands on just a *Marge*—a margin or a border—of snow, and it suits the *austerity* of his nature. *Awe* is a word of great significance in Dickinson's writing. She uses it twenty-three times in her poems alone. The Emily Dickinson Lexicon gives these wide-ranging meanings:

AWE (-s) n
A. Reverence; sublimity; veneration; respectful fear.
B. Terror; fright; trepidation; feeling of apprehension.
C. Admiration; wonder; amazement.

It is the first set of meanings that seems to fit this poem. The awe embodied by the Hemlock must be sought by *men* in *Wilderness* and *desert*. Few if any reading these lines in nineteenth-century Massachusetts would have failed to think instantly of Moses leading his people out of the Wilderness to the Promised Land, as told in the Bible's Book of Exodus. *Cloy* today is most often heard in its adjectival form, "cloying," meaning an excess of sweetness, richness, or sentiment. From ED's dictionary:

CLOY′ING, ppr.
Filling; filling to satiety, or disgust

CLOY, v.t.
1. Strictly, to fill; to glut. Hence, to satisfy, as the appetite; to satiate. And as the appetite when satisfied rejects additional food, hence, to fill to lothing [sic]; to surfeit. Who can cloy the hungry edge of appetite/By bare imagination of a feast?—Shak.

To comfortable citizens in satin vests, the Hemlock is of no account, but to those young and hardy dwellers around the Don and Dnieper rivers, both in the cold climes of Russia, the mighty Hemlock and all of the virtues he embodies is a familiar part of life.

Opposite the north on the compass, the south represents opposite kinds of experience. A south wind brings a breath of warmth to the heart as well as to the body, especially welcome after a season of cold days and colder nights. Here, the poet makes of that a metaphor for life lived to the fullest.

I think To Live - may be a Bliss
To those who dare to try -
Beyond my limit to conceive -
My lip - to testify -

I think the Heart I former wore
Could widen - till to me
The Other, like the little Bank
Appear - unto the Sea -

I think the Days - could every one
In Ordination stand -

And Majesty - be easier -
Than an inferior kind -

No numb alarm - lest Difference come -
No Goblin - on the Bloom -
No start in Apprehension's Ear,
No Bankruptcy - no Doom -

But Certainties of Sun -
Midsummer - in the Mind -
A steadfast South - upon the Soul -
Her Polar time - behind -

The Vision - pondered long -
So plausible becomes
That I esteem the fiction - real -
The Real - fictitious seems -

How bountiful the Dream -
What Plenty - it would be -
Had all my Life but been Mistake
Just rectified - in Thee
—J646/F757/M350

The poet imagines what *Bliss* one might find were one to try. Why does it require daring? "Life shrinks or expands in proportion to one's courage," Anais Nin once wrote.[10] The poet imagines that her *Heart* is capable of expanding to so great a capacity that her former heart would look as small then as the mere *Bank* of the *Sea* would appear to the entire sea. She only imagines this. She elaborates further on what such a wonderful state would be like with the interesting expression, C*ertainties of Sun*. A clue to what she is saying lies in the final verse of another poem:

The Robin is the One
That speechless from her Nest
Submit that Home - and Certainty
And Sanctity, are best
—J828/F501/M488

Dickinson places *Certainty* on the same level of value as sanctity and her beloved home. To be certain is to be free of doubt, a state she likens to *Midsummer—in the Mind*—conveying a feeling of the warmth of the *South* wind, felt not upon the body, but inwardly. She contrasts that condition to a previous *Polar time*, employing a stand-in term for the North's cold and privation. The blissful vision turns poignant in the final two stanzas, as we hear the poet's longing for such a state. All could be set right—*rectified*—by the person addressed as *Thee,* but this person is apparently not available. Some read the poem as addressed to an unavailable love, some as an unknowable God. The poet has left that question open, so you may make the poem your own.

Dickinson may also evoke the South and all that it stands for indirectly, for example, by naming a geographical location in a more southerly part of the world from New England. At Naples and to the south, volcanoes and earthquakes tell of hidden passion and power.

> A still - Volcano - Life -
> That flickered in the night -
> When it was dark enough to do
> Without erasing sight -
>
> A quiet - Earthquake Style -
> Too subtle to suspect
> By natures this side Naples -
> The North cannot detect
>
> The Solemn - Torrid - Symbol -
> The lips that never lie -
> Whose hissing Corals part - and shut -
> And Cities - ooze away -
>
> —J601/F517/M253

This is not the only poem in which Dickinson has a volcano.[11] Often the volcano appears to be a metaphor for her own passionate nature. It may be so in this poem, or it may be that of another person whom she has observed or that she imagines. As is so often the case, she does not specify, leaving it for the reader to find her own best reading. Try reading this poem as if *you* are the speaker; it can be a very rewarding and meaningful approach to a Dickinson poem.

On the original manuscript, Dickinson had first written "A still - Volcanic - Life" in the first line. She crossed it off and changed it to *Volcano.* It appears from this that she wants the word *volcano* to function as an adjective describing *Life.* We read the line, then, not as "Life is like a volcano," but as referring to a particular volcano-like life, potentially explosive. So far, yes, the volcano is *still.* The subject's *style* is like an *Earthquake,* but an outwardly quiet one—the tremors of this quake register subtly on the Richter scale, *too subtle* in fact, for people whose natures are cold—those from "*The North*"—even to suspect that they exist. No, only those from the warm south, familiar with hot passion, will feel and recognize those subtle tremors. The slumbering volcano, which, when it opens its lips—those *hissing corals*—burying cities in *oozing* lava, symbolizes those passions.

If the South can claim all the warmth and passion then, what might Emily have been communicating when she wrote that her brother, Austin, married and went East? "The Lord God planted a garden eastward in

Eden" (Genesis 2:8). The Garden of Eden—Paradise—was located in the East according to the Old Testament of the Bible. As already noted, when Adam and Eve were exiled, they were driven out of the garden eastward, away from God. When the Israelites were exiled in Babylon, they were exiled eastward, to spend years in suffering and hardship. The East, then, has both positive and negative associations from the Bible. We hear the latter in a letter from ED to a new friend, Kate Scott Turner (Anthon), a brilliant woman whom she loved and admired.

> Dare you dwell in the *East* where we dwell? Are you afraid of the sun? - When you hear the new violet sucking her way among the sods, will you be resolute? All *we* are *strangers* - dear - the world is not acquainted with us, because we are not acquainted with her. And Pilgrims! - Do you hesitate? And *soldiers* oft - some of us victors, but those I do not see tonight, owing to the smoke. We are hungry, and thirsty sometimes - We are barefoot - and cold -"[12]

In this letter, Emily was inviting Kate, already acquainted with Susan Dickinson, into the inner circle of her own select company, which included brother Austin and Susan. We may not know what circumstances she is describing in this figurative language, but it isn't an Eden. What would it be like to be banished from the Garden, from Paradise? That is perhaps impossible to put into words—unless you're Emily Dickinson.

> The lonesome for they know not What -
> The Eastern Exiles - be -
> Who strayed beyond the Amber line
> Some madder Holiday -
>
> And ever since - the purple Moat
> They strive to climb - in vain -
> As Birds - that tumble from the clouds
> Do fumble at the strain -
>
> The Blessed Ether - taught them -
> Some Transatlantic Morn -
> When Heaven - was too common - to miss -
> Too sure - to dote upon!
>
> —J262/F326 /M156

A psychic or spiritual state of longing is described in terms of travel. The expression *Eastern Exiles* evokes the gravitas of the aforementioned biblical exiles. The A*mber line* describes the breaking of dawn in the East. What has been lost and who has lost it Dickinson leaves unstated, for you to supply from your own life. What has been lost is irretrievable. Like trying to climb the *purple Moat* of the night sky, it is all *in vain.* She is reminded of birds tumbling *from the clouds* who can no longer sing the song—the *strain*—that *The Blessed Ether taught them.* Ether was thought in earlier times to permeate the universe as an invisible substance and in some traditions was considered spirit and associated with divinity. Because the story of the "Expulsion from Paradise," was so familiar to nineteenth-century Americans, the language cited here would have evoked the biblical story of man's fall from grace and banishment from the Garden of Eden. Dickinson employs the full weight of this narrative to measure the pain of loss. We have seen, however, that the east may also signify rebirth and new life. It may stand for warmth, passion, light, freedom. Note how very differently the East appears in the following poem:

Her Losses make our Gains ashamed -
She bore Life's empty Pack
As gallantly as if the East
Were swinging at her Back.
Life's empty Pack is heaviest,
As every Porter knows -
In vain to punish Honey -
It only sweeter grows -
—J1562/F1602/M727

When laboring against some adversity under especially advantageous conditions, we may speak of having "the wind at our back," aiding our efforts rather than opposing them. Here again, in this poem, the particular adversity is an experience of loss, a loss that leaves a feeling of emptiness. Emptiness, implying loneliness, is the hardest of all conditions to bear, the speaker implies, and so paradoxically, the *empty pack* feels *heaviest*. Yet *She*, the subject of this poem, *bore* it as if the warm wind of freedom were *swinging at her back*. The word "swinging" as used here is an example of Dickinson's strikingly original and effective use of common vocabulary. There is a free and easy feeling to this pulsating, assisting easterly wind.

Finally, we turn our gaze westward. In one simple elegant quatrain, Dickinson makes of the setting sun a metaphor for life's last hours and the end of time, and, for Dickinson, the end of time, as noted above, is eternity.

Look back on Time, with kindly eyes -
He doubtless did his best -
How softly sinks that trembling Sun
In Human Nature's West -
—J1478/F1251/M559

This is not a hard poem to interpret. *Human Nature's West* is surely the end, or toward the end, of life. The speaker looks back over the time now past, attributing to time the ability to act on its own, having *done his best*. She recognizes that it wasn't all perfect, and kindly assumes a charitable attitude toward time. "Well, you did your best," we may say in common parlance to a friend or neighbor whose disappointed efforts beg consolation. Because the poem is fairly easy to "get," we have a key to similar language appearing in other poems. Even without prior knowledge of how Dickinson uses the words *east* and *west*, however, it might be possible to glean it from the next poem alone:

> Said Death to Passion
> "Give of thine an Acre unto me."
> Said Passion, through contracting Breaths
> "A Thousand Times Thee Nay."
>
> Bore Death from Passion
> All His East
> He - sovereign as the Sun
> Resituated in the West
> And the Debate was done.
>
> —J1033/F988/M454

Youth has its passions as do the later stages of life. Passion may take form in the boundless enthusiasms of youth, powerful commitment to a belief in a cause developed over time, romantic love, or the joy of spiritual increase. In this poem, *Death* demands some territory from *Passion*. Passion will not yield, remaining steadfast in the face of death. Death then takes from passion everything belonging to the early stages of life—*His East*—as death does to all mortals who live long enough. The word *resituated* in the second verse is key. To resituate is to take a voluntary action. It implies conscious choice, and has an almost calculating flavor, like a move in chess. Passion is not coerced in this narrative. If I were to get out of the way of an oncoming bus, I probably wouldn't say that I had resituated myself onto the sidewalk unless I was trying to be funny. No, I'd say that I jumped, or that I got out of the way, or any one of a number of other expressions. In this verse, Passion, unsubdued in the face of relentless death, *resituates* in the last stage of life—*the West*—and a fine sunset.

Latitude, Degree, Meridian

Another of Emily Dickinson's special words, also related to geography, is "latitude." Her Webster's dictionary gives several definitions, one of which is "In geography, the distance of any place on the globe, north or south of the equator." The Emily Dickinson Museum in Amherst Massachusetts, for instance, is at latitude 42.375996. But *latitude* has other meanings as well, one of which is "Breadth; width; extent from side to side." We might say, for example, that certain parents allow their teenage son or daughter wide latitude in his or her activities, or we might ask our employer for some latitude in choosing how to complete a project. We have encountered this word previously in two poems: "'Tis not that Dying hurts us so" and "Conjecturing a Climate" (both in Chapter 2). In both poems, *latitude* is used in its literal geographical sense, or close to it. Not quite so in "Forever - is composed of Nows," another of Dickinson's better-known poems, which extends that word to a more figurative meaning.

> Forever - is composed of Nows -
> 'Tis not a different time -
> Except for Infiniteness -
> And Latitude of Home -
>
> From this - experienced Here -
> Remove the Dates - to These -
> Let Months dissolve in further Months -
> And Years - exhale in Years -
>
> Without Debate - or Pause -
> Or Celebrated Days -
> No different Our Years would be
> From Anno Dominies -
> —J624/F690/M334

Forever and *now* are temporal terms, and this poem is a meditation on time. Dickinson used the word forever in eleven poems, always in the sense of endless time. *Latitude of Home* must be an expression about time, then, not distance, and not about eternity either, since eternity is outside of time. We must go to our alternate definition of latitude as width, breadth, or extent. Indeed, forever is time of infinite extent. Dickinson creates a sense of a vast expanse of endless time by beginning with the particular, *Nows, experienced here,* and expanding out to the unimaginable *Forever composed of* Nows. *Home* is always here, now.

The Magna Carta was signed in AD 1297, a *celebrated day*. In much of the western world, the dates of great events in history are so recorded. But strip the dates away from our lives, the poet tells us, and let the *months* and *years* pass ever away. Then, our days would be no different from any other, and just as great as any *Anno Domini. Latitude of Home* expresses perfectly that enlarged value of the present.

In a lesser-known poem the word *latitude* again applies to something more than geographical distance.

> Delight is as the flight -
> Or in the Ratio of it,
> As the Schools would say -

The Rainbow's way -
A Skein
Flung colored, after Rain,
Would suit as bright,
Except that flight
Were Aliment -

"If it would last"
I asked the East,
When that Bent Stripe
Struck up my childish
Firmament -
And I, for glee,
Took Rainbows, as the common way,
And empty Skies
The Eccentricity -

And so with Lives -
And so with Butterflies -
Seen magic-through the fright
That they will cheat the sight -
And Dower latitudes far on -
Some sudden morn -
Our portion-in the fashion -
Done -

—J257/F317/M151

The *Delight* that we have in our experiences in life is in proportion to how quickly they take flight. "Sweeter than a vanished frolic/From a vanished green!" Dickinson wrote in an early poem.[13] A rainbow lasts only a short while, so we prize it the more. A ball of colored yarn—*A Skein*—would delight us just as much as a rainbow except for the rainbow's short duration. The rainbow is food for the soul.

AL´I-MENT, n.
That which nourishes; food; nutriment; any thing which feeds or adds to a substance, animal or vegetable, in natural growth

In the second verse, she remembers how, as a child, she thought that the rainbow, that *Bent Stripe*, might *last. Butterflies* live for only a week or two and all *Lives*, including those of the ones we love, are brief in the grand scheme of things. These beloved lives look magical to us in our fear that they too—*some sudden morn*—will be gone. Some species of butterfly migrate seasonally to other latitudes, and, in nineteenth-century America, vast in territory, when someone moved away it might well mean a friend removed permanently. When lives themselves are gone however, the *latitudes* that they occupy are not geographical. The *magic* of those lives is bestowed elsewhere. Among the several definitions for *dower,* a favorite word of Emily Dickinson, we have:

DOW′ER n
4. Endowment; gift.

Although Webster defined *dower* as a noun, Dickinson employs it here as a verb. It appears in fifteen Dickinson poems in both forms. See, for example, *Precious to Me—She still shall be* - (J727/F751/M377) for a noun usage.

Latitude is measured in degrees.[14] There are ninety degrees of latitude between the equator and each of the earth's poles. The circumference of a circle, our equator for instance, is divided into 360 degrees. Here are the first two of nine definitions given.

DE-GREE′, n
1. A step; a distinct portion of space of indefinite extent; a space in progression; as, the army gained the hill by degrees; a balloon rises or descends by slow degrees; and figuratively, we advance in knowledge by slow degrees. Men are yet in the first degree of improvement. It should be their aim to attain to the furthest degree, or the highest degree. There are degrees of vice and virtue.
2. A step or portion of progression, in elevation, quality, dignity or rank; as, a man of great degree. We speak of men of high degree, or of low degree; of superior or inferior degree. It is supposed there are different degrees or orders of angels.

Temperature, of course, is also measured in degrees. Water freezes at 32 degrees Fahrenheit, 0 degrees Celsius, for example. So this word can mean many things, and maybe that's why Dickinson liked it. She used it in eighteen poems.

The Moon is distant from the Sea -
And yet, with Amber Hands -
She leads Him-docile as a Boy -
Along appointed Sands -

He never misses a Degree -
Obedient to Her Eye
He comes just so far-toward the Town -
Just so far-goes away -

Oh, Signor, Thine, the Amber Hand -
And mine-the distant Sea -
Obedient to the least command
Thine eye impose on me -
—J429/F387M206

Degree as a measurement of distance on the globe certainly applies in this case, and, to this reader, with no ambiguity or suggestion of other meaning. The tides of the sea are moved along the latitudes and longitudes exactly as the gravitational force of the moon dictates, although the poet suggests the sea has an active role with the word *obeys,* and in noting that he *never misses*, as if there were some choice in the matter. The poet gives the moon an alliterative *Amber Hand* to move her *Sea,* an image that pleases the ear as well as the mind's eye. When low in the sky and under certain atmospheric conditions the moon can look the color of amber. As noted in Chapter 1, *Hand* can mean to manage or to conduct. In common parlance, "Let me give you a hand" is an offer to assist or to help. Thus the poet's *Amber Hand* conveys both the appearance and the action of the moon. In the first two stanzas, the moon is *She* and *Her,* while the sea is *Him,* and *He.* In the final stanza, she addresses a *Signor* as her moon, and she his sea, reversing the genders of the two parties. Who is leading whom, one wonders. For a similar questioning of gendered roles, see "In lands I never saw - they say" (J124/F108/M77).

In letters and poems Emily Dickinson strongly questioned the gender roles prevalent in her day. In the above poem, she does so with a gentle, almost coy, tone. In the next poem, the tone is very different. It is in the sense of personal elevation that the word *degree* appears in "Title divine - is mine!" but with a sharply ironic qualification.

Title divine - is mine!
The Wife - without the Sign!
Acute Degree - conferred on me -
Empress of Calvary!
Royal - all but the Crown!
Betrothed - without the swoon
God gives us Women -
When you - hold - Garnet to Garnet -
Gold - to Gold -
Born - Bridalled - Shrouded -
In a Day -
Tri Victory
"My Husband" - women say -
Stroking the Melody -
Is this - the way?
—J1072/F194/M701

Certainly in this poem we have a *degree* of "elevation, quality, dignity or rank," as given in definition two above. This is an *acute* degree, however, suggesting the pain of *Calvary* rather than elevation to the rank of *Empress.*

A-CUTE′, a.
1. Sharp at the end; ending in a sharp point; opposed to blunt or obtuse. An acute angle in geometry, is one which is less than a right angle, or which subtends less than ninety degrees. An acute angled triangle is one whose three angles are all acute, or less than ninety degrees each.
4. An acute disease, is one which is attended with violent symptoms, and comes speedily to a crisis, as a pleurisy; opposed to chronic.

She is an Empress without a crown, a *wife* without the *sign*, which many readers take to mean a wedding ring. She doesn't even get to experience the exhilarating *swoon* of the earthly bride, when wedding rings are exchanged. Garnet was in fact a popular gemstone for wedding rings in the mid–nineteenth century. But it will not be her fate to be *born* into new life (with a pun on being borne away by a man)—*bridalled* (made a bride with a pun on the bridle use to control a horse)—and *shrouded*—suggesting both the bridal vail and the burial shroud.

There is yet another word used for geographical location which Emily Dickinson favored:

> ME-RID′IAN, n.
>
> 1. In astronomy and geography, a great circle supposed to be drawn or to pass through the poles of the earth, and the zenith and nadir of any given place, intersecting the equator at right angles, and dividing the hemisphere into eastern and western. Every place on the globe has its meridian, and when the sun arrives at this circle, it is mid-day or noon, whence the name. This circle may be considered to be drawn on the surface of the earth, or it may be considered as a circle in the heavens coinciding with that on the earth.
>
> 2. Mid-day; noon.
>
> 3. The highest point; as, the meridian of life; the meridian of power or of glory.
>
> 4. The particular place or state, with regard to local circumstances or things that distinguish it from others. We say, a book is adapted to the meridian of France or Italy; a measure is adapted to the meridian of London or Washington. *Magnetic meridian*, a great circle, parallel with the direction of the magnetic needle, and passing through its poles

Emily Dickinson drew on the second and third definitions of meridian in poems, and in letters as well. When her beloved eight-year-old nephew Gilbert ("Gib") died in October of 1883, she sent the boy's mother, Susan Dickinson, a series of extraordinary condolence messages. In one of them, which one biographer declared "perhaps the finest she ever wrote to anybody,"[15] she wrote: "I see him in the star, and meet his sweet velocity in everything that flies - his life was like the bugle, which winds itself away, his elegy an echo - his Requiem ecstacy - Dawn and Meridian in one."[16]

In the following poem, a *surpassing sun* at the *Meridian* serves as metaphor for a "highest point," a "meridian of life," but is that what the speaker is claiming for herself?

> I see thee better - in the Dark -
> I do not need a Light -
> The Love of Thee - a Prism be -
> Excelling Violet -
>
> I see thee better for the Years
> That hunch themselves between -
> The Miner's Lamp - sufficient be -
> To nullify the Mine -

And in the Grave - I see Thee best -
Its little Panels be
Aglow - All ruddy - with the Light
I held so high, for Thee -

What need of Day -
To Those whose Dark - hath so - surpassing Sun -
It deem it be - Continually -
At the Meridian?

—J611/F442/M222

The speaker expresses a love that transcends all. She likens it to a light that, shining upon her beloved, enables her to see her friend more clearly. Her love is a prism which yields the entire visible spectrum, more abundant light than the most vivid violet. It has been years since they were last together the second stanza continues, with the image of the *Miner's Lamp* representing her love. The *Years That hunch themselves between* the pair would be as dark as inside a mine were it not for this light. The third stanza reveals the reason; the beloved is dead. The speaker will not abandon her love even so, claiming, heartbreakingly, that it is better this way. The love-light *nullifies* not only *the Mine*, but the very grave and death itself. Recall from the preface of this book that a mine, although a place of darkness, may also be a place where riches are found, and Dickinson does take advantage of that connotation in her poetry. In Dickinson's time, hand-held lanterns were used to see one's way in darkness. Stanza three ends with the image of her love as a lantern, which she *held high*, shining its light to make the *ruddy Panels* of the coffin or sepulchre *Aglow*. The poem ends with a triumphant rhetorical question. *What need* does one have *of Day*, which must inevitably wane into darkness, whose *Dark* is filled with the light of love that keeps one constantly and always at the highest point—*At the Meridian*? Each stanza mentions darkness—*the Dark, The Mine, the Grave.* Each also contains a more fully realized expression of light. In the structure of the poem, light dominates,

The word *noon* can stand in for meridian as well, meaning "Zenith, highest point of life" (EDL), as in this verse, from "I envy seas whereon he rides":

I envy Light - that wakes Him -
And Bells - that boldly ring
To tell Him it is Noon, abroad -
Myself - be Noon to Him -

—J498/F368/M195

She, the speaker, wants to be *Noon*, the high point of life, all that is desirable and good to him.

Film

Thomas Wentworth Higginson wrote of "That sensation we poor mortals often have, of being just on the edge of infinite beauty, yet with always a lingering film between, never presses down more closely than on days like this."[17] It was in this sense of the word *film* that Emily Dickinson wrote to friend, "I hope you are glad - Mary - no pebble in the Brook - today - no film on noon."[18] A film between us and a source of brightness, or a film on an otherwise transparent surface, obscures our view, and, for Dickinson, the word carries with it the association of the film that forms upon the eyes in death. To some readers, the next poem sounds like praise for the power of a poet's words. The first line, *She dealt her pretty words like Blades*, calls up images of dazzling artistry, perhaps. But the *film* in the third stanza, not to mention the *grimace* in the second, suggests a very different interpretation.

She dealt her pretty words like Blades -
How glittering they shone -
And every One unbared a Nerve
Or wantoned with a Bone -

She never deemed - she hurt -
That - is not Steel's Affair -
A vulgar grimace in the Flesh -
How ill the Creatures bear -

To Ache is human - not polite -
The Film upon the eye
Mortality's old Custom -
Just locking up - to Die.
—J479/F458/M230

The speaker of this poem has witnessed a cruel tongue in action. The word *pretty* is used sardonically. Words, like blades, can cut. As Shakespeare put it, "They that dally nicely with words may quickly make them *wanton*."[19] To *wanton* is to act excessively, and carelessly or loosely. (*Wanton* is seldom heard today its verb form, as ED is using it here.) The subject of the poem is unconcerned—not even fully aware—of the *Ache* that she is causing, seeing the resulting *grimace* as simply *impolite.* Among other poems where Dickinson uses the word film in this sense are "'Twas like a Maelstrom, with a notch" (J414/F425/M169), and in its verb form, "You see I cannot see - your lifetime" (J253/F313/M149). Reading the word *film* in these poems can prepare us for its even more figurative use in the final stanza of "You know that Portrait in the Moon," a poem of separation.

And when - Some Night - Bold - slashing Clouds
Cut Thee away from Me -
That's easier - than the other film
That glazes Holiday -
—J504/F676/M418

Someone, prefigured in earlier stanzas by the moon, has been cut away from her. When Christmas, Thanksgiving, and other holidays arrive, and friends and family gather together, the special someone is missed all the more acutely, which casts a shadow—a *glaze*—a *film*, over all. All of this is easier to bear than *the other film,* that final separator, death. The word glaze is especially effective in amplifying the import of the film, as we speak of eyes "glazing over," when we become detached from proceedings around us, and also of eyes glazing over in death. Both implications are present together.

Although a film can obscure vision, as a film on a window, for example, obscures the view to the outside, in the next short poem, Dickinson turns that meaning on its head.

The thought beneath so slight a film -
Is more distinctly seen -
As laces just reveal the surge -
Or mists the Appenine -
—J210/F203/M119

The film acts as an aid to perception now. A thought expressed in a slightly oblique or vailed manner may in fact make the underlying meaning more unmistakably recognizable. The heaving breast is more readily discernible thanks to the thin film of lace that covers it. The mighty *Appenine* (Apennine)mountain range looms more majestically in the mist than in the clear light of the sun.

Physiognomy

Physiognomy is generally considered a pseudo-science today, but belief in it dates back to the ancient Greek philosophers. It fell into disrepute during the Middle Ages, and then enjoyed something of a revival with English Romantic writers, including Charles Lamb (1775–1834) and Samuel Taylor Coleridge (1772–1834) which lasted into the late nineteenth century. It was founded on the belief that one could assess a person's character by a methodical examination of the person's physical features. More broadly defined, physiognomy could apply not only to persons, but to anything in the natural world. The broader definition of physiognomy was expressed by Sir Thomas Browne (1605–1682), whom Dickinson once named as particularly important to her:[20]

> And truly I have observed that those professed Eleemosynaries [anyone having to do with charitable giving, including those receiving the charity], though in a crowd or multitude, do yet direct and place their petitions on a few and selected persons: there is surely a Physiognomy, which those experienced and Master Mendicants [beggars] observe, whereby they instantly discover a merciful aspect, and will single out a face wherein they spy the signatures and marks of Mercy. For there are mystically in our faces certain Characters which carry in them the motto of our Souls, wherein he that cannot read a, b, c, may read our natures. I hold moreover that there is a Phytognomy, or Physiognomy, not only of Men, but of Plants and Vegetables; and in every one of them some outward figures which hang as signs or bushes [Bushes were hung out as signs before tavern doors] of their inward forms. The Finger of GOD hath left an Inscription upon all His works, not graphical or composed of Letters, but of their several forms, constitutions, parts, and operations, which, aptly joined together, do make one word that doth express their natures.[21]

It is in this wider sense of the word physiognomy that we read of another spider and his admirable web work.

> A Spider sewed at Night
> Without a Light
> Upon an Arc of White.
>
> If Ruff it was of Dame
> Or Shroud of Gnome
> Himself himself inform.
>
> Of Immortality
> His Strategy
> Was Physiognomy.
> —J1138/F1163/M705

Here again Dickinson employs a homely creature, a spider, and the homely activity of sewing, to address no less a subject than immortality. As will be explored in the next chapter, the question of what awaits us after death was an urgent one for Dickinson. It occupied her all her life. In sharp contrast to her own absorbing uncertainty, our spider goes about his task apparently confident in his *Strategy* for attaining it. Commonly, one would say that the spider spun his web rather than *sewed* it. The finished web might suggest something woven, but probably not something sewn. The unusual choice of the word *sewed,* a strictly human, usually feminine, activity tends to anthropomorphize the spider, aligning our sympathies more with the tiny creature. Dickinson seems to have admired spiders. This spider-artist achieves a kind of immortality through his work—his web work. He counts on the *Physiognomy* of his glorious, ingenious web to testify, in shimmering arcs of white, to his immortal art. Whether the great purpose of his work be *Ruff* (Frill; lace collar; fine-spun border; circular white edge of a neckline) *of Dame* or *Shroud of Gnome*, or something else, he *informs* only himself. The tone of the poem is one of detached admiration for the spider's self-sufficiency and independence.

In the first two stanzas of another poem the poet seems to be saying, "Sometimes Browne's 'finger of GOD' is not discernible to human eyes."

A Dew sufficed itself -
And satisfied a Leaf
And felt "how vast a destiny" -
"How trivial is Life!"

The Sun went out to work -
The Day went out to play
And not again that Dew be seen
By Physiognomy
—J1437/F1372/M519

The "science" of physiognomy, apparently, is not infallible. The vanished *dew* has left no trace of its existence. Normally we speak of "the dew" or "a drop of dew" but not "a dew." ED is not so constrained, however, and gives this particular drop of dew its own singular identity by recognizing it apart from the collective "dew."

Dickinson's Italic

The word italic means "Relating to Italy or its characters." Italic style characters first appeared in an edition of Virgil printed in Venice in 1501. When we write in italics, *like this,* the letters sloping toward the right, we are usually emphasizing the word or words italicized, drawing the reader's special attention to them. The italicized letters—characters—stand out from the surrounding text. The same may be said of human characters. Emily's niece wrote in praise of her father Austin Dickinson, Emily's brother,

> Not physically robust himself, but with a tremendous will; not rich, too tender of heart yet domineering at times; generous beyond all reason, honest to the last cent in money matters, and somehow, with Susan's help, always making his rather audacious ends meet, he seemed to us to live in italics to the eclipse of most of the plain print about him.[22]

Similarly, the mind's apprehensions may sometimes "stand out" from surrounding thought and experience, magnified by powerful circumstances.

In the first two verses of a longer poem, someone has died, and the awful import of the death has magnified consciousness.

The last Night that She lived
It was a Common Night
Except the Dying - this to Us
Made Nature different

We noticed smallest things -
Things overlooked before
By this great light upon our Minds
Italicized - as 'twere.
—J1100/F1100/M491

The word "death" has appeared many times in these pages. In Emily Dickinson's New England, death was an all too frequent visitor. Tuberculosis, home childbirth, typhoid fever and horse accidents combined with primitive medical care to take a heavy toll on its inhabitants. The dying person would lie in a room in the house, and the "death watch" would begin. In order that the person not be left alone, friends, neighbors, and family members would take turns sitting with her while she passed. In such circumstances, the impending loss, the inevitable fact of death, seems to magnify everything one sees and hears, and *smallest things* are *italicized, as 'twere.*

In the following poem, physiognomy is not mentioned, but the speaker applies something like it in assessing the inner condition of a man by examining closely his features. We are not told what happened to the man to cause him pain, but its ravages have left their marks upon his features. Because she does not explain the cause of that pain, or identify the sufferer, it could be anyone, anywhere, and you the reader may recognize someone whom you have known in this description. Make the poem your own.

The Hollows round His eager Eyes
Were Pages where to read
Pathetic Histories - although
Himself had not complained.
Biography to All who passed
Of Unobtrusive Pain
Except for the italic Face
Endured, unhelped - unknown.
—J955/F1071/M481

An *eager* expression is usually attractive, a sign of positive anticipation in the features. *Hollows* around the eyes are not, rather indicating illness or a long-troubled soul. In this strikingly original description, Dickinson combines the two, lending a forlorn, aspect to the eagerness; it is eagerness born of desperation. The sufferer is eager for relief, for respite. The speaker can read the man's *pathetic histories* in his face as though she were reading the pages of a book or a letter. We've seen this adjective, pathetic, before (Chapter 2).

> PA-THET'IC, or PA-THET'IC-AL, a.
> Affecting or moving the passions, particularly pity, sorrow, grief or other tender emotion; as, a pathetic song or discourse; pathetic expostulation

The speaker is moved to pity or sorrow by what she sees in this man's face, although the man himself has not complained. Nevertheless, passers-by could read that face like a *biography*. You can read the last four lines at least two somewhat different ways:

1. All who passed could read the biography of this unobtrusive pain. (Unobtrusive because it doesn't willfully thrust itself forward in front of others.) If it weren't for the italic face, the pain would not only be endured and unhelped, but it would also be unknown to others.
2. All who passed could read the biography of this pain, which would be unobtrusive except for the italic face. The pain has been endured, unhelped, and unknown to others.

This apparent ambiguity results from the lack of punctuation, and is a regular poetic practice of Dickinson's. In this way, the poem gives, or suggests, both readings at the same time, something that many readers find vexing. So often, it's best not to try to nail Dickinson down absolutely literally. In either case, however, the man's face is like a notice written in italics to emphasize his condition of enduring pain

One more note on this poem. Speaking grammatically we would say "He had not complained," but Dickinson substitutes the reflexive pronoun, "Himself." This, too, is a regular practice of Dickinson's, and we saw an instance of it in "A Spider sewed at Night" in the previous section. There are theories on why the poet used reflexive pronouns (itself, herself, ourselves, etc.) in this unconventional and ungrammatical way, but she never told us why herself. It is certain that she found similar usages in her reading, though. From her much loved *Aurora Leigh (First Book),* by Elizabeth Barrett Browning (Barrett Browning's portrait hung in the poet's bedroom) for instance.

> For me, I wrote
> False poems, like the rest, and thought them true
> Because myself was true in writing them.

And, from her King James Bible: "Himself took our infirmities, and bare our sicknesses" (Matthew 8:17).

As declared in the introduction to this book, one of the strategies that we will use to gain fuller appreciation of Emily Dickinson's poetry will be to consider her vocabulary and literary tropes in the context of the entire body of her work, including material from her letters. This chapter has relied particularly on that strategy. As the reader encounters the private vocabulary that we have introduced here, a fuller appreciation of the poetry must follow.

Dickinson's poems and her letters too, are replete with quotes from and allusions to the King James Bible. We explore this source in a later chapter. First, however, a survey of the religious landscape of nineteenth-century New England should prove enlightening.

Four

The Second Great Awakening

> "Last winter there was a revival here. The meetings were thronged by people old and young. It seemed that those who sneered loudest at serious things were soonest brought to see their power, and to make Christ their portion. It was really wonderful to see how near heaven came to sinful mortals. Many who felt there was nothing in religion determined to go once and see if there was anything in it, and they were melted at once."—L10, 31 January 1846

Emily Dickinson's Religious Heritage

The material in this chapter and the next contains keys that open many doors of meaning in Emily Dickinson's world, which she assures us is "superior for Doors."[1] Her vocabulary is laden with terms that were heavy with religious import in nineteenth-century America that is not generally recognized today. We will identify these terms and what they mean. Images in the poems are often drawn from scripture. These doors, too, we will open. And perhaps most importantly, we will get a sense of the spiritual and social forces that were at work during her lifetime, which in turn should help us grasp more fully their profound significance in much of her work. This book makes no attempt to identify or even speculate on Emily Dickinson's personal religious beliefs, but the influence on her writing of the religious forces acting in her time can hardly be overestimated.

Nathaniel Dickinson crossed the Atlantic Ocean with John Winthrop in a fleet led by the flagship *Arbella* in 1630. Winthrop helped found the Massachusetts Bay Colony in New England and served as its governor. Nathaniel was Emily Dickinson's direct ancestor. He was an English lawyer, a Puritan, and he came to the New World to help found a "City on a Hill," to be looked up to by the rest of the world as the model for true Christian worship and community.[2] These early settlers left comfortable lives in England to begin anew in the wilderness that was then North America. They were met with scarcity, harsh, bitter winters, and the ever-present threat of attack by hostile natives. The Puritans who so ventured were unwilling to compromise with the church practices then prevalent in England. Their sole motive was to live a Godly life and practice their form of Christianity as they deemed necessary.

Reformed Protestantism, or Calvinism, held that the Bible is the sole source and authority for religious guidance. According to their Doctrine of Total Depravity, no aspect of human nature is uncontaminated by original sin. The Doctrine of Unconditional Election held that from the beginning God has elected some mortals for salvation and others for damnation, and that there is nothing an individual can do—no prayer, no sacrament, no good works—that can save them. Only by the grace of God is one saved. Generations later, words such as *elect* and *grace* will still carry the weight of their theological meanings into Emily Dickinson's poetry.

The second and third generations of Massachusetts colonists were different from their parents and grandparents. Born in the New World, they had no memory of or allegiance to the old. They found themselves in a land with abundant resources and, in the eyes of their elders, pursued worldly gain and comforts to the neglect of religion. The literature dating from 1660 and thereafter sounds a ceaseless lament for the falling away from the original mission of the Massachusetts pilgrims to found "A City on a Hill."[3] It was under these circumstances that Protestant ministers undertook to reignite the religious fire that burned in earlier generations, and it can be seen as part of a movement in the Protestant world at large against the rationalism of the Age of Enlightenment. Itinerant preachers such as George Whitefield (or Whitfield, 1714–1770),[4] an English Anglican cleric, delivered fervid, heartfelt sermons both in England and in the American colonies, sermons aimed at bringing listeners to a "conversion experience" in which they would throw themselves on the mercy of God and accept Jesus Christ as their savior. Terrifying descriptions of the eternal suffering of lost souls were heard. Emotional audiences, anxious for their salvation, would weep and moan aloud. Huge crowds would gather to hear some of the famous preachers, where grown men would fall to the ground writhing in agony. This was the First Great Awakening, and it came to Massachusetts in the 1740's, where Jonathan Edwards (1703–1758), America's greatest Calvinist theologian, preached from the pulpit in Northampton Massachusetts, only a few miles from Amherst.

After the American Revolution (1775–1783), another falling away from religion was perceived by many ministers, as the Age of Enlightenment stressed reason over faith with increasing influence, and a geographically expanding population made it ever more difficult to get to church from the frontier, or otherwise hear the gospel preached. This lead to more itinerant preachers, often known as "circuit riders," ministering to settlers in remote areas, and it also lead to a new phenomenon, the camp meeting.

Most often held in the open air, camp meeting revivals aimed at mass conversions. People would travel by horse and wagon for as long as four days to hear several preachers and pray for a sign of salvation. The first of these took place in July1800 at Gaspar River, Kentucky, led by a Scotch-Irish Presbyterian minister named James McGready, where some fell to the ground crying out in despair that they were surely damned. About forty-five people were converted at Gaspar River over the course of three days, and some historians mark this event as the beginning of the Second Great Awakening. Others mark it with a greater revival at Cane Ridge, Kentucky, in August of 1801. Led by Barton Stone, another Presbyterian minister, it attracted a crowd estimated by some who were there at least 10,000 and perhaps as many as 25,000. The stakes could not be higher for believers. They would spend eternity either united with their loved ones in heaven or in the fire and sulfur of hell. The leading revivalist preacher and theologian in Dickinson's lifetime was Charles Grandison Finney (1792–1875).

It was the duty of all good Christians to strive to save others by helping them to their own conversion. Emily Dickinson's grandfather, Samuel Fowler Dickinson, a Puritan like his forebears, was zealous in the cause of saving souls. At great cost to himself, he helped found Amherst College to train men for the ministry, especially for missionary work. His son Edward, Emily's father, converted later in life, though he had been an active member of the church parish prior to that.

Early Struggles

The earliest records that we have touching on Emily Dickinson's attitude toward religion come in letters to young friends. At age fifteen, she wrote to schoolmate Abiah Root.

> Although I feel sad that one should be taken and the others left, yet it is with joy that Abby[5] & I peruse your letter & read your decision in favor of Christ & though we are not in the fold yet I hope when the great shepherd at the last day separates the sheep

> from the goats we may hear his voice and be seated with the lambs on the right hand of God.[6] I know now that I ought to give myself to God & spend the springtime of life in his service for it seems to me a mockery to spend life's autumn & summer in the service of Mammon & when the world no longer charms us, "When our eyes are dull of seeing & our ears of hearing, when the silver cord is loosed and the golden bowl broken,"[7] to yield our hearts, because we are afraid to do otherwise & give to God the miserable recompense of a sick bed for all his kindness to us. Surely it is a fearful thing to live & a very fearful thing to die & give up our account to the supreme ruler for all our sinful deeds and thoughts upon this probationary term of existence."[8]

Two years later she is still struggling, seemingly more intensely, with "the all-important subject." Again, to Abiah Root, written from Mount Holyoke Female Seminary, where she attended and resided in 1847 and 1848.

> Abiah you may be surprised to hear me speak as I do knowing that I express no interest in the all-important subject, but I am not happy, and I regret that last term, when the Golden opportunity was mine, that I did not give up and become a Christian. It is not now too late, so my friends tell me, so my offended conscience whispers, but it is hard for me to give up the world. I had quite a long talk with Abby while at home and I doubt not she will soon cast her burden on Christ. She is sober, and keenly sensitive on the subject, and says she only desires to be good. How I wish I could say that with sincerity, but I fear that I never can.[9]

Mount Holyoke Female Seminary was an institution of higher education for women where religion was paramount. Biographer Cynthia Griffin Wolff writes, "At Mount Holyoke the religious influence was far from coercive, but it was unrelenting."[10] The pressure from those around her to accept Christ as Savior may have been at its most intense during this time.

The pressure did not entirely abate when she returned home to Amherst however. In 1850, one of many religious revivals took place there. These revivals, unlike the raucous, demonstrative camp meetings in the west, were subdued and intensely serious affairs. An Amherst College president wrote of it:

> In the winter and spring of 1850, there was another general revival, in which there were over thirty "hopefuls" among the students, and which made no small addition to the numbers and the strength of the church. Including some from the families of the faculty, there were thirty-three persons who together presented themselves at the altar, almost filling the broad aisle of the chapel, all in the bloom of youth, and who now for the first time dedicated themselves by their voluntary consecration to the service of their Maker, Redeemer and Sanctifier.[11]

It was during the spring of that year that ED wrote once more to friend Abiah Root.

> I presume that you have heard from Abby, and know what she now believes - she makes a sweet, girl Christian, religion makes her face quite different, calmer, but full of

> radiance, holy, yet very joyful. She talks of herself quite freely, seems to love Lord Christ most dearly, and to wonder, and be bewildered, at the life she has always led. It all looks black, and distant, and God, and Heaven are near. She is certainly very much changed. She has told you about things here, how the "still small voice is calling,"[12] and how the people are listening, and believing, and truly obeying - how the place is very solemn, and sacred, and the bad ones slink away, and are sorrowful - not at their wicked lives - but at this strange time, great change. *I* am one of the lingering *bad* ones, and so I do slink away, and pause, and ponder, and ponder, and pause, and do work without knowing why - not surely for *this* brief world, and more sure it is not for heaven -

Later in the same year, we can detect a dawning resolve replacing former doubt.

> The shore is safer Abiah, but I love to buffet the sea - I count the bitter wrecks here in these pleasant waters, and hear the murmuring winds, but oh, I love the danger. You are learning control and firmness. Christ Jesus will love you more I'm afraid he don't love me *any*![13]

The Language of the Church

There is always a danger in presuming that anything described or related in Emily Dickinson's poetry is necessarily biographical—in assuming that she is necessarily describing her own personal experience or mental outlook. On the subject of religious faith the poems express quite conflicting and contradictory points of view. Nevertheless, religious referents permeate much of her writing, and familiarity with the vocabulary of biblical scripture, Calvinist theology, and revivalism gives us a much fuller understanding of the poems and letters, as clearly evinced in the letters already quoted. An end-of-summer poem, a copy of which ED referred to as "My Cricket," offers a fine example.

> Further in Summer than the Birds
> Pathetic from the Grass
> A minor Nation celebrates
> Its unobtrusive Mass.
>
> No Ordinance be seen
> So gradual the Grace
> A pensive Custom it becomes
> Enlarging Loneliness.
>
> Antiquest felt at Noon
> When August burning low
> Arise this spectral Canticle
> Repose to typify.
>
> Remit as yet no Grace
> No Furrow on the Glow

Yet a Druidic - Difference
Enhances Nature now
—J1068/F895/M534

Here we have another poem of Indian summer (Chapter 2)—far enough into the season that *Birds* have begun to migrate away. The word *pathetic* may sound puzzling to us in this context, but the sound of the crickets seems to have affected the poet deeply. In 1884 she wrote to a friend, "The cricket sings in the morning, now, a most pathetic conduct."[14] By comparing the sound to a sacred *Mass* (A Roman Catholic term, not Protestant, hence a different *Nation*) she conveys her sense of reverence for what she hears. Extending the metaphor, she tells us that, *so gradual* is the divine process at work—*the Grace* -that *no Ordinance be seen*. Ordinance is another word for sacrament. The sacraments recognized by her church were *ordained* by Jesus Christ as recorded in the Bible, and were thought of as external signs of an inner relationship with God. No external signs are seen that would signal the slow seasonal change taking place. *Antiquest* is ED's coined word for "most antique." Crickets in central Massachusetts chirp mostly at night. If the night is cold however, some species will chirp instead during the day, and this would most probably happen late in the season as winter is approaching. Hearing the sound at *noon*, then, the poet feels most keenly the antiquity of this ancient *Custom* of nature, signaling impending winter. The mood has changed from one of celebration in the first stanza to one of enlarged *Loneliness*.

A canticle can be any song, but people in Dickinson's church would have understood *Canticle* to refer to, or at least suggest, the biblical Song of Solomon, or Song of Songs, which is joyous and exalted poetry. The Canticles in this poem however are *spectral,* moving us another step away from the celebratory tone of the Mass. Note how the mood changes through the course of the poem, enacting within itself the slow, gradual change of the seasons which it describes. More, these Canticles typify (anticipate) the *repose* of winter, when natural processes sleep, or, as Dickinson puts it in another cricket poem, which we examine in the next chapter, "When Nature's Laugh is done." A chill is felt in this suggestion of winter's death-like sleep, removing us yet again another step away from the life in the grass. The word *typify* refers to the Christian reading of the Old Testament of the Bible as prefiguring persons and events in the New Testament. For example, Jerusalem, or Zion in the Old Testament, typifies the church and then heaven of the New. (The source of this belief is found in Galatians 4:25, 26 and Hebrews 12:22.) Moses was a prophet and leader of his people, and led them out of slavery. As such he was a "type of," or typical of, the Lord Jesus who leads his people out of the slavery of sin (Deuteronomy 18:15; Acts 3:22; 1, Corinthians 10:2; Galatians 3:27; 3:19; and 1 Timothy 2:5).

TYPE, n.
1. The mark of something; an emblem; that which represents something else.
2. A sign; a symbol; figure of something to come; as, Abraham's sacrifice and the paschal lamb, were types of Christ. To this word is opposed antitype. Christ, in this case, is the antitype.

TYPI-FY, v.t.
To represent by an image, form, model or resemblance, The washing of baptism typifies the cleansing of the soul from sin by the blood of Christ. Our Savior was typified by the goat that was slain.

No grace—again, this divine process at work—need not be remitted—that is, given up or returned—*yet!* The glow of the hour is not yet disfigured by any furrow-like mark or condition.

FUR′ROW, n.
1. A trench in the earth made by a plow.
2. A long narrow trench or channel in wood or metal; a groove.
3. A hollow made by wrinkles in the face.

We also may speak of furrowing the brows in displeasure or anger. No such sign is apparent presently, but something has changed. *A Druidic Difference enhances Nature now.* How much Emily Dickinson knew about the Druids, an ancient Celtic religious class in Britain, is not certain, but she would have read of their fierce practices, such as human sacrifice, in her Latin texts. (Romans encountered Druids in Britain and wrote about them). It may be that Dickinson is engaging in one of her signature poetic devices, purposefully combining contradictory terms (For example, *revolting bliss*, in "The waters chased him as he fled" J1749/F1766/M694 or, *sumptuous despair*, in "I would not paint a Picture" J505/F348/M184). Otherwise, how could a Druidic difference enhance nature in the familiar sense of that word? The Druids, like Emily herself, were close to nature in practice and belief. Possibly she was taking the fourth definition of that word in her dictionary, no longer heard, shown below.

EN-HANCE, v.t
1. To raise; to lift; applied to material things by Spenser, but this application is entirely obsolete.
2. To raise; to advance; to highten; applied to price or value.
3. To raise; applied to qualities, quantity, pleasures, enjoyments, &c.
4. To increase; to aggravate.

By moving step by step from the sacred to the nearly diabolical the poem continues to enact its very subject—the sense of impending loss—the slow slide from the life of summer to the death of winter.

The Dickinson family attended Amherst's First Congregational Church ("Congregational" denotes the church polity, not its theology.) which stipulated eleven "Articles of Faith." Article number three was: "You believe that the scriptures of the Old and New Testaments are the word of God, revealed as holy men were moved by the Holy Ghost, and that they are our only rule of faith and practice."[15]

Emily Dickinson's playful take-off would have bordered on the blasphemous in the view of some of her townsfolk!

> The Bible is an antique Volume -
> Written by faded Men
> At the suggestion of Holy Spectres -
> Subjects - Bethlehem -
> Eden - the ancient Homestead -
> Satan - the Brigadier -
> Judas - the Great Defaulter -
> David - the Troubadour -
> Sin - a distinguished Precipice
> Others must resist -
> Boys that "believe" are very lonesome -
> Other Boys are "lost" -
> Had but the Tale a warbling Teller -
> All the Boys would come -
> Orpheus' Sermon captivated -
> It did not condemn -
>
> —J1545/F1577

To call the Bible *antique,* rather than ancient, is to imply that it is outdated, perhaps even a curiosity. To refer to *Holy Spectres*, in the plural rather than the Holy Spirit, in the singular, is to suggest a weaker source of inspiration for the Bible's authors than was believed by church members. (Spectre is an alternate spelling of specter—a ghost or apparition.) The *ancient Homestead*, the *Brigadier*, the *Great Defaulter*, and the *Troubadour* (a minstrel-poet) are recognizable character types from nineteenth-century Gothic novels, which ED and her contemporaries read enthusiastically. Here, major biblical figures become these character types, turning the Bible into an entertaining novel-like story. Characters in Gothic novels might find themselves in danger of falling over a cliff—or a *Precipice*—here equated with the danger that Christians face—*sin. Others must resist* sin, but implicitly not the teller of the *Tale! All the Boys* do not *come to listen* to him, but if his tale had *a warbling* tone, they would.

WAR´BLE, v.i.
1. To quaver a sound or the voice; to modulate with turns or variations
2. To cause to quaver.
3. To utter musically; to be modulated.

Orpheus of Greek mythology charmed all living things with his music. The Teller's sermons are not pleasant to hear—not very inviting at all! Those boys who do come then—the ones *who believe*—are lonely, because they are not joined by their implicitly more numerous peers. According to Reformed Protestant theology, we are saved by faith alone—in other words we are saved when we *believe*.[16] Those who do not believe are *lost* souls.

Signs and Emblems

Growing up, Emily Dickinson heard and read incessant instruction on how a good Christian was to scrutinize the "Book of Nature"[17] for signs of divine intent. There, one would find signs of God's truth and purpose. Specific natural phenomena had quite definite meanings, and books of emblems were published to help seekers identify them.

Dr. Edward Hitchcock (1793–1864), an ordained Congregationalist Pastor and president of Amherst College (1845–1854) where he was a professor of geology, chemistry, natural history and natural theology,[18] was the dominant intellectual force in the Amherst of Dickinson's youth. A series of lectures that he gave during the period are an extended exercise in reading the Book of Nature as a Christian. The figure below shows an image from the frontispiece of a book of Hitchcock's collected lectures.

In the first lecture in the series, titled *The Resurrection of the Spring*, Hitchcock states,

> In the first place, the Bible distinctly announces the fact that there will be a resurrection of the dead at the end of the world.
>
> Natural theology, then, as it seems to me, harmonizes fully with the revealed doctrine of the resurrection; nay, it throws some light on the meaning of scripture, and silences the skeptical objection.
>
> It is in the spring, also, for the most part, that we witness what has long been thought an illustration of this subject; I mean the metamorphosis of the insects. Enveloped in his silken shroud, the chrysalis has passed the wintry months in some obscure plot, apparently almost as lifeless as a man in the grave. But in the vernal season it bursts forth from its prison endowed with new life and beauty.[19]

CHRYS´A-LIS, n.
The particular form which butterflies, moths, and some other insects assume, before they arrive at their winged or perfect state.

"Emblems of the Resurrection" (from Edward Hitchcock, *Religious Lectures on Peculiar Phenomena of the Four Seasons* [Amherst, MA: J.S. and C. Adams, 1851], courtesy Amherst College).

We saw in our discussion of Circumference that Dickinson recognized a limit to what could be known. What lies beyond death—the promise of resurrection and the question of immortality—she called her "flood subject,"[20] usually interpreted to mean that she found it overwhelming. In "My Cocoon tightens - Colors teaze -" (Dickinson's spelling of *tease*) she contemplates her condition from both inside and outside the cocoon.

My Cocoon tightens - Colors teaze -
I'm feeling for the Air -
A dim capacity for Wings
Demeans the Dress I wear -

A power of Butterfly must be -
The Aptitude to fly
Meadows of Majesty concedes
And easy Sweeps of Sky -

So I must baffle at the Hint
And cipher at the Sign
And make much blunder, if at last
I take the clue divine -
—J1099/F1107/M494

Her cocoon seems to *tighten* because she is growing within it! We are there with her as she becomes gradually more aware of a much greater, wider, dazzling world beyond her silken shroud. She becomes aware of a latent *power* in herself ready to burst forth. The drab cocoon—her plain *Dress*—is *demeaned*, is made to look shabby by comparison with the coming glory. As a butterfly, she must yet *baffle at the hint* of the new life to come. As a mortal human being, she must *cipher at the Sign* of that new life presented her by the cocoon. Cipher most commonly meant writing or using figures, but additionally, from her Webster's dictionary, "To have, or to learn a cipher, is to be able to interpret it." There will be mistakes and missteps—*much blunder if at last* she truly *takes* the *divine clue* of metamorphosis offered to her by nature.

From her earliest letters and verses and throughout her life, Emily Dickinson questioned the possibility of immortality, and regarded questions of what might await us after death as beyond her Circumference. Regarding it as her "flood subject," however, did not prevent her from going there in her imagination, and writing poems from the point of view of someone already dead. In the last verse of one of her after-death poems, the chrysalis emblem represents her earthly life as seen after her joyous arrival in the afterlife.

Three times - we parted - Breath -and I -
Three times - He would not go -
But strove to stir the lifeless Fan
The Waters - strove to stay.

Three Times - the Billows threw me up -
Then caught me - like a Ball -
Then made Blue faces in my face -
And pushed away a sail

That crawled Leagues off - I liked to see -
For thinking - while I die -
How pleasant to behold a Thing
Where Human faces -be -

The Waves grew sleepy - Breath - did not -
The Winds - like Children -lulled -
Then Sunrise kissed my Chrysalis -
And I stood up - and lived -

—J598/F514/M251

In the fourth stanza, the speaker stands up and lives after dying in the third. We now recognize this apparent paradox as an imagined resurrection to new life after death, as discussed of above.

There is an old saying that a drowning man rises up three times before sinking for the last time. Dickinson must have heard it; another poem begins, "Drowning is not so pitiful/As the attempt to rise/Three times, 'Tis said, a sinking man/Comes up to face the skies" (J1718/F1542/M662).

She imagines the back-and-forth fight between herself and the ocean's billows for survival. *Billows* can and did sometimes refer to clouds or to anything inflated by the wind. We may speak of billowing sails, for example. Dickinson is using it in an extended sense, including water as well as wind, as defined in her 1844 dictionary:

BIL´LOW, n.
A great wave or surge of the sea, occasioned usually by violent wind. It can hardly be applied to the waves of a river, unless in poetry, or when the river is very large.

As noted in Chapter 3, the sunrise in the east was another sign of the promised resurrection. The sunset in the west was a sign of going home to God the Father in heaven. Dickinson wrote of nature's signs of heaven explicitly. Without prior knowledge of the particular religious meaning of the word *sign*, one would probably miss the tone of confident independence in this next poem. The speaker senses the existence of *Heaven,* not from what she's been told of by others to look for, but from the splendors of nature that she sees around her.

"Heaven" has different Signs - to me -
Sometimes, I think that Noon
Is but a symbol of the Place -
And when again, at Dawn,

A mighty look runs round the World
And settles in the Hills -
An Awe if it should be like that
Upon the Ignorance steals -

The Orchard, when the Sun is on -
The Triumph of the Birds
When they together Victory make -
Some Carnivals of Clouds -

The Rapture of a finished Day -
Returning to the West -
All these - remind us of the place
That Men call "paradise" -

Itself be fairer - we suppose -
But how Ourself, shall be
Adorned, for a Superior Grace -
Not yet, our eyes can see -
—J575/F544/M297

Knowing that *Noon* stood for the highpoint of experience in Dickinson's private vocabulary, we will not be surprised to find it here as a sign of *Heaven*, along with birdsong, dawn and sunrise. *The Orchard when the Sun is on*—is a line probably best illuminated by something she wrote to a friend in a letter:

> My dying Tutor[21] told me that he would like to live till I had been a poet, but Death was much of a Mob as I could master - then - And when far afterwards - a sudden light on Orchards, or a new fashion in the wind troubled my attention - I felt a palsy - the Verses just relieve.[22]

In the final verse she *supposes* that heaven will actually be *fairer* than any of its signs, but she cannot imagine how she herself will be changed to fit her new home. Although there may be a slight note of doubt in this final reflection—she supposes, she isn't certain—the tone of the poem is otherwise grounded in a jubilant here and now, with the word *Heaven* in the first line surrounded by quotation marks. The speaker views the world around her, beholds a *mighty look* on nature's features, and feels a sense of awe. The effect of sunlight on the *Orchards* transports her. The singing birds, to her ears, sound *triumphant. Clouds* present *carnivals* and the day finishes in *rapture*, all part of this world, not the next.

As already noted, Dickinson poems are open to interpretation. I have a friend, a deep appreciator of Dickinson's poetry, who wonders if the poem *Will there really be a "Morning"* might be about insomnia! Maybe. It is fun to read it that way. However, in the light of what we have learned about *Morning* as a sign, how do you read it?

> Will there really be a "Morning"?
> Is there such a thing as "Day"?
> Could I see it from the mountains
> If I were as tall as they?
>
> Has it feet like Water lilies?
> Has it feathers like a Bird?
> Is it brought from famous countries
> Of which I have never heard?
>
> Oh some Scholar! Oh some Sailor!
> Oh some Wise Men from the skies!
> Please to tell a little Pilgrim
> Where the place called "Morning" lies!
> —J101/F148/M87

The promised resurrection, of which the rising sun of morning is a sign; is referred to by some Christians as "The New Day."

> Doubtless at the dawning of the New Day- the approaching new dispensation—the language of the human family will be one of the things reconstituted, and over the oracles of divine truth, old and new, the bitterness of controversy will be exchanged for a sympathetic oneness of adoration at the clearness and the glory of things made known (Henry Deacon, 1865).

Furthermore, *Morning* and *Day* are within quotation marks, indicating something spoken of but not certainly known, thus compounding the uncertainty inherent in the question that the first stanza poses. Will such a thing as The New Day ever come? If she could see further, as from tops of *mountains*, could she descry an it? How would she recognize it? *Feet like Water lilies* has been interpreted variously as the footprint-like appearance of the lily-pad on the surface of the water, as a reference of the *feet* of water through which the plant must grow to reach the surface, and as an allusion to Jesus' feet as He walked on water.[23] Can anyone tell her *where "Morning" lies?"* Perhaps a *Scholar* can, who has learned much through his studies, or a *Sailor*, who, having traveled to so many places, may have learned of it, or *Wise Men from the skies*, who must have the greatest view of all from their lofty realm. One more clue as to what *Morning* she refers is that the speaker is a *Pilgrim:*

PIL'GRIM, n

1. A wanderer; a traveler; particularly, one that travels to a distance from his own country to visit a holy place, or to pay his devotion to the remains of dead saints. [See Pilgrimage.]
2. In Scripture, one that has only a temporary residence on earth.

In in another poem, "At last - to be identified -," we recognize *Day* as again possibly referring to more than simply tomorrow. Members of the church believed that when the Holy Spirit baptized them they were *identified* with Jesus Christ in His death, burial, resurrection, and ascension into heaven. An intimate relationship or union was formed with Christ so that one became identified with Him. This belief is grounded in several passages in the New Testament, including Galatians 2:20: "I have been crucified with Christ; and it is no longer I who live, but Christ lives in me; and the life which I now live in the flesh I live by faith in the Son of God, who loved me and gave Himself up for me."

It might be easy to read "At last - to be identified -" as a description of a dark and difficult time in her life that the speaker has passed through, were it not for the special application of the word *identified* in the theology of the church. And, it would be hard to appreciate the poem fully without that association.

At last - to be identified -
At last - the Lamps upon your side -
The rest of life - to *see* -

Past Midnight - past the Morning Star -
Past Sunrise -
Ah, What leagues there *were* -
Between our feet - and Day!

—J174/F172/M99, 226

The past tense in line five tells us that the journey is over and that *Day* has arrived. The poem is addressed to someone (*Upon your side*), but she doesn't say whom. By omitting specific referents, she creates a poem that can carry at least three readings at once. If the person addressed is Christ, then the speaker of this poem has received the Holy Spirit, been baptized into Christ and is now able to exclaim, "*At last - to be identified.*" If the person addressed is a mortal person who has died, then this would be another after-death poem, and she has been reunited with him or her on the other side. If the poem is addressed to a living mortal, she is making an analogy between her relationship with that person and a mystical union with Christ—actually, and perhaps surprisingly, a not uncommon practice between romantic couples in mid–Victorian times. Historian Karen Lystra writes:

> One woman wrote to her husband in a private poem on married love, "Thou art my church and thou art my book of psalms!!" she also addressed him "Toi! Qu'en mon coer seul je nomme,/je te vois partout et, en toi, je vois Dieu." ["You! who alone has my heart/I see you everywhere, and in you I see God."]
>
> [....] The emphasis on romantic love as sacramental was not merely metaphorical convenience. The process of mutual identification encouraged by nineteenth-century courtship nurtured self-expression, self-knowledge, and thus self-development. Consequently the use of the metaphor of salvation or rebirth had an experiential dimension in the deepening and expanding awareness of selfhood that was created through romantic love.[24]

And, here is Emily Dickinson's brother, Austin, writing to his paramour, Mable Loomis Todd:

> You are my world and my Christ. I say it most reverently, and if there is a heaven for me, you are that—God pity such love. Of one man for one woman. The mystery and the might of it! Yes, and the shining glory! The consummate flower—and final triumph of Divine achievement. Love, which is creation itself.[25]

In this light, Dickinson's employment of the language of the church in a love poem would not be unique, blasphemous, or particularly unusual for her time.

I would like to repeat something stated earlier. This book makes no attempt to identify or even speculate on Emily Dickinson's personal religious beliefs. I do not claim or imply that she saw or claimed to see signs of God's promise in nature. I am claiming that her poetry is deep in the vocabulary and imagery of her religious heritage and surroundings, including that of Christian Signs and Emblems. In "A Science - so the Savans say," she contemplates a single flower still blooming after a snowfall, and reads in it a sign almost oppositely from how her Christian neighbors would have.

> A science - so the Savans say,
> "Comparative Anatomy" -

By which a single bone -
Is made a secret to unfold
Of some rare tenant of the mold,
Else perished in the stone -

So to the eye prospective led,
This meekest flower of the mead
Upon a winter's day,
Stands representative in gold
Of Rose and Lily, manifold,
And countless Butterfly!
—J100/F147/M87

To begin with, Emily Dickinson was familiar with the science of comparative anatomy as applied to fossil remains. Dr. Edward Hitchcock was one of the first dinosaur track experts. The Beneski Museum of Natural History at Amherst College still holds his collected fossils. His *Elementary Geology*, with a chapter titled "Palaeontology [sic], or the Science of Organic Remains," was in the Dickinson family library. *Savans* is derived from the French. In English today it is usually written as Savants:[26]

SA'VANT, n. [plur. Savans. Fr. *savan.*]
A man of learning; in the plural, literary men.

In the first verse of the poem, a learned paleontologist comes upon a single fossilized bone or footprint. From that small clue, he is able to identify the species, or, if the species is an unknown one, deduce some of the features of the animal. Likewise, someone long taught to see evidence of the divine in nature, coming upon a flower blooming in winter, would recognize it as a sign of God's promise of eternal life. Contrarily, Dickinson sees it as the lone reminder of the millions of roses, lilies, and butterflies that no longer exist!

In the third lecture of the aforementioned series, entitled "Euthanasia[27] of the Autumn," Dr. Hitchcock expands on that season as a sign of the promise of new life after the death of winter. He focuses on the bright leaves of the New England autumn as "signals of joy" prefiguring the joy of the life to come. Who in modern times, however, would share the sentiment suggested in the first sentence of the following excerpt?

The gay splendor of our forests, as autumn comes on, may seem to some inappropriate, when we consider that it is the precursor of decay and death. But when we remember that the plant still lives, and after a season of inaction will awake to new and more vigorous life, and that the apparent decay is only laying aside a summer robe, because unfit for winter, is it not appropriate that nature should hang out signals of joy rather than of sorrow? Why should she not descend exultingly, and in her richest dress, into the grave, in hope of so early and so glorious a resurrection?

Emily Dickinson expresses a very different point of view in the following poem:

> Nature - sometimes sears a Sapling -
> Sometimes - scalps a Tree -
> Her Green People recollect it
> When they do not die -
>
> Fainter Leaves - to Further Seasons -
> Dumbly testify -
> We - who have the Souls
> Die oftener - Not so vitally -
> —J314/F457/M230

The emblem of the tree blackened by lightening was a familiar one in the visual arts. Writing of the renowned painter of American landscapes Thomas Cole, with whose work Dickinson was familiar, Judith Farr explains:

> Cole's synthesizing image for both the violence implicit in nature and its endurance—a proof of the benevolence of God—was the blasted or quartered tree. In well-known landscapes like *The Cove, Catskills* , (ca. 1827) and *The Oxbow* (ca. 1836), this devastated tree appears at the left margin on the canvas. It was adopted by Cole's followers as a metaphor for conquered suffering. If trees could survive lightening and storm, so could human beings transcend pain and social disorder.[28]

The power of the emblem lies in the fact that the tree is still alive, though stricken by lightning or perhaps blasted in war. *Her Green People recollect it*, as green leaves yet cling to the branches. If it continues to survive—*When they do not die*—still viable branches would grow and new green shoots would appear to replace and increase the lost parts of the tree. Thus we have an emblem of hope and triumph over adversity.

The *Fainter Leaves* are those of late autumn, having faded from their earlier glory described by Dr. Hitchcock. They *Dumbly testify* to the cycle of decay and rebirth into *further seasons* of summers. Leaves are dumb in that they do not speak, but the word can have pejorative connotations from association with expressions like "dumb animal," and "dumb luck." Had Dickinson wanted to offer an uplifting message in harmony with that of Dr. Hitchcock, she would probably have found a more elevating word. The leaves die just once a year and most trees are never blasted. *We - who have the Souls Die oftener.* As already noted, Emily Dickinson saw her friends and neighbors die with alarming regularity. They will not spring back to life like the tree, nor will there be further seasons for any one of them, at least not here on Earth.

Argument from Design

Edward Hitchcock, though a champion of science, examined the geological record for evidence to support tenets of Christianity. For example, he believed that soil is produced by decaying and crumbling rocks. Without soil, there could be no plant life and therefore no animal life either. In this he found proof of Divine intent.[29]

Referred to often as "argument from design," (also as the "teleological argument") the idea was that an intelligent creator could be inferred by examining the evidence all around us in the natural world. Though the idea is traceable back to the ancient Greeks, Hitchcock had a more immediate predecessor in the English theologian William Paley (1743–1805), who famously wrote:

> In crossing a heath, suppose I pitched my foot against a stone and were asked how the stone came to be there, I might possibly answer that for anything I knew to the contrary it had lain there forever; nor would it, perhaps, be very easy to show the absurdity of this answer. But suppose I found a *watch* upon the ground, and it should be inquired how the watch happened to be in that place, I should hardly think of the answer which I had given, that for anything I knew the watch might have always been there.[30]

Paley goes on to say that because the watch is composed of parts that work together to achieve a specific purpose, an intelligent designer must be at work. He continues to develop the argument for some four hundred pages.

We find in Dickinson's writing once again a contrary view that sees no concern for human beings, benevolent or otherwise, in nature. See for example "Of Bronze - and Blaze" (J290/F319/M152) or "I watched the Moon around the House" (J629/F593/M270) in addition to the following poem:

> Four Trees - upon a solitary Acre -
> Without Design
> Or Order, or Apparent Action -
> Maintain -
>
> The Sun - upon a Morning meets them -
> The Wind -
> No nearer Neighbor - have they -
> But God -
>
> The Acre gives them - Place -
> They - Him - Attention of Passer by -
> Of Shadow, or of Squirrel, haply -
> Or Boy -
>
> What Deed is Theirs unto the General Nature -
> What Plan
> They severally - retard - or further -
> Unknown -
>
> —J742/F778/M382

Viewing the scene, she sees no *Design*. The trees are simply there, standing in the meadow. They *Maintain* themselves apparently without need of a pre-existing design. Dickinson does not specify for us what it is that the trees maintain; she has once again left that part out; a signature literary device of hers, one that is key to understanding her poetry, and a topic to which we will devote more attention in a later chapter. Certainly though, it is apparent that these trees are maintaining themselves. In lines five and six, *The Sun—upon a Morning meets them,* and so does *The Wind.* The morning sun and the wind are near neighbors of the four trees, but God is nearer. The Acre gives the trees a place to maintain themselves, and the trees attract the attention of people passing by. The trees also give the acre some shade, and may attract a squirrel or a boy who might like to climb there. The poet sees no *design*, but she sees a mutual exchange between the four trees and the acre, from which each of them gains. All is in harmony. *What Deed is Theirs*—what do they *unto the General Nature*—in the great scheme of things is unknown. *What Plan* each individual member of this scene advances or retards is also unknown. Today, the word *several* is almost always used to mean more than two, but not a great many. In this poem, it carries an earlier and more primary meaning:

> SEV′ER-AL, a. [from sever.]
> 1. Separate; distinct; not common to two or more; as, a several fishery; a several estate. A several fishery is one held by the owner of the soil, or by title derived from the owner. A several estate is one held by a tenant in his own right, or a distinct estate unconnected with any other person.
> 2. Separate; different; distinct.
> 3. Divers; consisting of a number; more than two, but not very many.
> 4. Separate; single; particular. Each several ship a victory did gain.—Dryden.
> 5. Distinct; appropriate. A joint and several note or bond, is one executed by two or more persons, each of whom is bound to pay the whole, in case the others prove to be insolvent

The word several has its origins in the word *sever*, which means to cut away from the main body or divide into parts (usually by force). What each separate, individual member in the scene, the acre and each of the four trees, does to *further or retard* any Plan is unknown.

Another word heard less often in modern times is *haply.*

> HAP′LY, adv.
> 1. By chance; perhaps; it may be.
> 2. By accident; casually.

The harmonious participants in the scene and the nearness of God impart a sublime feeling, yet, we are left at last confronting the unknown, often disquieting, or at least somewhat disturbing, to contemplate. How can we reconcile these seemingly disparate aspects of the poem? A line in a letter from Emily to two favored cousins may provide a clue: "It is true that the unknown is the largest need of the intellect, yet for it, no one thinks to thank God."[31]

One of the keys to grasping Dickinson's poetry is to recognize and accept the value, and the intellectual primacy that she places on the unknown. She holds that what is knowable, at least here in this life, is finite, delimited by Circumference. Beyond that lies Awe.

FIVE

The King James Version

"[...] my knowledge of housekeeping is of about as much use as faith without works, which you know we are told is dead. Excuse my quoting from the scripture dear Abiah, for it was so handy in this case that I couldn't get along very well without *it.*"—L8, 25 September 1845

Biblical Allusion, Christian Typology and a Pagan Goddess

In the early letter to friend Abiah Root quoted above, Emily Dickinson, age fourteen, alludes to the epistle of James in her Bible.[1] This chapter establishes that she was intimately familiar with scripture and could assume that her readers and correspondents were similarly familiar. There were several Bibles in the Dickinson home, and her father read a chapter aloud to the family every morning when he was home. She attended a Sabbath school once a week, and Sunday church services ran for the entire day. Residents of Amherst in the nineteenth century heard scripture read and quoted every day, and throughout the day. There is no single source more frequently quoted or alluded to in Dickinson's poems, or in her letters, than the King James Version of the Bible. The following poem cannot be read with full comprehension without an understanding of its biblical and typological referents:

The murmuring of Bees, has ceased
But murmuring of some
Posterior, prophetic,
Has simultaneous come.
The lower metres of the Year
When Nature's laugh is done
The Revelations of the Book
Whose Genesis was June.

Appropriate Creatures to her change
The Typic Mother sends
As Accent fades to interval
With separating Friends
Till what we speculate, has been
And Thoughts we will not show
More intimate with us become
Than Persons, that we know.
—J1115/F1142/M540

Here is another poem of Indian summer like poems reviewed in Chapter 2. The murmuring honey bees and bumble bees of summer have returned to "those dim countries where they go" (See "I dreaded that first Robin, so" in Chapter 2) and now another *murmur* is heard—that of the crickets. The sound of the crickets arrives later in time than that of the bees—*Posterior-* and *prophetic*, because, as we saw in "'Twas later when the summer went" (Chapter 2) it is a sign that foretells the coming end of summer. *The lower metres of the Year are* lower, probably, because of the pulsating nature of the collective sound. The pitch of the cricket's sound is actually higher than that of the bees. *Revelations* refers to *The Revelation of Saint John the Divine*, the last book in the King James Bible. Indian summer is the last chapter in the book of summer; *June* is the first, as *Genesis* is the first book in the Bble. These *Creatures,* the crickets, that *the typic Mother sends* are appropriate to the *Change* of season. Here again is the language of biblical typology used to express exactly the same thing that it does in "Further in Summer than the Birds." *Mother* Nature (not God) *sends* the crickets to typify—to anticipate—the coming autumn. But here we have a further implication. A *Mother* is going through a *Change*. Menopause, or the "change of life," or simply "the change," was also described as the "Indian Summer" of a woman's life, as historian Carroll Smith-Rosenberg has found:

> If a woman had followed a sound regimen throughout life and had no predisposition to malignant disease, menopause could bring with it a golden age of health and freedom from the periodic inconvenience, pain, and depression of menstruation. The menopausal period could just become the "Indian Summer" of a woman's life—a period of increased vigor, optimism, and even of physical beauty.[2]

The crickets, these *Creatures* are *appropriate* in another sense than the simple seasonal one. A further implication lies in part in Dickinson's use of the word *Accent*, which she employs in ten poems. By considering that word within the body of her work, we form a more sure idea of what she intends. Another poem, *Where I have lost, I softer tread* for example, contains the lines,

Whom I have lost, I pious guard
From accent harsh, or ruthless word -
—J104/F158/M88

"Don't speak ill of the dead" is the commonly heard expression of this imperitive. Accent is a quality of the human voice, and as such can stand for the human voice itself. The subsiding sounds in the grass remind the poet of *separating friends,* as they begin to hear from each other only at *intervals*. She deems it appropriate to the coming *Change*. Friends may separate for reasons other than that one of them is moving away. When a friend dies, or when an especially beloved friend does move away, it is like summer fading into chilly autumn, followed inevitably by the silence of winter.

In this state of transition the speaker tells of *Thoughts we will not show*. Smith-Rosenberg goes on to explain that, in nineteenth-century America, communication between mother and daughter regarding the change from childhood to puberty could be so repressed, that the daughter was often left to contend with what would most likely be a traumatic experience under any circumstances, entirely alone.[3] These changes would indeed be accompanied by thoughts we do not show.

In the previous poem, the accents fading to intervals between separating friends convey a gentle, slightly melancholy tone. In "These saw visions," Dickinson manages to turn the same image into a much sharper, even painful one. This time it is indeed death that has forced the separation.

These - saw Visions -
Latch them softly -
These - held Dimples -
Smooth them slow -
This - addressed departing accents -
Quick - Sweet Mouth - to miss thee so -

This - We stroked -
Unnumbered Satin -
These - we held among our own -
Fingers of the Slim Aurora -
Not so arrogant - this Noon -

These - adjust - that ran to meet us -
Pearl - for Stocking - Pearl for Shoe -
Paradise - the only Palace
Fit for Her reception - now

—J758/F769/M357

The poem is spoken by someone at the open casket of a departed friend. She passes a last fond gaze over the body, beginning at the eyes. It is the job of the mortician to fasten the eyes closed.[4]

These saw Visions
Latch them softly -

The viewer's gaze falls next onto the cheek. She asks that the mortician, who must smooth the features to a repose-like state, to remove traces of the precious, vanished dimples slowly.

These held Dimples -
Smooth them slow -

The gaze falls next to the mouth which so recently spoke in the familiar voice and now is heard no more. *Quick* has two meanings. Applied to the word *miss,* we read "How quickly I miss hearing those accents!" Applied to *sweet mouth*, we read that the she misses that mouth that was once sweetly alive and animated. By not applying standard punctuation, Dickinson has left us with both meanings.

This - addressed departing accents -
Quick - Sweet Mouth - to miss thee so -

Now, the viewer lingers on the hair, the hair that she used to stroke lovingly, strands too numerous to count. The allusion is probably to Matthew 10:30, "But the very hairs of your head are all numbered"[5] Omniscient God knows the very numbers of those hairs, the speaker of the poem does not.

This - We stroked -
Unnumbered Satin -

And now, we come to the hands. Once the viewer held these fingers among her own. She likens the departed friend to the goddess Aurora. The word *arrogant* seems to have had some positive connotations, for Dickinson. She wrote to a correspondent, thanking him for a photograph of himself, "Your Face is more joyful, when you speak-and I miss an almost arrogant look that at times haunts you—but with that exception, it is so real I could think it you."[6]

Fingers of the Slim Aurora -
Not so arrogant - this Noon -

AU-RO′RA, n.
1. The rising light of the morning; the dawn of day, or morning twilight.
2. The goddess of the morning, or twilight deified by fancy. The poets represented her as rising out of the ocean, in a chariot, with rosy fingers dropping gentle dew.

At last, we arrive at the feet, which once ran to meet her friend, in their shoes and stockings. They must be set just so. Tears fall and lie glistening like pearls adorning the stocking and the shoe.

These - adjust - that ran to meet us -
Pearl - for Stocking - Pearl for Shoe -

We have surveyed the body from head to feet, with a vivid and reverent memory at every stopping-place. We step back at last for a final look upon the departed friend, taking in the whole, and note that only God's heaven is fit for her now.

Paradise - the only Palace
Fit for Her reception - now

"In my Father's house are many mansions: if *it were* not *so*, I would have told you. I go to prepare a place for you" (John 14:2).

In the next poem of separation it is not necessarily death that has caused the pain. The language of the poem, and the direct address to a *Savior* in the third stanza, suggest separation from the beloved now in *Heaven*, but the possibility that she is allowing this language to stand as metaphor for a separation from a loved one on Earth, cannot be entirely ruled out. I will argue that it doesn't matter. The poem leaves us with an experience of unspecified, but concentrated regret, and it does so in part by not tying the experience to a particular person—divine or otherwise—or circumstance.

I should have been too glad, I see -
Too lifted - for the scant degree
Of Life's penurious Round -
My little Circuit would have shamed
This new Circumference - have blamed -
The homelier time behind.

I should have been too saved - I see -
Too rescued - Fear too dim to me
That I could spell the Prayer
I knew so perfect - yesterday -
That Scalding One - Sabachthani -
Recited fluent - here -

Earth would have been too much - I see -
And Heaven - not enough for me -
I should have had the Joy
Without the Fear - to justify -
The Palm - without the Calvary -
So Savior - Crucify -

Defeat - whets Victory - they say -
The Reefs - in old Gethsemane -
Endear the Coast - beyond -
'Tis Beggars - Banquets best define -
'Tis Thirsting - vitalizes Wine -
Faith bleats to understand!

—J313/F283/M346

In the first verse, we find two words in Dickinson's special vocabulary that we have already encountered—*degree* and *Circumference.* The *new Circumference* that she has missed out on, a missed chance for love or a postponed heaven, is one of an expanded realm of existence. It is contrasted with another circle image, her *little circuit,* the *homelier* life left to her.

Emily Dickinson wrote to a valued friend, "Of our greatest acts we are ignorant - You were not aware that you saved my life."[7] She may have meant it figuratively, or she may have meant it literally, but the verb *saved* has a direct object in this letter, *my life.* When one is simply *saved*, however, it carries a greater force and suggests the saving of the soul, albeit often hyperbolically. Had she been *too saved*, she tells us, she would have forgotten yesterday's prayer. In the theological sense of the word; there are no degrees of salvation. You are either saved or you are damned. *Too saved,* then, we read as the poet's way of emphasizing the vastness of the discrepancy between her lost salvation and her present state. The *scalding prayer* that she recites is *sabachthani*—"And about the ninth hour Jesus cried out with a loud voice, saying, Eli, Eli, lama sabachthani?[8] That is to say, my God, my God, why hast thou forsaken me?" (Matthew 27:46).

The intensity continues in verse three. She would have preferred this *Earth* to *Heaven* had she received here on Earth the unnamed blessing. She would have had heavenly *joy* without the *Fear* of God to *justify* it. Justify, in the language of the Church, meant "set right before God." This would be very familiar language to Emily Dickinson's contemporaries from a foundational tenet of Calvinism, alluded to in the previous chapter, "Justification by Faith Alone," which is grounded in scripture. (How theologians reconciled this article of faith with the doctrine of unconditional election, or that "Faith without works is dead" according to James, we happily set aside.) "But for us also, to whom it shall be imputed, if we believe on him that raised up Jesus our Lord from the dead; Who was delivered for our offences, and was raised again for our justification" (Romans 4:24–25) and:

> or all have sinned, and come short of the glory of God; Being justified freely by his grace through the redemption that is in Christ Jesus: Whom God hath set forth *to be* a propitiation through faith in his blood, to declare his righteousness for the remission of sins that are past, through the forbearance of God To declare, I say, at this time his righteousness: that he might be just, and the justifier of him which believeth in Jesus [Romans 3:23–26].

The Palm-without the Calvary- refers to Jesus' triumphal entry into Jerusalem during the Jewish Passover celebration, where he was greeted by throngs of people like royalty: "On the next day much people that were come to the feast, when they heard that Jesus was coming to Jerusalem,

Took branches of palm trees, and went forth to meet him, and cried, Hosanna: Blessed *is* the King of Israel that cometh in the name of the Lord" (John 12:12–13). A few days later Jesus was crucified on Calvary.[9] The speaker likens her own fate to that of Jesus, which fate was preordained and necessary for the fulfilment of his mission.

The final line of the stanza is an imperative, directed toward *Savior*. There are at least two ways to read this. If the speaker is addressing Christ, then she wants to be identified with Him in his crucifixion, in the way discussed in Chapter 4. If, however, the speaker is addressing a beloved person from whom she is separated, and whom she addresses as her *Savior,* then she, too, is fated to suffer a metaphorical "crucifixion," through him or her

The first line of the final stanza is reminiscent of another Dickinson poem, "Success is counted sweetest /By those who n'er succeed" (J67/F112/M69), which conveys the idea that deprivation magnifies the value of success, or victory. By ending the statement with *they say-*, she lets us know that she's not entirely convinced herself. Gethsemane, as noted previously, is the site of Jesus' final agony before crucifixion. Gethsemane was a garden; there could have been no *reefs* there. Ships are wrecked on reefs, though, often in site of the *coas*t and safety, a coast looking so much more precious now. *Banquets* seem most sumptuous to *Beggars*—those who have long been deprived of sustenance. *Wine* is most appreciated by those suffering from a *parching* thirst. These observations would suggest that her suffering may have a purpose and a value. It is this hopeful notion which *Faith bleats to understand.* Bleating is the sound that sheep make, that follow unquestioningly to wherever they are lead, and, in a second copy of this final verse, sent to ED's sister-in-law, the word *faith* is in quotation marks, indicating that it is from an external source and is not her own. "Faith is Doubt,"[10] she once wrote, and on this note of doubt the poem ends.

The Vail

We return now to the first stanza of poem J263/F293/M138, which we considered first in Chapter 1, where I promised to look more closely at the *vail* spoken of there. A factual knowledge of this particular vail helps to bring this poem and others into focus.

A single Screw of Flesh
Is all that pins the Soul
That stands for Deity, to Mine,
Upon my side the Vail -

The word vail (also spelled veil), when used metaphorically, may stand for an obscuring or hiding of something. A "vail," for example, can be said to exist between us and the afterlife, or between us and God. We may speak of a "veiled threat," when the danger is expressed indirectly. But Dickinson's contemporaries would have recognized another association—one to a physical vail which was believed indeed to stand between God and His people.

The Book of Exodus narrates a period of the Israelites "wandering in the wilderness" before arriving in the land that God had promised to their patriarchal ancestors. During their wandering their leader, Moses, meets God face-to-face on a mountain top and receives two tablets on which are written God's commandments to his people. By agreeing to abide by the commandments, the Israelites enter into a covenant with God. He will protect them as long as they obey His commands. God then commands Moses to direct his people to build a sanctuary: "And let them make a sanctuary for me that I might dwell among them" (Exodus 25:8). There follow detailed instructions on how to build the sanctuary, including all materials, dimensions, and furnishings. Dimensions are given in cubits,[11] a word that you will find in several Dickinson poems. The sanctuary, often called The Tabernacle ("tent" or "dwelling place"), will be God's dwelling place on earth: "Then I will dwell among the Israelites and be their God. They will know that I am the Lord their God, who brought them out of Egypt so that I might dwell among them" (Exodus 29:45–46).

The tabernacle was surrounded by four walls of fabric. One entered, by way of an aperture covered by a hanging cloth, into a courtyard. The walls were constructed so that no one could see into the courtyard from the outside, and only Israelites were permitted inside. Within the courtyard was a tent, which one entered by way of a vail into "The Holy Place." Once within The Holy Place, one would find another vail, behind which was a smaller space called The Holy of Holies. Here was kept the Ark of the Covenant, a chest containing the sacred tablets. This is the most sacred of places, and here God himself dwelt among his chosen people. Only the High Priest was permitted to enter therein, and he only once a year. It is this powerful image of The Holy of Holies behind the second vail[12] that lends the stanza its power.

In this poem, a vail exists between the speaker and someone who has died, but this someone is *The Soul that stands for Deity* to her soul. By calling to mind the second vail of the tabernacle, she lends to the departed person an association with *Deity*—with God. This should not startle us; we've seen that it was not an uncommon practice to assign divine attributes to a romantic love.

Keeping the image of the second vail of the tabernacle in mind makes the meaning of the last line of the following poem easy to appreciate.

The last of Summer is Delight -
Deterred by Retrospect.
'Tis Ecstasy's revealed Review -
Enchantment's Syndicate.

To meet it - nameless as it is -
Without celestial Mail -
Audacious as without a Knock
To walk within the Veil.
—J1353/F1380/M521

The delight of the last days of summer is *deterred*—discouraged, prevented—on looking back on the long days now passed away. As in "Summer begins to have the look" (Chapter 2) the speaker's *Delight* in summer is reduced somewhat as she *Reluctantly but sure perceives/A gain upon the backward leaves.* Etymologically, to *reveal* is to unveil, and a *review* is a look back or seeing again. *Syndicate,* in its verb form, is to publish severally (or manage). The delight of summer's last days is discouraged, or perhaps even prevented, on looking back. We know that we're coming to the end. It is the result of reviewing the *ecstasy* past.

For another example of a metaphoric vail, see "Faith - is the Pierless Bridge" (J915/F978/M451).

The Book of Revelation

In Chapter 1 we noted that ED seems to have been especially drawn to the last book of her Bible, the full title of which is The Revelation of Saint John the Divine (often shortened to "Revelation"). In Revelation, John[13] records what he saw and heard in visions given him by God, including spoken words of Jesus Christ. In this section we will see how Dickinson uses images from Revelation to express her own thoughts, ideas, and feelings. We begin our first example, however, in the Gospel According to St. Matthew: "Jesus, when he had cried again with a loud voice, yielded up the ghost. And, behold, the veil of the temple was rent in twain from the top to the bottom; and the earth did quake, and the rocks rent; And the graves were opened; and many bodies of the saints which slept arose, And came out of the graves after his resurrection, and went into the holy city, and appeared unto many" (Matthew 27:50–54). It is this day of the Resurrection to which Dickinson refers in the first stanza of the next poem, which is surely among her most passionate.

There came a Day at Summer's full,
Entirely for me -
I thought that such were for the Saints,
Where Resurrections - be -

The Sun, as common, went abroad,
The flowers, accustomed, blew,
As if no soul the solstice passed
That maketh all things new -

The time was scarce profaned, by speech -
The symbol of a word
Was needless, as at Sacrament,
The Wardrobe - of our Lord -

Each was to each The Sealed Church,
Permitted to commune this - time -
Lest we too awkward show
At Supper of the Lamb.

The Hours slid fast - as Hours will,
Clutched tight, by greedy hands -
So faces on two Decks, look back,
Bound to opposing lands -

And so when all the time had leaked,
Without external sound
Each bound the Other's Crucifix -
We gave no other Bond -

Sufficient troth, that we shall rise -
Deposed - at length, the Grave -
To that new Marriage,
Justified - through Calvaries of Love -
—J322/F325/M155

The poet has lived a day that seems to her as glorious as the day of the risen Jesus and the resurrection from the dead of saints, as told in Matthew. In the second stanza she draws from Revelation: "And God shall wipe away all tears from their eyes; and there shall be no more death, neither sorrow, nor crying, neither shall there be any more pain: for the former things are passed away. And he that sat upon the throne said, Behold, I make all things new. And he said unto me, Write: for these words are true and faithful" (Revelation 21:4–5).

She may have chosen the word "maketh" instead of "make" to fit the meter. The option would have been familiar to her from a hymn written by Sam Longfellow:

The freer step, the fuller breath,
The wide horizon's grander view,
The sense of life that knows no death,
The Life that maketh all things new!

In stanza three, *The Wardrobe of our Lord* is the physical body of Christ, which is not necessary at *Sacrament*, as He is there in spirit. Clothing as a metaphor for the physical body is found elsewhere in the Bible: "It is sown a natural body; it is raised a spiritual body. There is a natural body, and there is a spiritual body" (I Corinthians 15:44) and "For we know that if our earthly house of *this* tabernacle were dissolved, we have a building of God, an house not made with hands, eternal in the heavens. For in this we groan, earnestly desiring to be clothed upon with our house which is from heaven" (2 Corinthians 5:1–2). The "earthly house" to which Paul refers is the physical body. The "house not made with hands" is the spiritual body. The physical body as clothing was a familiar metaphor in the popular culture of the nineteenth century.

> Take them, O Grave! and let them lie
> Folded upon thy narrow shelves,
> As garments by the soul laid by,
> And precious only to ourselves!
> —Henry Wadsworth Longfellow, "Suspiria"

And, finally on this point, Dickinson used the body-clothes metaphor elsewhere in her work. *Perhaps they do not go so far,* she speculates about those who have passed beyond this mortal life. Might they not be closer than we realize now without their physical bodies, their *corporeal clothes*. Dickinson does not write "lack of" their corporeal clothes, as we might expect, but rather, *lapse of,* meaning in this case a falling, or a passing.

> Perhaps they do not go so far
> As we who stay, suppose -
> Perhaps come closer, for the lapse
> Of their corporeal clothes -
> —J1399/F1455/M608

The supper of the Lamb is a marriage supper. Jesus was, for humanity, as a sacrificial lamb unto God. The lamb in Revelation is Jesus Christ: "And he saith unto me, Write, Blessed *are* they which are called unto the marriage supper of the Lamb. And he saith unto me, These are the true sayings of God" (Revelation 19:9). To whom is the Lamb married? In the gospels, Jesus compares himself to a bridegroom of the faithful (Matthew 8:15, Mark 2:19, Luke 5:34). Husband and wife, *sealed* in marriage, are to each other as Christ is to his Church. In the language of the New Testament, the church is not a building or collection of buildings. The church is the community of faithful believers.

> For the husband is the head of the wife, even as Christ is the head of the church: and he is the saviour of the body. Therefore as the church is subject unto Christ, so *let* the wives *be* to their own husbands in every thing. Husbands, love your wives, even as

Christ also loved the church, and gave himself for it; That he might sanctify and cleanse it with the washing of water by the word, That he might present it to himself a glorious church, not having spot, or wrinkle, or any such thing; but that it should be holy and without blemish [Ephesians 5:23–27].

The speaker in Dickinson's poem, however, experiences no such final union. The two must part. The image is of two persons, each on the *deck* of a different ship. The ships are sailing away from each other toward separate destinations, while the two look back towards each other as the distance between them grows. The final stanza offers a particularly dense combination of biblical allusions. *Sufficient troth, that we shall rise* alludes to the promise of the resurrection. *Deposed - at length, the Grave* - relies on God's word that there shall be no more death: "He will wipe every tear from their eyes. There will be no more death' or mourning or crying or pain, for the old order of things has passed away" (Revelation 21:4).

Jesus taught that marriage between persons does not exist in the afterlife.[14] The last line of the poem contains language with which we are now familiar—*Justified - through Calvaries of Love*—set right before God through pain and suffering, in the image of the crucifixion.

In Chapter 2 of Revelation Jesus says to John: "Fear none of those things which thou shalt suffer: Behold, the devil shall cast some of you into prison, that ye may be tried; and ye shall have tribulation ten days: Be thou faithful unto death, and I will give thee a crown of life" (Revelation 2:10). Emily Dickinson responds to Jesus' offer in a way that the pastor of her church would not have approved.

"Faithful to the end" Amended
From the Heavenly Clause -
Constancy with a Proviso
Constancy abhors -

"Crowns of Life" are servile Prizes
To the stately Heart,
Given for the Giving, solely,
No Emolument.

—J1357 (Version 1)/F1386/M591

"Faithful to the end" Amended
From the Heavenly clause -
Lucrative indeed the offer
But the Heart withdraws -

"I will give" the base Proviso -
Spare Your "Crown of Life" -
Those it fits, too fair to wear it -
Try it on Yourself -

—J1357 (Version 2) (Johnson includes this second version in his reader's edition)

ED rejects this particular crown because it comes with a *Proviso;* she is promised it *provided* that she remains *faithful to the end.* But, her *constancy*—her continued and constant faith—would require no such promise. She abhors the very notion of being bribed for faithfulness. The second stanza offers a good example of lines that may be read in more than one way. Read:

"Crowns of Life" are servile Prizes
To the stately Heart

Read also:

To the stately Heart,
[constancy is] Given for the Giving, solely

E-MOL′U-MENT, n.
1. The profit arising from office or employment; that which is received as a compensation for services, or which is annexed to the possession of office, as salary, fees and perquisites.
2. Profit; advantage; gains in general.

She would ask nothing in return for her devotion. She finds the *Proviso* implying that she would require a reward *base.*

BASE, a.
1. Low in place. [Obs.]
2. Mean; vile; worthless; that is, low in value or estimation; used of things.

Emily Dickinson lived in a family of lawyers. She heard the language of the law around her home growing up; her poems contain a lot of it.

PRO-VI′SO, n.
An article or clause in any statute, agreement, contract, grant or other writing, by which a condition is introduced; a conditional stipulation that affects an agreement, contract, law, grant, &c. The charter of the bank contains a proviso that the legislature may repeal it at their pleasure

Some Very Different Crowns

There are other "crowns" in Emily Dickinson's vocabulary. A favorite word of hers, *diadem,* is a kind of crown with entirely different connotations. (It appears in fourteen of her poems).

DI′A-DEM, n.
2. In modern usage, the mark or badge of royalty, worn on the head; a crown; and figuratively, empire; supreme power.

In the this sense, the wearer of the diadem crown is as someone endowed with nobility, high station, and of rare privilege; Moreover, Roman soldiers placed a crown of thorns on Jesus' head before crucifying him.[15] Used in this other sense, the crown of thorns becomes a general symbol for inflicted suffering. Dickinson contrasts both crowns in the final two stanzas of *Rearrange a "Wife's" affection!*

Burden - borne so far triumphant -
None suspect me of the crown,
For I wear the "Thorns" till *Sunset* -
Then - my Diadem put on.

Big my Secret but it's *bandaged*
It will never get away
Till the Day its Weary Keeper
Leads it through the Grave to thee.
—J1737/F267/M132

Emily Dickinson revered English poet Elizabeth Barret Browning well enough to have an engraved portrait of the English poet on her bedroom wall. In Browning's *Aurora Leigh,* the poet playfully fashions a poet's crown for herself (see Appendix A). Dickinson seems to have liked the idea and adopted it for herself in "The face I carry with me - last," our next poem, and in others as well. She wrote to friend, apparently after receiving a book of poems from him, "My crown indeed! I do not fear the King, attired in this grandeur. Please send me gems again. - I have a flower. It looks like them, and for it's bright resemblance, receive it"[16] (ED refers to her poems as her flowers). And so the heavenly crowns are not always spurned.

The face I carry with me - last -
When I go out of Time -
To take my Rank - by - in the West -
That face - will just be thine -

I'll hand it to the Angel -
That - Sir - was my Degree -
In Kingdoms - you have heard the Raised -
Refer to - possibly.

He'll take it - scan it - step aside -
Return - with such a crown
As Gabriel - never capered at -
And beg me put it on -

And then - he'll turn me round and round -
To an admiring sky -
As one that bore her Master's name -
Sufficient Royalty!
—J336/F395/M211

Some of the language in this poem is perhaps becoming familiar now. Going *out of time* is to go from this life into eternity. When the speaker does so, she will be *in the west,* which may be associated with the end of life, eternity, and the unknown. One of fourteen definitions of *face* in her dictionary is

> FACE, n.
> 4. Countenance; cast of features; look; air of the face.

Today, after an attempt to soften the effects of some adverse circumstance, we might say, "We set the best face on it that we could." It is the face in this sense, which she associates with the person addressed, that she will take with her to present *to the Angel.* The face will be proof of her former *degree* on earth, in the understanding of this word that we have also noted, "A step or portion of progression, in elevation, quality, dignity or rank; as, a man of great degree."

And then the new arrival receives her heavenly crown.

> CA´PER, v.i.
> To leap; to skip or jump; to prance; to spring

One smiles at the thought of the great archangel Gabriel capering about like a overexcited child. Any tendancy to read the poem with grave solemnity is checked here.

The Symbolic White

Emily Dickinson famously began dressing in white at some point in the latter half of her life. Why she did so has been the subject of much speculation, ranging from self-appointed nun (Bride of Christ) through abandoned bride to reclusive priestess of high art. Still others suggest that white was a symbol of her death to the world. Whatever the reason may have been, white has special and varied significance in her writing. Charles Anderson wrote[17]: "To pin down the exact significance of White for Dickinson is impossible. It permeates her writing with several shades of meaning. She used it, for example, as the characteristic color of death in 'the White Exploit,' and God in 'The White Creator.'"[18]

In the next poem, "Of Tribulation, these are They," the scriptural white seems most helpful, and so we turn again to Revelation: "Thou hast a few names even in Sardis that have not defiled their garments; and they shall walk with me in white, for they are worthy. He that overcometh the same shall be clothed in white raiment; and I will not blot out his name from the book of life, but I will confess his name before my father, and before his angels" (Revelation 3:4–5). "And after this I beheld, and lo, a great multitude, which no man could number, of all nations and kindreds, and people and tongues, stood before the throne, and before the lamb, clothed with white robes, and palms in their hands" (Revelation 7:9). "And to her [the bride of the lamb] was granted that she should be arrayed in fine linen, clean and white: for the fine linen is the righteousness' of saints" (Revelation 19:8).

Of Tribulation, these are They,
Denoted by the White.
The Spangled Gowns, a lesser Rank
Of Victors, designate -

All these - did conquer -
But the Ones who overcame most times -
Wear nothing commoner than Snow -
No Ornament, - but Palms -

"Surrender" - is a sort unknown -
On this Superior soil -
"Defeat" - an Outgrown Anguish -
Remembered, as the Mile

Our panting Ancle barely passed -
When Night devoured the Road -
But we - stood - whispering in the House -
And all we said - was
"SAVED"!

—J325/F328/M157

Those arrayed in white robes have come out of great *Tribulation*. Here again is Dickinson's theme of a purifying suffering necessary to yield the highest perfection, as in, for example, *Essential Oils—are wrung*—(Chapter 1). Those arrayed in *Spangled Gowns,* richer and more luxurious than plain white ones, are nevertheless of a *lesser rank*, although they *did conquer;* they are *victors* because they, too, are among the *saved. Snow* is another way of indicating white, in the sense of purity.

> And one of the elders answered, saying unto me, What are these that are arrayed in white robes? and whence camest they? And I said unto him, Sir, thou knowest. And he said to me, these are they which came out of great tribulation., and have washed their robes, and made them white in the blood of the lamb. Therefore are they before the throne of God, and serve him day and night in his temple: and he that sitteth on the throne shall dwell among them [Revelation 7:13–15].

In addition to S*now*, Dickinson also used words such as bone, marble, alabaster, and pale to connote whiteness, depending on what shade of meaning she intended.

Continuing on to stanza three with Revelation still our guide, we must ask, "to what have these superior souls not surrendered?" Is it loss of faith perhaps? Unbelief? Or despair, *When Night devoured the Road*? Whatever it was, those who endured and were "faithful to the end" are now *Saved!* This is perhaps not a poem of a particular triumph of perseverance, but rather a universal message of faith given in the language of Revelation.

Dickinson sent this poem to Thomas Wentworth Higginson. At the bottom of the page she wrote, "I spelled Ankle - wrong." "Ancle," however, is a British spelling of the word, and she certainly saw that spelling in her Bible.[19]

In the next poem, "Mine - by the Right of the White Election!," "white" has been read by many scholars as alluding to a bridal dress. However, brides did not customarily wear white in the United States until in the late 1870s,[20] and the poem is dated by editors to 1862. White was the color of a northern European background associated with purity and excellence,[21] but Dickinson does not appear to have applied it in that sense either. However, in the 1850s and 60s, white was the color of royalty, of order and tradition against the red of republicanism,[22] and there is perhaps a glance at that meaning here.

Mine - by the Right of the White Election!
Mine - by the Royal Seal!
Mine - by the Sign in the Scarlet prison -
Bars - cannot conceal!

Mine - here - in Vision - and in Veto!
Mine - by the Grave's Repeal -
Titled - Confirmed -
Delirious Charter!
Mine - long as Ages steal!

—J528/F411/M219

Understanding the significance of the word *Election* as denoting God's favor and promise of salvation, and having found whiteness in abundance in Revelation, encourages us to interpret the first line of the poem scripturally. In the second line, we find an association of white with royalty, as noted above, and also in Revelation, we find a coherent meaning for the *Seal*: "And I saw another angel ascending from the east, having the seal of the living God: and he cried with a loud voice to the four angels, to whom it was given to hurt the earth and the sea, Saying, Hurt not the earth, neither the sea, nor the trees, till we have sealed the servants of our God in their forehead" (Revelation 7:2–3). Those receiving the seal in their foreheads are none other than the elect of God. The poem is an imaginative projection into that spiritual salvation of which the speaker is certain. She is certain by her election, by having received the seal, and by a sign that she knows is in her heart, the scarlet prison of mortality. In the words of John Calvin, "As it is not for us to penetrate into God's secret council, to seek there assurance of our salvation, he specifies signs or tokens of our election which should suffice us for the assurance of it."[23]

With Charles Anderson's words in mind about the impossibility of pinning down Dickinson's White, consider the following poem.

> Why - do they shut Me out of Heaven?
> Did I sing - too loud?
> But - I can say a little "Minor"
> Timid as a Bird!
>
> Wouldn't the Angels try me -
> Just - once - more -
> Just - see - if I troubled them -
> But don't - shut the door!
>
> Oh, if I - were the Gentleman
> In the "White Robe" -
> And they - were the little Hand - that knocked -
> Could - I - forbid?
>
> —J248/F268/M133

Here the poet imagines herself shut out of heaven for an unknown offense. Dickinson often spoke of her writing of poetry as *singing,* which explains the word *say* in the third line. One does not *say* music, but one does say poetry. The association of singing and saying permits a pun on the word *Minor*, as referring both to a smaller, quieter voice and to a minor key in music. In the poet's scenario, it is the angels in heaven who have shut her out. For the *Gentleman in the "White Robe"* we return to Matthew: "And behold, a severe earthquake had occurred, for an angel of the Lord descended from heaven and came and rolled away the stone and sat upon it. And his appearance was like lightning, and his clothing as white as snow" (Matthew 28:2–3). The incident described follows the crucifixion of Jesus. A different version of the same incident appears in the The Gospel According to Saint Mark: "And entering into the sepulchre, they saw a young man sitting on the right side, clothed in a long white garment; and they were affrighted. And he said to them, 'Do not be amazed; you are looking for Jesus the Nazarene, who has been crucified. He has risen; He is not here; behold, here is the place where they laid Him'" (Mark 16:5–6). In both scenarios the white-robed visitor is an angel. "Could she forbid the angel entry into heaven, should he knock?" she asks herself. The question is rhetorical; she knows that she could not forbid.

Intimate with the Gospels

In a letter to two dear friends, Emily wrote, "If prayers had any answers to them, you were all here to-night, but I seek and I don't find, and knock and it is not opened. Wonder if God is just - presume He is, however, and 'twas only a blunder of Matthew's."[24] The allusion is to Matthew 7:7: "Ask, and it will be given to you; seek, and you will find; knock, and it will be opened to you." Emily knew that her letter's recipients would recognize the allusion instantly, as any other one of her circle or the wider community would have. This small example indicates just how intimate these people were with the four biblical Gospels, Matthew, Mark, Luke, and John. Of these, the most important to Dickinson was Matthew, followed by John.[25] Without familiarity with the Gospel of John, the identity of Philip in the following final two stanzas of "The Frost was never seen" would be unknown, and much of the import of the poem would be missed.

> Unproved is much we know -
> Unknown the worst we fear -
> Of Strangers is the Earth the Inn
> Of Secrets is the Air -
>
> To analyze perhaps
> A Philip would prefer
> But Labor vaster than myself
> I find it to infer.
>
> —J1202/F1190/M554

In John, Jesus tells his disciples that the way to God the Father[26] is through himself, and that anyone who has known him, Jesus, has also known the Father. The disciple Philip asks Jesus to show them the Father: "Jesus saith unto him, Have I been so long time with you, and yet hast thou not known me, Philip? He that hath seen me hath seen the Father; and how sayest thou *then*, Shew us the Father" (John 14:9).

The Earth houses strangers, the poet tells us, and the air is full of secrets. She will not, as *A Philip* would, subject these mysteries to the curiosity of the intellect, satisfied to rest in the belief that to do so would be a labor *vaster* than herself, that is, beyond her circumference. Again, as in "Four Trees - Upon a solitary Acre" (Chapter 4), the mind comes to rest in the unknown. Keeping this "greatest need of the intellect" always in mind is key to grasping the profound meaning for Dickinson of the unknowable. It is not anxiety producing; quite the opposite, it is necessary for sanity and is where peace may be found.

For Christians looking for signs of God's divine intent in natural phenomena, spring was a sign of God's promise of a new life after death. In the following poem, Dickinson describes changes that she observes as spring approaches, and ends with a triumphant reflection on her "flood subject."

An altered look about the hills -
A Tyrian light the village fills -
A wider sunrise in the morn -
A deeper twilight on the lawn -
A print of a vermilion foot -
A purple finger on the slope -
A flippant fly upon the pane -
A spider at his trade again -
An added strut in Chanticleer -
A flower expected everywhere -
An axe shrill singing in the woods -
Fern odors on untravelled roads -
All this, and more I cannot tell -
A furtive look you know as well -
And Nicodemus' Mystery
Receives its annual reply!
—J140/F90/M64

As spring is just beginning, the poet notes the change in the light that comes with it.

TYR'I-AN, a.
1. Pertaining to the ancient Tyre.
2. Being of a purple color.

The EDL provides a fuller explanation for Dickinson's particular use of this adjective than her dictionary offers.

TYRIAN, proper adj. [see Tyrian, n.]
Mediterranean; Middle Eastern; pertaining to Tyre; of the port in Southern Lebanon on the Mediterranean Sea; capital of purple dye industry in the ancient world; [fig.] royal; majestic; [metaphor] purple; scarlet; violet.

Changing light, creatures stirring to life, human activity resuming, the fragrant odors of reappearing plants, *and more,* announce the arrival of the welcome new season, all in seeming *reply* to *Nicodemus' mystery.* The reference is to John Chapter 3. Jesus has explained to Nicodemus that he, Nicodemus, must be born again (or, "born from above" in other translations). Nicodemus asks how a man can be born again. Jesus tells him: "Marvel not that I say unto ye that ye must be born again. The wind bloweth where it listeth, and thou hearest the sound thereof, but canst not tell whence it cometh, and whither it goeth: so is every one that is born of the Spirit. Nicodemus answered and said unto him, How can these things be?"

(John 3:7–9). "How can a person be born again?" poor Nicodemus asks. He receives his *annual reply* in the rebirths witnessed in nature, the signs of God's intent for us. The gospels of Matthew, Mark, and Luke all relate how Jesus selected a number of his disciples from among fishermen. In the ancient near east fishermen were simple working men, generally illiterate, but the disciples of Jesus occupied high "degree," in Emily's language. In nineteenth-century America, a fisherman was also a hard-working man not of particularly high social status, or as the poet puts it in the next poem, he was of *freckled human nature*, and not at all saintly.

What Soft - Cherubic Creatures -
These Gentlewomen are -
One would as soon assault a Plush -
Or violate a Star -

Such Dimity Convictions -
A Horror so refined
Of freckled Human Nature -
Of Deity - ashamed -

It's such a common - Glory -
A Fisherman's - Degree -
Redemption - Brittle Lady -
Be so - ashamed of Thee -
—J401/F675/M418

ED is taking a satirical look at the less admirable traits in some of her female neighbors. *Dimity* is a kind of white cotton cloth, sheer, lightweight, and inexpensive. Using the adjective form of the word, Dickinson transfers the properties of lightweightedness and insubstantiality to the *Gentlewomen's convictions.* Among those convictions is an expressed *Horror* at *freckled Human Nature.* Freckles were often seen as imperfection in the human complexion. See, for example, "Themself are all I have" (J1094/F1054/M473).Here freckles are metaphorically applied to human nature itself, suggesting imperfections in character and behavior. Dickinson implies that having such an attitude is like being ashamed of *Deity.* They see the surface freckles, but not the *Glory* within. See "This dirty - little - Heart" (J1311/F1378/M521) for example. Simple human nature is so *common,* yet Jesus' disciples, some no more than common fishermen, were men of the highest *degree* and regarded as saints, "And Jesus, walking by the sea of Galilee, saw two brethren, Simon called Peter, and Andrew his brother, casting a net into the sea: for they were fishers. And he saith unto them, Follow me, and I will make you fishers of men. And they straightway left *their* nets, and followed him" (Matthew 4:18–20).

We have encountered the words "saved" and "salvation" before, in the sense of being saved by the grace of God for eternal life. Another expression for the same condition is *Redemption.* Jesus is often called the Redeemer.

> RE-DEMP'TION, n.
>
> 6. In theology, the purchase of God's favor by the death and sufferings of Christ; the ransom or deliverance of sinners from the bondage of sin and the penalties of God's violated law by the atonement of Christ.
>
> Paul, in his epistle to the Ephesians, indicates that mortals can cause the Deity to be ashamed of them by speaking ill.

"Let no corrupt communication proceed out of your mouth, but that which is good to the use of edifying, that it may minister grace unto the hearers. And grieve not the Holy Spirit of God, whereby ye are sealed unto the day of redemption" (Ephesians 4:29:30).

The *Soft Cherubic Creatures* at the start of the poem are *Brittle Ladies* at the end. It's as if we begin with a charitable, if superficial, appraisal of the ladies, and are lead through further scrutiny to the opposite view.

Dickinson will often enclose words from scripture in quotation marks. In fact, quotation marks are a good clue that the words enclosed might be from the Bible, which can be helpful when in doubt.

> You're right - "the way is narrow" -
> And "difficult the Gate" -
> And "few there be" - Correct again -
> That "enter in -thereat" -
>
> *'Tis* Costly - So are *purples*!
> 'Tis just the price of *Breath* -
> With but the "Discount" of the Grave -
> Termed by the *Brokers* - *"Death"*!
>
> And after *that* - there's Heaven -
> The *Good* Man's - *"Dividend"* -
> And Bad Men - "go to Jail" -
> I guess -
>
> —J234/F249/M122

The speaker seems either to converse with someone quoting scripture to her in conversation, or she is addressing her Bible itself. The tone is that of a jaunty conversation. The first stanza draws from a well-known verse in Matthew. Jesus teaches: "Enter ye in at the strait gate: for wide *is* the gate, and broad *is* the way, that leadeth to destruction, and many there be which go in thereat: Because strait *is* the gate, and narrow *is* the way, which leadeth unto life, and few there be that find it" (Matthew 7:13–14).

The second stanza begins with an allusion to The Acts of the Apostles: "And a certain woman named Lydia, a seller of purple, of the city of Thyatira, which worshipped God, heard *us*: whose heart the Lord opened, that she attended unto the things which were spoken of Paul" (Acts 16:14). The city of Thyatira[27] was famous for its dyes. The purple dye was of high value and, as a seller of purple dye and fabrics, Lydia was a successful business woman who gave aid and succor to Paul and other early disciples.

The way to salvation is narrow and difficult, and what is at journey's end—heaven—is purchased at the *price of Breath,* which must be given up in order to attain it. The price is *Discounted,* though, by *the Grave,* which promises to bring the narrow way to an eventual end in *Death*, freeing us from further obligation. The language of trade and commerce, applied to the serious subject of death and the afterlife, extends the conversational tone that began the poem to one of ironic irreverence. In the words *Good Man's* and *Bad Men* there is an echo of the kinds of admonitions directed at children, making the proposition of *Heaven* itself seem a bit fanciful. The poem ends abruptly, in doubt, with the final stanza abbreviated and sounding incomplete, reflecting, within the structure of the verse itself, that the speaker has not completed her engagement with the question of what lies beyond this mortal life.

From the last two chapters, we can appreciate how important it is to understand Dickinson's Christian heritage and the main religious text—her Bible—on which she so steadily relied. There are at times more specific contexts, often of a personal nature, for individual poems as well. This is the subject of our next chapter.

SIX

The Poem in Context

"You and I did'nt[1] finish talking. Have you room for the sequel, in your vase?"—L270, about 20 July 1862

In the introduction, I explained that we would approach the poetry using three different strategies. In the preceding chapters, we focused on words that were available to her in her time and place in history, including language and usages with dominant religious or biblical connotations, and on her private and esoteric vocabulary. Now we will turn to poems that are connected to a certain person, object, or local condition that is often not apparent at all. We have seen one such poem, "If she had been the Mistletoe" (Chapter 1), sent to Mr. and Mrs. Samuel Bowles. These are poems, sent to friends and family members, that may relate to a specific event or relationship. There are poems that were never meant to stand alone on a page. They accompanied gifts, letters, or flowers or were connected to specific conditions or developments in the community. These poems can be especially enjoyable to read. Knowing to whom they were sent, and what that person or persons may have meant to Emily, knowing the circumstances and a detail or two about what might have accompanied the poem, we are brought back to the nineteenth century and seem to stand closer to this ever-fascinating poet.

"My Friends are my Estate"

The letter (L270) quoted above, to Emily's distant cousin Eudocia Flynt, included a flower for her cousin's vase. It also included a poem. Again, Emily Dickinson sometimes referred to her poems as her flowers. In the poem for her cousin, the flower and poetry are brought together in one image.

All the letters I can write
Are not fair as this -
Syllables of Velvet -
Sentences of Plush,
Depths of Ruby, undrained,
Hid, Lip, for Thee -
Play it were a Humming Bird -
And just sipped - me -
—J334/F380/M202

"This," in the second line, is the enclosed flower, which offers *velvet* and *plush* fairer than the *syllables* or *sentences* of any letter that she could write. The flower may have been a tea rose, or similarly shaped flower. The tea rose gets its name from the fact that when a person tilts the blossom to her nose to inhale the fragrance, the lower edge touches her lips, and it appears that she is drinking from a tea cup.

"It," in the next-to-last line, as some, including your author, reads it, refers to the person addressed, cousin Eudocia. Others have read "it" as referring to a specific hummingbird, and that the poem is concerned entirely with that hummingbird—a very good example of how widely differently even devoted Dickinson readers may interpret a poem. It was an occasional and peculiar practice of the poet's to substitute "it" where normally one would say "you" (or "he" or "she"). She is saying, "pretend you are a hummingbird as you bring the flower to your nose and lips and that you are sipping me!" Other examples of this unusual usage can be found in a draft letter to an unknown recipient (words in brackets are crossed out on the holograph, while words in parenthesis are written above the word preceding it):

Oh - did I offend it - [Did'nt it want me to tell it the truth] Daisy - Daisy - offend it - who bends her smaller life to his (it's) meeker (lower) every day[2]

And, in this verse from a longer poem:

If it had no pencil
Would it try mine -
Worn - now - and *dull* - sweet,
Writing much to thee.
—J921/F184/M527

ED sent the poem above to close family friend, the aforementioned Samuel Bowles. Bowles was one of the great journalists of the nineteenth century, travelled widely, and was by all accounts an energetic, charismatic man who drew people to him. He thought enough of Emily's poetry to print five of them in his influential newspaper, *The Springfield Republican* (anonymous, without her permission, and edited). Emily, a prolific letter writer, importuned her correspondents to write back to her soon and at length. She made no exception, apparently, for the busy and hardworking Bowles. She teased him about his perceived unresponsiveness with the poem above, which was accompanied by a worn stub of a pencil.

Here is a poem that ED sent to her young nephew Ned. Would you guess what this poem is "about" if you read it alone on the page?

Drab Habitation of Whom?
Tabernacle or Tomb -
Or Dome of Worm -
Or Porch of Gnome -
Or some Elf's Catacomb?
—J893/F916/M431

The poet's niece, Martha Dickinson Bianchi, wrote that ED sent a copy of this poem "with a cocoon to her little nephew."[3] Ned Dickinson, born in June of 1861, would have been three or four years old, so fortunately his Aunt Emily provided a clue. The playful sound of the poem, created by a series of five near-rhymes, would appeal to a child without the child's needing to understand it. Must you know that it is a description of a cocoon to enjoy the poem? Perhaps not. It might otherwise hint at some unformed mystery and left to our imagination. But knowing the little concomitant piece of history can add a certain pleasing perspective to the poem. It really is a marvelous description of a cocoon.

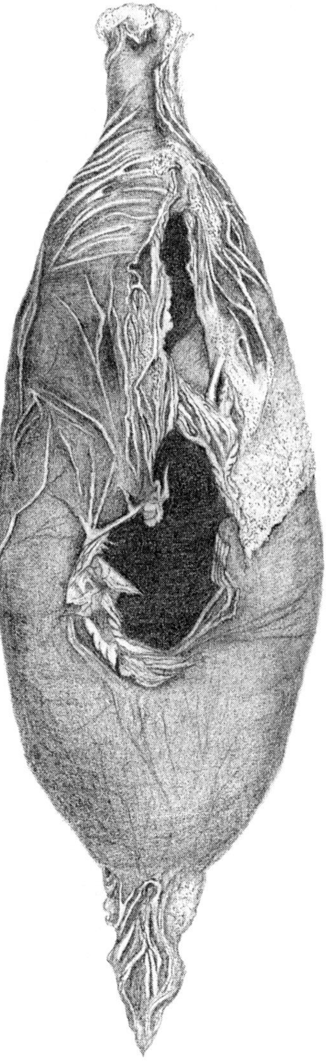

"Cocoon" (drawing by Julie Gough [UK]).

ED's "estate" included Kate Scott Turner (later Anthon), introduced earlier in this book (Chapter 3), who, in February of 1859, paid a visit to ED's sister-in-law, Susan, in Amherst. The two were dear friends, and Emily soon adopted Kate into her heart as Susan already had. Soon after that first visit, Emily expressed her feelings in a letter: "Distinctly sweet your face stands in its phantom niche - I touch your hand - my cheek your cheek - I stroke your vanished hair, Why did you enter, sister, since you must depart? Had not its heart been torn enough that you must add your shred?"[4] Emily knitted a pair of garters for Kate and sent them to her with a verse:

> When Katie walks, this simple pair accompany her side,
> When Katie runs unwearied they follow on the road,
> When Katie kneels their loving hands still clasp her pious knee -
> Ah! Katie! Smile at Fortune, with two so *knit to thee!*
>
> —J222/F49/M699

Emily Dickinson, a notorious recluse, would sometimes avoid even people close to her, a behavior that became more acute and frequent with the years. By the time she had reached middle age, few but the older residents of the village had ever seen her, and she eventually became known as "the myth." Why she behaved this way is the subject of more than one theory. She described it herself as "a cowardice of strangers I cannot resist."[5] The following poem, written about 1877, most likely addresses Kate Scott Anthon, who visited, or attempted to visit her, that year.

> I shall not murmur if at last
> The ones I loved below
> Permission have to understand
> For what I shunned them so -
> Divulging it would rest my Heart
> But it would ravage theirs -
> Why, Katie, Treason has a Voice -
> But mine - dispels - in Tears.
>
> —J1410/F1429/M601

The surviving holograph of this poem is in the form of a note, in pencil, signed "Emily." It is written on the first and third pages of a folded sheet of letter paper, but was never sent. It is a draft of a letter that may have been sent, but whether it was is unknown. On the fourth side of the paper ED wrote:

> We shun because we prize her Face
> Lest sight's ineffable disgrace
> Our Adoration stain
>
> —J1429/F1430M/601

She crossed out the word *sight's* and wrote *proof's* beneath. She wrote *mar* and also *flaw*, below *stain*, but did not cross off. She seems to be trying to explain why she failed to see Katie on one or more occasions. What, if she divulged it, would rest her heart but ravage theirs? The answer may lie in the lines on the fourth page, which might be rendered as, "I prize you to the point of adoration. You could not live up to my adoration in person, and I would esteem you less, then." *Treason* is willful betrayal, which requires *a voice.* The speaker, though, has no such voice. Her voice *dispels in tears.*

"A Hedge Away"—The View from Emily Dickinson's Bedroom West Window" (photograph by Jeff Morgan).

Although scholars caution against autobiographical readings of Dickinson's poems, you may feel safe with poems such as these. The speaker of "One Sister have I in our house," is certainly Emily Dickinson herself. She and her younger sister, Lavinia, lived together with their parents in the Dickinson homestead. Their brother Austin lived next door with his wife, Susan, and their three children, and the house still stands in Amherst today as part of The Emily Dickinson Museum. A single hemlock hedge, over three hundred feet in length, grew in front of both houses.

One Sister have I in our house,
And one, a hedge away.
There's only one recorded,
But both belong to me.

One came the road that I came -
And wore my last year's gown -
The other, as a bird her nest,
Builded our hearts among.

She did not sing as we did -
It was a different tune -
Herself to her a music
As Bumble bee of June.

Today is far from Childhood -
But up and down the hills
I held her hand the tighter -
Which shortened all the miles -

And still her hum
The years among,
Deceives the Butterfly -
Still in her Eye
The Violets lie
Mouldered this many May.

I spilt the dew -
But took the morn;
I chose this single star
From out the wide night's numbers -
Sue - forevermore!

—J14/F5/M46

Susan Dickinson was not only the poet's dearest friend and sister-in-law; as far as we know, she was also her closest literary confidante. She married Emily's brother, Austin, in 1856, but the two women were friends from their teenage years. Although letters that Emily sent to Susan often express love bordering on idolatry, friendships do have their rough spots sometimes, and it is evident from the *mouldering violets* and the *spilt dew* that this poem may have been written during or following such a time.

Life in Amherst

All was not violets, dew, and sweet country living in Amherst, however. On April 19, 1876, the following article appeared in a local newspaper:

> It appears that a week ago last Friday, Mr. Lothrop treated his wife rather roughly at table, and she was compelled to go to her room to recover from the effects of the ill-treatment. On this occasion his second daughter, Mary, 18 years of age, instantly protested against such brutality [...] Mr. Lothrop then knocked her down and pounded her with his slipper.[6]

A few years later, the Rev. J L Jenkins of the First Congregational Church, where the Dickinsons, excepting Emily, worshiped, recalled an episode that followed the above report.

> I was called down to the library on the afternoon of the 31st., where I found Mary sitting on the sofa. [...] The girl impressed me as being much cast down and in great

> trouble. She said to me, "I have come to you on a strange errand Mr. Jenkins' I have come to tell you that I hate my father!" She then drew up her sleeve, or held her hand out, and said that her father had struck her, and on her wrist, very plainly to be seen, were the marks of bruises that might have been made with a slipper.[7]

Following Mary's visit, the Rev. Jenkins consulted Emily's brother Austin and Dr. Edward Hitchcock for advice. The three men met with Lothrop but he denied the charges. Trial and the threat of excommunication followed. Lothrop later sued *The Springfield Republican* newspaper for libel based on their published report of the trial.

> The trial of Rev. Mr. Lothrop for cruelty to his family was begun before the First Church in secret session last evening, the accused not being present. The testimony covered the training of his three daughters, from their infancy up, and was of a most revolting character, involving brutal horsewhippings for trivial offences, systematic starving, the feeding of rotten meat, and positive dishonesty and faithlessness in his family relations.[8]

The Rev. C D Lothrop and family lived in Amherst, though he was at this time without a pulpit. He had already developed a sorry reputation in town. On the day that the notice of the trial appeared, Mrs. Julius Seelye, wife of the college president at the time, wrote to her husband: "The Lothrop matter is all out. On Saturday it was talked of through the streets and today the whole story is in the Republican."[9] The general attitude was summed up in a subsequent newspaper article: "It is hard to write calmly about such a man as Rev. Mr. Lothrop whose shocking cruelty to his family is elsewhere told."[10]

In 1879, Emily sent Susan Dickinson a poem headed "In Petto" (secret; private). At the bottom of the page she signed "Lothrop."

> A Counterfeit - a Plated Person -
> I would not be -
> Whatever strata of Iniquity
> My Nature underlie -
> Truth is good Health - and Safety, and the Sky.
> How meagre, what an Exile - is a Lie,
> And Vocal - when we die -
>
> —J1453/F1514/M722

One could read and enjoy this poem without knowing or guessing any of the story of Mr. Lothrop, but surely reading it in context lends it a mordant and bitterly ironic tone that we might not otherwise have heard. The reader now has some idea of how deep are the *strata of Iniquity* to which the poet alludes. The antidote is *Truth,* which Dickinson relates to *good Health,* anticipating the findings of modern medical research, to *Safety,* in that "the truth shall set you free," and to *the Sky,* symbolizing limitless freedom itself.

To lie is to separate oneself from others, making of one an *Exile*. In the final line, she may be echoing Shakespeare: "The Evil men do lives long after them. The good is oft interred with their bones" (Julius Caesar, Act 3, Scene 2).

The Great White Plague

Amherst, then, was not spared its portion of scandal, sordid events or bad behavior. Nor was it spared its share of the common diseases of the time, including pulmonary tuberculosis, known also as consumption, and, in Emily Dickinson's time, as the Great White Plague. In mid–nineteenth-century New England, it was responsible for about one in every four deaths. The victim wasted away, sometimes very quickly, but more often gradually over years or even decades. Among the symptoms were pain in chest and shoulders, fever, loss of weight, fatigue, and a worsening cough that eventually brought up blood from the lungs. In the beginning of Chapter 49 of his novel, *Nicholas Nickleby*, Charles Dickins leaves us a moving description of the "dread disease."

> There is a dread disease which so prepares its victim, as it were, for death; which so refines it of its grosser aspect, and throws around familiar looks unearthly indications of the coming change; a dread disease, in which the struggle between soul and body is so gradual, quiet, and solemn, and the result so sure, that day by day, and grain by grain, the mortal part wastes and withers away, so that the spirit grows light and sanguine with its lightening load, and, feeling immortality at hand, deems it but a new term of mortal life; a disease in which death and life are so strangely blended, that death takes the glow and hue of life, and life the gaunt and grisly form of death; a disease which medicine never cured, wealth never warded off, or poverty could boast exemption from; which sometimes moves in giant strides, and sometimes at a tardy sluggish pace, but, slow or quick, is ever sure and certain.[11]

In an 1873 letter to two younger cousins Dickinson wrote, "When I was a baby, Father used to take me to the mill for my health.[12] I was then in consumption!"[13] Fortunately for her and for the world, she did not succumb to the disease. Nevertheless, it was an ever-present threat. Death was a frequent visitor in Amherst, and Emily Dickinson saw friends and loved ones fall victim with alarming regularity, as the metronome of death ticked on.

So has a Daisy vanished
From the fields today -
So tiptoed many a slipper
To Paradise away -

Oozed so in crimson bubbles
Day's departing tide -
Blooming - tripping - flowing -
Are ye then with God?
—J28/F19/M39

Daisies don't go to paradise, but girls do, and if tuberculosis takes them there, one of the final signs of their going will be the *crimson bubbles* on their lips. Dickinson ends the poem with the central question of her "flood subject." As late as 1882, she wrote to Washington Gladden, a leading Congregationalist minister (1836–1918), asking anxiously, "Is immortality true?"[14]

Dickinson could use the imagery of tuberculosis to color a rendering of more general suffering as well.

A *wounded* Deer - leaps highest -
I've heard the Hunter tell -
'Tis but the Extasy of death -
And then the Brake is still!

The *smitten* Rock that gushes!
The *trampled* Steel that springs!
A Cheek is always redder
Just where the Hectic stings!

Mirth is the mail of Anguish -
In which it cautious Arm,
Lest anybody spy the blood
And "you're hurt" exclaim!
—J165/F181/M94

This poem may just as well have appeared in Chapter One under "Forgotten Words and Meanings." *Brake,* a term less often used in this way today, here means a thicket of brush. "Brake," as in a deceleration device, is a different word. *Extasy* is Dickinson's spelling of *ecstasy*. The key word in this poem, however, is *Hectic.* This was the name given to the telling red spot on the cheek that signaled the presence of tuberculosis.

HEC'TIC, n.
An exacerbating and remitting fever, with stages of chilliness, heat and sweat, variously intermixed; exacerbation chiefly in the evening; the sweats mostly in the night; pulse weak; urine with a natant [swimming or floating] furfuraceous [Scaly; branny; scurfy; like bran] cloud.

Note that *hectic* is defined as a noun here, now archaic. In modern usage it is an adjective. In his *Dictionary of Word Origins,* John Ayto writes, "The use of *hectic* for referring to great haste or confusion is a surprisingly recent development, not recorded until the first decade of the twentieth century."

Mail usually refers to letters and packages sent through the post office.

As she did in *A single Screw of Flesh* (Chapter 1), Dickinson draws on another definition:

> MAIL, n.
> 1. A coat of steel net-work, formerly worn for defending the body against swords, poniards, &c. The mail was of two sorts, chain and plate mail; the former consisting of iron rings, each having four others inserted into it; the latter consisting of a number of small lamins [Thin plates or scales] of metal, laid over one another like the scales of a fish, and sewed down to a strong linen or leathern jacket.
> 2. Armor; that which defends the body

Outwardly, laughter and mirth are evidence of good humor, but may also cover an inner *anguish*, like a protective coat of mail. Similarly, the highest leap of the deer, while resembling an expression of joy, may really be a leap of pain. A rock gushing life-giving water is indeed miraculous, but the rock must first be *smitten,* a biblical allusion to Moses' causing water to spring from a rock by striking it with his rod.[15] A steel trap springs with quick energy, but not until it is *trampled* on. Usually we would speak of stepping on a trap rather than trampling on one, but with the cumulative effect of the words *wounded, smitten,* and *trampled* we are left with a feeling of something quite violent implied.

The American Civil War

"Sorrow seems to me more general than it did, and not the estate of a few persons, since the war began; and if the anguish of others helped with ones [sic] own now would be many medicines."[16] So wrote Emily Dickinson to two younger cousins during the war years (1861–1865). She could not fail to be touched by the war, not only through her daily reading of newspapers and journals, but acutely through its effects on the people around her. About 618,000 Americans died in the Civil War, more than in the American Revolutionary War, the War of 1812, the Mexican American, the Spanish American War, the two World Wars, and the Korean War combined. Among the dead were Dickinson's friends and neighbors. She wrote poems that tell of the losses acutely.

> When I was small, a Woman died -
> Today - her Only Boy
> Went up from the Potomac -
> His face all Victory
>
> To look at her - How slowly
> The Seasons must have turned
> Till Bullets clipt an Angle
> And He passed quickly round -

If pride shall be in Paradise -
Ourself cannot decide -
Of their imperial Conduct -
No person testified -

But, proud in Apparition -
That Woman and her Boy
Pass back and forth, before my Brain
As even in the sky -

I'm confident that Bravoes -
Perpetual break abroad
For Braveries, remote as this
In Scarlet Maryland -
—J596/F518/M253

The Army of the Potomac was the largest Union Army in the Eastern Theater of the American Civil War, and takes its name from the Potomac River, which flows through the nation's capital. The woman's son was part of the army of the Potomac, but is no longer, having gone up from there, presumably to heaven. *Clipt* is Dickinson's spelling of the word "clipped." Why the alternate spelling? She did not need it to fit the meter; both clipt and clipped scan the same. There are many, however, who see in Dickinson's manuscripts a visual component. In choosing the spelling that she did, she has clipped the very word itself, and so rendered in the holograph an embodiment of the word's meaning.

Maryland was a slave state and a border state between the opposing sides, North and South. Many bloody battles were fought there. Because Maryland and the Potomac are named in the poem, it would be hard to interpret it as referring to anything but the Civil War. That, however, is unusual in a Dickinson poem. It is, in fact, a hallmark of her work that she avoids specific referents and will leave whatever inspired the poem unspoken. The reader is left with the effect of the inspiration, or an emotion, rather than a fixed idea of what the poem is "about."

A good example of the latter case is "They dropped like Flakes." This poem has been read by some as describing something in nature, such as seeds wind-blown from pods, although this is not so of all readers, and in in fact it was first published under the title "The Battlefield" in 1892,[17] so given by an editor who had indeed seen combat in the war, and who understood what he was reading. Despite her reclusiveness, Emily Dickinson was not cut off from the world around her. Her prolific letters reveal a very well-informed, knowledgeable and highly educated woman.

They dropped like Flakes -
They dropped like Stars -

Like Petals from a Rose -
When suddenly across the June
A Wind with fingers - goes -

They perished in the Seamless Grass -
No eye could find the place -
But God can summon every face
On his Repealless - List.

—J409/F545/M298

On reading this poem, someone familiar with the history of the war might well recall eyewitness accounts of the fighting in the battles, accounts such as these of the battle of Fredericksburg, Virginia: "The Union troops-over forty thousand strong-launched a series of suicidal attacks across open ground. They were mowed down by a scythe of shot; none got closer than forty yards from the stone wall" and "They melted like snow on the ground—wave after wave of Federal soldiers charging uphill across an open muddy plain." Other eyewitnesses to the same terrible battle likened the falling troops to a field of wheat, falling in waves, under the mower's scythe. Such accounts have a poetic cadence in contrast to the brutal nature of what is described. We hear that contrast in Dickinson's poems as well. *Repealless,* meaning "without repeal," is another Dickinson word coining. The *List* is the list of names of those elected by God for salvation, as explained in Chapter 4, concerning the Calvinist Doctrine of Unconditional Election.

Besides giving this poem a title, the first editors regularized punctuation, removed internal capital letters and changed the second stanza to get an exact rhyme.

They perished in the seamless grass,
No eye could find the place;
But God on his repealless list
Can summon every face.

It would have been very easy for Dickinson to have done the same, certainly. This is a clear indication that she did not want the poem to end with an exact rhyme. If she ever explained why she chose as she did, that explanation has been lost, but as Dickinson wrote it, the poem ends without the final confidence that the exact rhyme would have lent it, and that was perhaps her intent.

He scanned it - staggered has been read as a poem about a suicide. We will offer a different interpretation.

He scanned it - staggered -
Dropped the Loop
To Past or Period -

Union and Confederate Dead at Fort Mahone, Petersburg, Virginia, 1865 (Library of Congress).

Caught helpless at a sense as if
His Mind were going blind -

Groped up, to see if God was there -
Groped backward at Himself
Caressed a Trigger absently
And wandered out of Life
—J1062/F994/M456

What did *he scan* before *he staggered*? Again, the poet leaves that unsaid. Here, however, is historian Shelby Foote, describing civil war battlefield action: "And you'll see pictures of the dead on the battlefield with their clothes in disarray, as if someone had been rifling their bodies. That was the men themselves tearing their clothes up to see where the wound was, and they knew perfectly well that if they were gut-shot, they'd die."[18]

Lines 2 through 7 of the poem describe, as perhaps no one but Dickinson could, desperate swings of the mind following the terrible blow. As the soldier begins to *wander out of life*, the one hand that is still holding onto his rifle drops to his side. As he falls, he squeezes the trigger, firing randomly. It's doubtful that someone about to shoot himself pulls the trigger *absently*. Here again, in the word *caresses*, we find that distressing contrast between the beauty of the poetry and its subject matter.

The Trove, the Herbarium and the Vault

Emily Dickinson had her "wars," too, and she laid them away in books.

My Wars are laid away in Books -
I have one Battle more -
A Foe whom I have never seen
But oft has scanned me o'er -
And hesitated me between
And others at my side,
But chose the best - Neglecting me - till
All the rest, have died -
How sweet if I am not forgot
By Chums that passed away -
Since Playmates at threescore and ten
Are such a scarcity -
—J1549/F1579/M637

What Dickinson meant by the first line of this poem is perhaps best illuminated by turning to Ralph Waldo Emerson (1803–1882), writing at a time when literacy levels were historically high, a condition having its roots in the Puritan settlers of the seventeenth century requiring that all children be taught to read so that they could read the Bible. A famous essayist, Emerson exulted in observing that private thoughts and questions could now be submitted to diaries or worked out in verse by ordinary people, in contrast with a not too distant past:

> The philosophy of the day has long since broached a more liberal doctrine of the poetic faculty than our fathers held, and reckons poetry the right and power of every man to whose culture justice is done. […]. the practice of writing diaries is becoming almost general; and every day witnesses new attempts to throw into verse the experiences of private life.
>
> […] The poet is compensated for his defects in the street and in society, if in his chamber he has turned his mischance into noble numbers. Is there not room then for a new department in poetry, namely, *Verses of the Portfolio*?[19]

By the time Dickinson wrote *My Wars are laid away in Books,* the idea of "Verses of the Portfolio" had taken hold. After the poet's death, her sister,

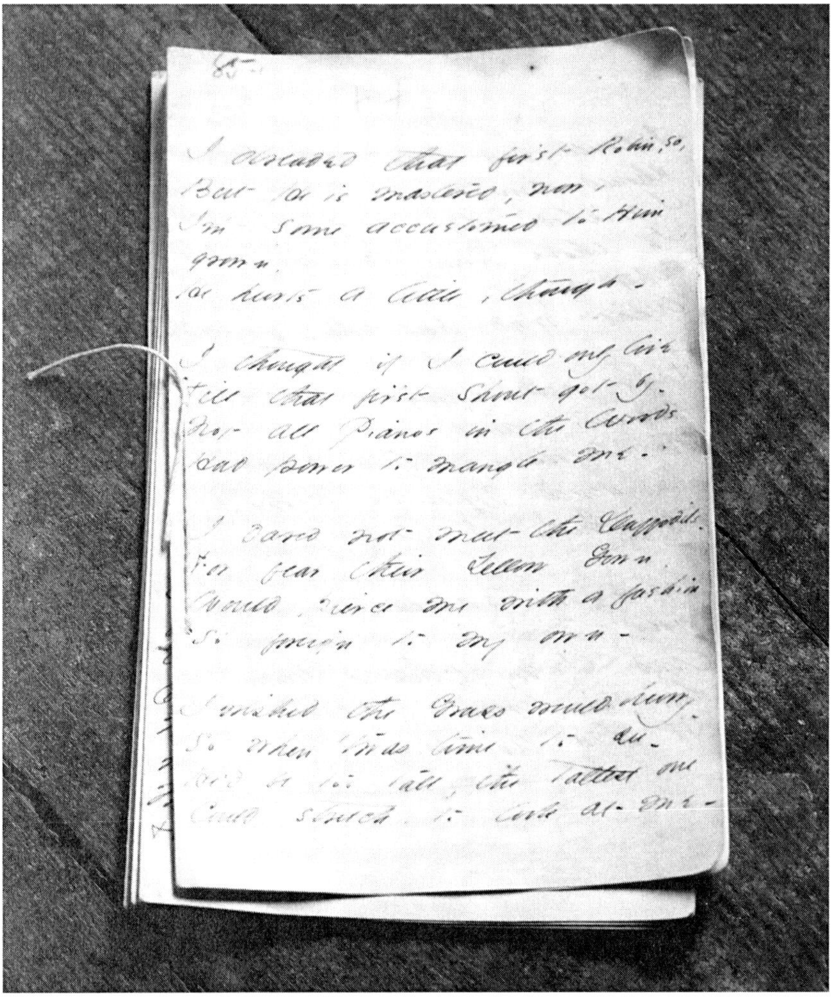

"An Emily Dickinson Fascicle" (photograph by Michael C. Medeiros).

Lavinia, found forty hand-sewn books, known to Dickinson scholars as "fascicles," in a trove that also included hundreds of poems on loose sheets and scraps of paper. These books were evidently the poet's private copies, as Lavinia had been unaware of their existence even though the two lived in the same house for most of their lives. They are written in ink on good writing stationary pre-folded by the stationer, which Dickinson stacked and bound with string passed through two pin holes. There are more than 800 poems in this form alone, where Emily Dickinson laid her wars away.

A modern dictionary definition of *chum* is "a close friend." Earlier, it had a more specific and limited meaning.

> CHUM, n
> A chamber fellow; one who lodges or resides in the same room: a word used in colleges.

Amherst was, by the time Emily Dickinson was born, a college town. The definition above would have been familiar to her. In this earlier definition, we find an association with youth. Dickinson's *chums* have this same aura of youth about them, and the speaker of the poem is old. *Three score and ten* (70) is not an age that the poet herself ever reached, dying in May 1886 age 55.

As a teenager, Emily began work on another kind of book. At age fourteen she wrote to her schoolmate Abiah Root: "Have you made an herbarium yet? I hope you will if you have not, it would be such a treasure to you; most all the girls are making one."[20] Emily Dickinson's herbarium of 66 pages contains 400 well-preserved pressed flowers and plants, artistically arranged, meticulously displayed, with the Latin name for each written beneath. She gathered most of her specimens in the woods and hills near her home and elsewhere in Massachusetts. In "I robbed the Woods," the speaker imagines the trees looking on after one of her forages and wonders how they regard her activities.

> I robbed the Woods -
> The trusting Woods.
> The unsuspecting Trees
> Brought out their Burs and mosses
> My fantasy to please.
> I scanned their trinkets curious
> I grasped - I bore away -
> What will the solemn Hemlock -
> What will the Oak tree say?
> —J41/F57

This poem poses no challenges to interpretation. "Because I could not stop for Death" certainly does, and though it may be the most widely anthologized, and therefore perhaps the best-known, of all Dickinson poems, many widely disparate interpretations of these familiar lines are found among its legion commentators.

> Because I could not stop for Death -
> He kindly stopped for me -
> The Carriage held but just Ourselves -
> And Immortality.
>
> We slowly drove - He knew no haste
> And I had put away

My labor, and my leisure too,
For His Civility -

We passed the School, where Children strove
At Recess, in the Ring -
We passed the Fields of Gazing Grain -
We passed the Setting Sun -

Or rather - He passed Us -
The Dews drew quivering and chill -
For only Gossamer my Gown -
My Tippet - only Tulle -

We paused before House that seemed
A Swelling of the Ground -
The Roof was scarcely visible -
The Cornice—in the Ground -

Since then - 'Tis Centuries - and yet
Feels shorter than the Day
I first surmised the Horses' Heads
Were toward Eternity

—J712/F479/M239

Questions abound. Where is the speaker at the end of the poem? Is she speaking from beyond the grave, or is she still in the carriage, heading toward eternity?—the same carriage that you are in at this moment, dear reader. Why would she be so seemingly willing to climb in? Does she have a choice? Can grain gaze? At what? Early editors deleted the fourth stanza—why? These questions have all been asked many times, and they have been answered differently by different readers. You may ponder them on your own or read from the volumes that have been written on them.[21] Our purpose here is to situate the poem in its time and place.

First, there is a pair of words in stanza four that will be unfamiliar to many readers. *Tulle* is a soft, fine silk or cotton material like net, used for making vails and dresses. Still in use today, this word was not in ED's dictionary; *tippet* was:

TIP'PET, n.
A narrow garment or covering for the neck, worn by females. It is now made of fur, though formerly of some kind of cloth.

Perhaps most misunderstood is the image in the fifth verse. What is she describing? Is it something real, or imagined? From a north window of a home that she occupied during an early period in her life, Emily Dickinson looked out over the town cemetery, which would have been clearly visible from her upper rooms. Before mechanized means were available to break through the frozen winter ground, bodies were stored in an unheated tomb within the cemetery. A concrete room, covered with soil and planted

"Amherst Town Tomb" (photograph by Jeff Morgan).

with grass, was used to store bodies during the cold of winter until the ground thawed and could be opened for the burial. The Amherst town tomb is still there in West Cemetery, where the poet is buried.

We paused before House that seemed
A Swelling of the Ground -
The Roof was scarcely visible -
The Cornice - in the Ground -

This stanza, as in all but one stanza in the poem, is in perfect hymn meter, so called because it matches the metrical form of a great body of Christian hymns—quatrains of alternating eight and six-syllable lines (or three and four "beats"). Emily Dickinson heard these hymns sung regularly growing up, not only in church, but in the home as well. They were the soundtrack of her life. The familiar meter of the hymns was imprinted early and deeply in her brain. The one stanza that violates the form somewhat is the fourth—the stanza that the early editors omitted. The first line, *Or rather - He passed Us*, is six syllables rather than the usual eight, three beats rather than four, and the second line is eight syllables rather than the usual six, four beats rather than three. The missing beat in the first line brings us up short, creating the very unexpectedness of the mood change taking place at this point in the narrative. This must have been intentional; she could have sustained the standard meter without changing a single word by writing:

Or rather - He passed Us - the Dews
Drew quivering and chill -
For only Gossamer my Gown -
My Tippet - only Tulle -

So often, as in this instance, a seeming irregularity in a Dickinson poem reveals purposeful design on closer examination. Editors have regularized the line breaks in almost all of the poems in print. On the manuscript of this poem, Dickinson placed the word *Us* on a separate line, then began the following line with *The Dews*.

The First Congregational Church in Amherst relied greatly on the hymns of Isaac Watts, and there were three Watts hymnals in the Dickinson family library.[22] Among the very familiar hymns was one, "There Is a Land of Pure Delight," which enumerates the pleasures that await the faithful in Heaven. Dickinson, in a humorous reworking of this theme, has applied it wishfully to her home town, and imagines her own Heaven there…

Where bells no more affright the morn -
Where scrabble never comes -
Where very nimble Gentlemen
Are forced to keep their rooms -

Where tired Children placid sleep
Thro' Centuries of noon
This place is Bliss - this town is Heaven -
Please, Pater, pretty soon!

"Oh could we climb where Moses stood,
And view the Landscape o'er"
Not Father's bells - nor Factories,
Could scare us any more!
—J112/F114/M70

Thomas H. Johnson focuses specifically on the final verse as a free rendering of the fourth stanza of the Isaac Watts hymn named above:

Could we but climb where Moses stood,
And view the landscape o'er,
Not Jordan's stream, nor Death's cold flood,
Should fright us from the shore.

"Father's Bells" would seem to imply that Edward Dickinson roused the family for breakfast by ringing a bell. Factory whistles were unwelcome alarms which sounded every workday morning at six o'clock. As a college town, Amherst had more than a small village's customary share of "very nimble Gentleman."[23] Like college students today, they could be rowdy and noisy at times. In Emily Dickinson's heaven, they keep to their rooms. Her peace in not interrupted by bells or whistles.

> SCRAB'BLE, v.i.
>
> 1. To scrape, paw or scratch with the hands; to move along on the hands and knees by clawing with the hands; to scramble; as, to scrabble up a cliff or a tree. [A word in common popular use in New England, but not elegant.]
>
> 2. To make irregular or crooked marks; as, children scrabble when they begin to write; hence, to make irregular and unmeaning marks

The line *Where scrabble never comes*, evokes the particularly North American expression, *hardscrabble,* meaning having poor soil or having harsh and difficult living conditions because of poverty. In such circumstances one must, figuratively speaking, scrape, paw or scratch out one's living from whatever scant resources are available. Emily's heaven suffers no such deprivation.

Seven

Secrets of the Temple

Specialized Vocabularies

"I have a brother and a sister—My Mother does not care for thought—and Father, too busy with his Briefs to notice what we do"—L260, 25 April 1862

The Law, Commerce and Politics

As explained in Chapter 5, living in a family of lawyers, Emily Dickinson heard the language of the law all around her. In cases involving commercial transactions she heard the vocabulary of commerce as well. Among the visitors to the Dickinson home were partners in her father's law practice, travelling attorneys and judges, with some of whom young Emily developed enduring friendships. Her father was also a politician, serving in the state legislature and in the United States House of Representatives. It is not surprising, then, to find legal, commercial, and political terminology in her poetry, but it is surprising to see what she does with it. We begin by returning to a poem that we have already considered in another context (Chapter 5).

Mine - by the Right of the White Election!
Mine - by the Royal Seal!
Mine - by the Sign in the Scarlet prison -
Bars - cannot conceal!
Mine - here - in Vision - and in Veto!
Mine - by the Grave's Repeal -
Titled - Confirmed -
Delirious Charter!
Mine - long as Ages steal!
—J528/F411/M219

There are legal and/or political terms in every line of this poem but the last. We understand from our previous reading that the *Election* is a state of grace, in the language of the church. Election is also a state of elevation in the language of politics; one is elected to office by way of processes established in law. Because she doesn't say what *Mine* refers to, both divine and earthly possibilities are present together.

In addition to marking the elect of God in their foreheads, *seals* were used in all manner of business.

> SEAL, n
> 1. A piece of metal or other hard substance, usually round or oval, on which is engraved some image or device, and sometimes a legend or inscription. This is used by individuals, corporate bodies, and states, for making impressions on wax upon instruments of writing, as an evidence of their authenticity. The king of England has his great seal and his privy seal. Seals are sometimes worn in rings.

A *Royal Seal* must be the grandest and most binding of all then.

Prisons and *Bars* enter into the legal world when the law is broken. Also, some readers have detected an allusion to bars in another sense:

> BAR, n.
> 1. A piece of wood, iron or other solid matter, long in proportion to its diameter, used for various purposes, but especially for a hinderance or obstruction; as, the bars of a fence or gate; the bar of a door or hatchway.
> 2. Any obstacle which obstructs, hinders or defends; an obstruction; a fortification. —
> 3. The shore of the sea, which restrains its waters.
> 4. The railing that incloses the place which counsel occupy in courts of justice. Hence the phrase, at the bar of the court, signifies in open court. Hence also licensed lawyers are called barristers; and hence the whole body of lawyers licensed in a court, are customarily called the bar. A trial at bar, in England, is a trial in the courts of Westminster, opposed to a trial at Nisi Prius, in the circuits.
> 5. Figuratively, any tribunal; as, the bar of public opinion. Thus the final trial of men is called the bar of God.

A bar, then, can be any obstruction, or, understood in the legal sense, the machinations of the legal system which in this case cannot *conceal* what has been confirmed by a *Royal Seal*. It is hers *in Vision*, that is, by spiritual insight. It is also hers *in Veto*, even if banned or prohibited by some authority. Someone seeking membership in the church could be vetoed by the deacons and the minister of the church. Being out of the church meant that you were not considered to be among the elect. Even so, the poet declares, *Mine!* Whatever it is that she is claiming as hers, it is hers whether she is among the elect of the church or not. This reading argues against reading "Election" in the religious sense of the word, and may be why many readers understand her to be claiming her election to the *Title* of Poet.

To *Repeal* in law is to revoke or nullify a particular statute. In this poem, is the grave itself that is repealed, or is the grave repealing something? The dual possibilities allow us to read the line two ways. If it is the grave that is repealed, couching the promised resurrection in legal terms, then *Mine!* is the New Life that awaits beyond. Or is the grave offering her repeal from this mortal life, to be joined with a departed love in heaven? Or will she achieve another kind of immortality, through her poetry?

Titled! Examining this word closely, we find again a range of meanings, any of which can work within the poem.

> TI'TLE, n.
>
> 1. An inscription put over any thing as a name by which it is known.
> 2. The inscription in the beginning of a book, containing the subject of the work, and sometimes the author's name.
> 3. In the civil and canon laws, a chapter or division of a book.
> 4. An appellation of dignity, distinction or pre-eminence given to persons; as duke, marquis and the like.
> 5. A name; an appellation.
> 6. Right; or that which constitutes a just cause of exclusive possession; that which is the foundation of ownership; as, a good title to an estate; or an imperfect title.

If the speaker is claiming Godly election (ED herself never joined the church), her title in the church would be "Saint." Generally speaking, to be *Confirmed!* is to be established and validated. The word also has a religious meaning of being "admitted to the full privileges of the church." Her new status is confirmed by a *Charter*, a solemnly executed instrument conferring exclusive right and title in perpetuity. However, her charter is *Delirious!* Delirious defined literally means a straying mind, having wild disconnected ideas, and possibly being unaware of one's surroundings. Figuratively it means extremely happy, and lighthearted rather than lightheaded. One may be delirious with joy, for example.

What has the speaker found to make her so deliriously happy? Is it certainty of election to God's favor? Does she anticipate a union with a departed earthly love in the afterlife? Is she triumphantly proclaiming her rank among poets? All these and other interpretations as well have been written and published. As with so much of Dickinson's writing, different meanings seem to co-exist in a single work. If the poet intended any single one, she doesn't tell us. It is good to keep some words of Robert Weisbuch had in mind: "It is Perfectly natural for us to ask as a first question of any poem what it is about, and yet this is exactly the wrong question to pose to almost any Dickinson lyric."[1]

Nor does the speaker in the next poem identify the "*Circumstance*" to which she refers in the first line, although a rather satisfying interpretation has been advanced. But first, the poem.

Alone and in a Circumstance
Reluctant to be told
A spider on my reticence
Assiduously crawled

And so much more at Home than I
Immediately grew
I felt myself a visitor
And hurriedly withdrew

Revisiting my late abode
With articles of claim
I found it quietly assumed
As a Gymnasium
Where Tax asleep and Title off
The inmates of the Air
Perpetual presumption took
As each were special Heir -
If any strike me on the street
I can return the Blow -
If any take my property
According to the Law
The Statute is my Learned friend
But what redress can be
For an offense nor here nor there
So not in Equity -
That Larceny of time and mind
The marrow of the Day
By spider, or forbid it Lord
That I should specify.

—J1167/F1174/M549

During the Victorian era, people took rules of propriety very seriously. Public modesty was enjoined on all. It would be against all social rectitude to talk about an outhouse (privy), or anything associated with activities undertaken therein, in public. A widely accepted interpretation of this poem is that the *Circumstance* in which the speaker finds herself is, indeed, the family outhouse. Under this particular circumstance her aforementioned admiration for the spider is apparently curtailed.

The poet finds herself confronting a spider in the outhouse. The spider crawls upon her *reticence,* defined in ED's dictionary as "concealment by silence." One is quite naturally silent when alone in this private circumstance. He seems so much more *at home* there than she does, that she feels like it is she who is the visitor, and she withdraws. The poet casts the events that follow in terms of a property rights dispute. When she returns, she bears *articles of claim,* which, in legal terms would be a demand for money or property, or an assertion that one is entitled to, or has the perceived or actual right to receive, money or property. Emily's "articles" in this case are more likely a broom and a dustpan. But when she opens the door now, she finds it *quietly assumed*

AS-SUME′, v.t.
1. To take or take upon one. It differs from receive, in not implying an offer to give.
2. To take what is not just; to take with arrogant claims; to arrogate; to seize unjustly; as, to assume haughty airs; to assume unwarrantable powers.

Unspecified insects have arrogantly and unjustly occupied the property. The word *gymnasium* does not appear in Dickinson's Webster's dictionary, but it is defined in the EDL:

GYMNASIUM, n
Site for exercises in climbing, leaping, stretching, balancing, swinging, and so forth; place for practice in athletic exercises.

The flying insects—*inmates of the air*—that she sees are cavorting about in all manner of ways. Today, the word inmate is used to describe prisoners or others held against their will, such as patients in an asylum. These inmates of the air, however, are there of their own accord.

IN′MATE, n. [in or inn and mate.]
1. A person who lodges or dwells in the same house with another, occupying different rooms, but using the same door for passing *in* and out of the house.
2. A lodger; one who lives with a family, but is not otherwise connected with it than as a lodger.

There enters into the narrative now a legality known popularly as "squatter's rights," by which someone can gain legal possession of real property merely by having occupied that property unchallenged for a specified length of time or longer. The original owner may lose legal *Title* to the property. One occupies a privy only occasionally. Because of her absence, the insects are "squatting" on the property, and, according to the law, are able to do so in perpetuity (*perpetually*); Of course, the insects obey natural law; there is no man-made law to protect her from them. An owner can also lose title to a property by not paying the real estate T*ax*. *Tax asleep*[2] is the poet's way of saying that the long-unpaid tax may have put her property rights in jeopardy. In occupying the property, the squatters claim perpetual *presumption*, noun form of the verb presume:

PRESUME, v.
1. Guess; assumption; speculation; conjecture; supposition.
2. Liberty; license; perceived right; self-granted privilege; audaciously claimed prerogative.
3. [Fig.] estimation; beginning; taste; sample; portion; part; specimen; brief vision.

Definition 2 fits the situation here.

A *special Heir*, as defined in old English and Scottish law, is one that is not determined solely by primogeniture, by which the first born son inherits the estate. Dickinson cleverly assumes the right of primogeniture for herself, assigning the role of usurpers to the unwelcome trespassers.

She can invoke no law to rescue her, as she can if any *strike* her *on the street.* If anyone takes her property, she knows that there is a *Statute*—a written law—to protect her. *Learned Friend* was a respectful form of address among lawyers, sometimes applied sardonically. But there is no law to *redress* the *offence* done to her. There is no law broken *here* in the present circumstance, *nor there* in the written law. Moreover, to say that something "is neither here nor there" in daily speech is to say that it doesn't matter, that it's not relevant to the matter at hand. One can dismiss an argument with a simple "Well, that's neither here nor there." Our speaker is having trouble making her case before the law.

Equity has taken on new meaning since Dickinson used it.[3] Her dictionary gives five definitions; they all concern the law:

> EQ´UI-TY, n.
> 1. Justice; right. In practice, equity is the impartial distribution of justice, or the doing that to another which the laws of God and man, and of reason, give him a right to claim. It is the treating of a person according to justice and reason. The Lord shall judge the people with equity. Ps. xcviii. With righteousness shall he judge the poor, and reprove with equity. Is. xi.[4]
> 2. Justice; impartiality; a just regard to right or claim; as, we must in equity allow this claim.
> 3. In law, an equitable claim.
> 4. In jurisprudence, the correction or qualification of law, when too severe or defective; or the extension of the words of the law to cases not expressed, yet coming within the reason of the law. Hence a court of equity or chancery, is a court which corrects the operation of the literal text of the law, and supplies its defects, by reasonable construction and by rules of proceeding and deciding, which are not admissible in a court of law. Equity then is the law of reason, exercised by the chancellor or judge, giving remedy in cases to which the courts of law are not competent.
> 5. Equity of redemption, in law, the advantage, allowed to a mortgager, of a reasonable time to redeem lands mortgaged, when the estate is of greater value than the sum for which it was mortgaged.

Alas, there is no law to redress the stealing of her time—*the marrow of the Day.* The laws of men do not apply to a *Spider.* May the *Lord forbid* that she should be so un-genteel as to have to specify by name any of the other creatures she has encountered!

The legal subtleties of this poem could not have been accessible to anyone outside the legal profession. Its humorous irreverence and oblique indelicacy suggest that it may have been written for a person of her own generation, rather than that of her parents, someone well acquainted with the vocabulary of the law.

There is another poem in which Dickinson, again using legal vocabulary, contrasts manmade law with natural law.

> The Rat is the concisest Tenant.
> He pays no Rent.
> Repudiates the Obligation -
> On Schemes intent
>
> Balking our Wit
> To sound or circumvent -
> Hate cannot harm
> A Foe so reticent -
> Neither Decree prohibit him -
> Lawful as Equilibrium.
> —J1356/F1369/M590

The poem begins with a simple statement, yet perhaps a puzzling one, and not for any legal language, but for the familiar word, *concise. Concisest is* Dickinson's coined word for "most concise."

> CON-CISE, a.
> Brief; short, applied to language or style; containing few words; comprehensive; comprehending much in few words, or the principal matters only;

How is The Rat the most concise of tenants? The word in question, according to ED's dictionary, derives from the "Latin *concisus*, cut off, brief, from *concido*; *con* and *cædo*, to cut." The rat is "cut off" from the rest of the household. *He pays no Rent.* Payment of rent is a legal *Obligation* only among humankind. Among the definitions of an obligation are:

> OB-LI-GA´TION, n.
> 1. The binding power of a vow, promise, oath or contract, or of law, civil, political or moral, independent of a promise [...].
> 4. In law, a bond with a condition annexed and a penalty for non-fulfillment.

The Rat is *intent* on *Schemes* which, because he is separate from the other residents in the house, those other residents are unable to *sound* or *circumvent*.

> SOUND, v.t.
> 3. To try; to examine; to discover or endeavor to discover that which lies concealed in another's breast; to search out the intention, opinion, will or desires.

> CIR-CUM-VENT´, v.t.
> Literally, to come round; hence, To gain advantage over another, or to accomplish a purpose by arts, stratagem, or deception; to deceive; to prevail over another by wiles or fraud; to delude; to impose on.

The wily Rat seems to have the best of us. *Hate* him though we may, our hatred *cannot harm/A Foe so reticent* as he. *Reticent,* the adjective form of *reticence,* was encountered in the previous poem, defined as "concealment by silence," but by extension it here implies unprovoked and therefore beyond our influence. The rat does not respond at all to our hatred of him.

Neither Decree prohibit him. In the legal context, a decree is a judicial decision, or determination of a litigated cause. The Rat is beyond the reach of this kind of decree, just as Emily's unwelcome outhouse invaders were beyond the reach of any statute. In another kind of decree, however, the Rat is perhaps confirmed and validated. A decree may also be, "In theology, predetermined purpose of God; the purpose or determination of an immutable Being, whose plan of operations is, like himself, unchangeable." The Divine Decrees were and are central to Calvinism, and would have been utterly familiar to the parishioners of Amherst. God's decree to redeem the elect and not others, His decree to create man, His decree to allow for the fall of Man in Adam and Eve, and His decree to send Christ as the redeemer are all established tenets of Calvinism. Although it is certainly within His power to do so, God makes no decree that *prohibits* the Rat from going about his business. On the contrary, the Rat obeys natural law, the laws of God's creation. There seems to exist, in the balance of power between the Rat and the household, an *Equilibrium* which is itself an expression of natural law. According to James Guthrie, "Dickinson's almost proprietary interest in nature prompted her to sympathize with her nonhuman protagonists, despite their occasional repulsiveness. [...] who lives according to an idiosyncratic set of rules as consistent as the laws of physics. While he abides by them, he remains immune to criticism. He, like the spider, enjoys a legitimate claim to the premises that laws and decrees cannot erode."[5]

Dickinson often used legal language, as well as impressive-sounding Latinate words, in humorous context, as in *Alone and in a Circumstance.* In the following poem she is again involved in a property dispute, but this time against an unbeatable opponent.

> I had some things that I called mine -
> And God, that he called his,
> Till, recently a rival Claim
> Disturbed these amities.
>
> The property, my garden,
> Which having sown with care,
> He claims the pretty acre,
> And sends a Bailiff there.

The station of the parties
Forbids publicity,
But Justice is sublimer
Than arms, or pedigree.

I'll institute an "Action"-
I'll vindicate the law-
Jove! Choose your counsel-
I retain "Shaw"!

—J116/F101/M72

Emily has cultivated her flowers and God has made other plants to grow in and around her garden as well—friendly arrangements between her and God, which she describes as *amities* (singular amity[6]) defined as "Friendship, in a general sense, between individuals, societies or nations: harmony; good understanding"; The amities, however, have been disturbed by God's *Bailiff*. Bailiffs were officers appointed by the Sherriff for many purposes, such as to arrest persons, serve summonses, and other quite specialized services. In English law, for example, there might be serving under a landlord a bailiff (spelled with a single letter "f" in ED's dictionary) of forests and of manors, who would direct the husbandry. It may be such a metaphorical bailiff that God has sent to ED's garden. Because she addresses the Deity as *Jove,* the supreme God of the Romans also known as Jupiter, who could hurl thunderbolts from the sky, it is perhaps a lightning strike or a storm that *claims the pretty acre.*

Persons, or groups of persons, engaged against each other or involved in litigation, are opposing *parties. The station of the parties*, that is to say their positions in society, *forbids publicity.* One Dickinson biographer has observed "[…] among the gentility of the time, its obsessive aversion to publicity."[7] Members of the gentility would be able to boast of their *pedigree*, but it gains them no advantage before the law, and a legal solution is certainly preferable to resorting to *arms* to resolve a dispute. Justice is therefore *sublimer* (ED's coined word for "more sublime"). Trusting in justice then, ED begins legal proceedings against Jove—she *institutes an "Action"* against him, inviting him to *Choose* his *counsel*, as she emphatically chooses hers. Henry Shaw (about 1832–1887) was a day laborer in Amherst who would dig in the garden for ED,[8] and who happened to have the same surname as Lemuel Shaw (1781–1861), who served as Chief Justice of the Massachusetts Supreme Judicial Court (1830–1860).

In *I gave myself to Him*, Dickinson employs the language of commerce and the law to describe a marriage, quite askew of the prevailing sentiments of the romantic age.

I gave myself to Him -
And took Himself, for Pay,
The solemn contract of a Life
Was ratified, this way -

The Wealth might disappoint -
Myself a poorer prove
Than this great Purchaser suspect,
The Daily Own - of Love

Depreciate the Vision -
But till the Merchant buy -
Still Fable - in the Isles of Spice -
The subtle Cargoes - lie -

At least - 'Tis Mutual - Risk -
Some - found it - Mutual Gain -
Sweet Debt of Life - Each Night to owe -
Insolvent - every Noon -
—J580/F426/M170

Pay, Wealth, Purchaser, Depreciate, Merchant, buy, Cargoes, Risk, Gain, Debt, owe, Insolvent—total twelve terms of commerce. *Contract, ratified, prove,* add three terms of law. In America, marriage is a legal contract.

In George Bernard Shaw's play *Man and Superman,* the character Tanner says of Petrarch and Laura and of Dante and Beatrice, that "They never exposed their idolatry to the test of domestic familiarity." Expressing the same idea in general terms, Dickinson states that *The Daily Own - of Love/ Depreciate the Vision*. Dickinson definitely seems to challenge some of the Romantic notions of her time, in addition to conventions of the English language, turning the verb *Own* into a noun. We would likely express the thought something like, "The daily ownership of love depreciates the value of our original vision of it," but that wouldn't be poetry, would it?

Sweet Debt of Life refers to "the marriage debt," which, in the law of medieval Christendom, was the obligation of a married person to have sexual intercourse with his or her partner when asked (barring certain mitigating circumstances, such as illness). In which party's favor, husband or wife, this law was most likely written, enjoined, and enforced, the reader may surmise. After paying the debt *Each Night,* she is *Insolvent every Noon,*. Being insolvent is the condition of "not having money, goods, or estate to pay all debts."

The Language of Science

Emily Dickinson had a superior education, especially for a nineteenth-century American woman, which included the natural sciences. The Presence of Dr. Edward Hitchcock enriched the scientific enterprises undertaken at Amherst College, and his interest in comparative anatomy may have inspired at least one Dickinson poem. It is from the science of botany, however, that Dickinson draws much of her scientific terminology.

> The Lilac is an ancient shrub
> But ancienter than that
> The Firmamental Lilac
> Upon the Hill tonight -
> The Sun subsiding on his Course
> Bequeaths this final Plant
> To Contemplation - not to Touch -
> The Flower of Occident.
> Of one Corolla is the West -
> The Calyx is the Earth -
> The Capsules burnished Seeds the Stars -
> The Scientist of Faith
> His research has but just begun -
> Above his synthesis
> The Flora unimpeachable
> To Time's Analysis -
> "Eye hath not seen" may possibly
> Be current with the Blind
> But let not Revelation
> By theses be detained -
> —J1241/F1261/M562

What is the poet describing here? What is a *firmamental Lilac? Ancienter* is ED's coined word for "more ancient." The lilac is a flower, and also the name of the color of the purple lilac (lilacs may also be white). The sun, sinking into the west, casts a lilac hue across the sky, reflected on the *Hill.* We cannot *Touch* this lilac hue, but we may *contemplate* it. It is the *Flower of Occident*—of the west—where the sun sets. Then, the poet begins to describe this flower in botanical terms. *Corolla, Calix, Capsules, Seeds. The Scientist of Faith*—the natural scientist with his scientific vocabulary and faith either in scientific method or in natural theology, *has but just begun* his research. This *Flora unimpeachable,* however, is *Above his synthesis*—defined as "the combining of elements to form a new whole" (EDL).

IM-PEACH′A-BLE, a.
1. Liable to accusation; chargeable with a crime; accusable; censurable.
2. Liable to be called in question; accountable.

Although it is the first definition of impeachable that is familiar to most people today, it is the second that applies here. Charles Anderson writes: "The heavenly flower, she says, cannot be discredited by 'Times Analysis.' This is the phrase that lifts her poem above the conventional treatments of natural beauty as manifestations of God, and takes her view beyond contemporary science to the mathematical philosophers of today."[9] Anderson recognizes a point touched on earlier, that our earthly lives are trapped in time, as is the analysis of the natural scientist. Is the heavenly flower ever beyond our reach then? St. Paul tells us that there are some things which mortal eye will never behold: "But as it is written, Eye hath not seen, nor ear heard, neither have entered into the heart of man, the things which God hath prepared for them that love him" (1 Corinthians 2:9). That may be true for the blind, Dickinson continues, but she cites next the Revelation of St. John the Divine, who did indeed behold the "things which God hath prepared for those that love him,"[10] in spite of "theses."

> THE´SIS, n. [plural theses]
> 1. A position or proposition which a person advances and offers to maintain, or which is actually maintained by argument; a theme; a subject.
> 2. In logic, every proposition may be divided into thesis and hypothesis. Thesis contains the thing affirmed or denied, and hypothesis the conditions of the affirmation or negation.

Scientific and logical propositions are subject to argument. By casting Paul's statement as a thesis, Dickinson implies the possibility of doubt concerning its unquestionable truth. With a light tone and humorous use of the vocabulary of science, she disguises a quite subversive message.

In the 1830s, as the Second Great Awakening advanced into its third decade, a new spiritual movement emerged in New England, profoundly different from that of the Protestant revivals of the day. Called Transcendentalism, its adherents sought not a religious conversion experience, but direct contact with the divine through nature, independent of any clergy or scripture. God was a universal spirit, and it was through nature that the spirit communicated with human beings, not merely through signs and emblems, but directly. Nature was not so much to be studied with scientific objectivity, but rather experienced through the spirit. Transcendentalism, then, became not just a direct challenge to Protestant orthodoxy, but also "a revolt against the empiricism of Enlightenment science."[11]

This spirit of revolt surely animates *The Lilac is an ancient Shrub.* Where Dickinson employs scientific terminology, the same spirit of revolt is often discernible, usually combined with light-hearted humor, as in the following poem, which seems to treat the fervent convictions of the Transcendentalists rather playfully.

> "Arcturus" is his other name -
> I'd rather call him "Star."
> It's very mean of Science
> To go and interfere!

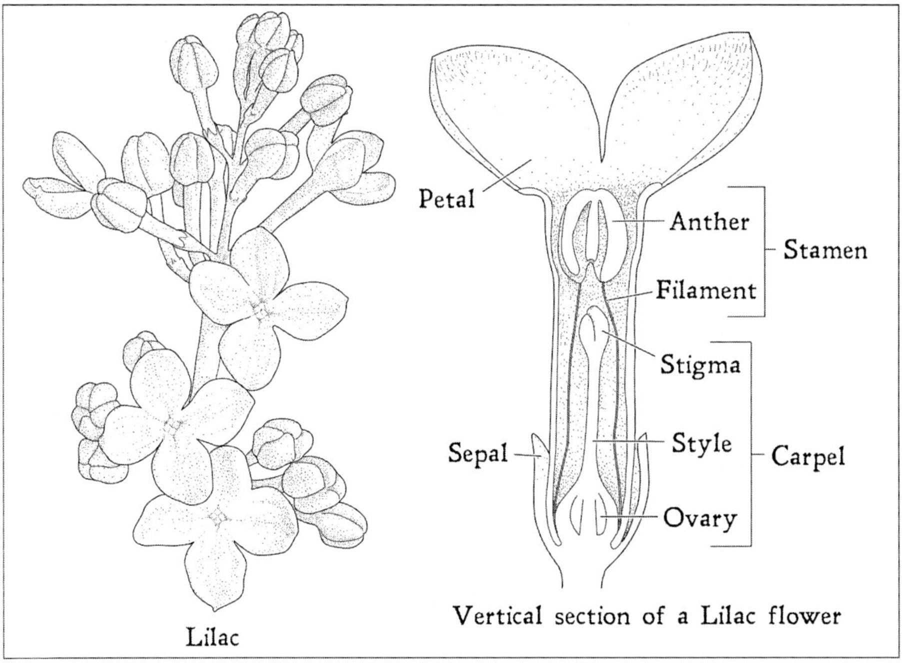

"Parts of a Flower" (drawing by Will Sillin).

I slew a worm the other day-
A 'Savan' passing by
Murmured "Resurgam" - "Centipede"!
"Oh Lord - how frail are we"!

I pull a flower from the woods-
A monster with a glass
Computes the stamens in a breath -
And has her in a "class"!

Whereas I took the Butterfly
Aforetime in my hat -
He sits erect in "Cabinets" -
The Clover bells forgot.

What once was "Heaven"
Is *"Zenith"* now -
Where I proposed to go
When Time's brief masquerade was done
Is mapped and charted too.

What if the poles should frisk about
And stand upon their heads!
I hope I'm ready for "the worst" -
Whatever prank betides!

Perhaps the "Kingdom of Heaven's" changed -
I hope the "Children" there
Won't be "new fashioned" when I come -
And laugh at me - and stare-

I hope the Father in the skies
Will lift his little girl -
Old fashioned - naughty - everything-
Over the stile of "Pearl."

—J70/F117/M73

"'*Arcturus*,' the brightest star in the norther sky. Isn't the name *Star* just fine by itself?" the poet seems to ask. Ralph Waldo Emerson, in his essay *Beauty*, expresses a similar sentiment, but the contrast in tones is unmistakable: "The boy had juster views when he gazed at the shells on the beach, or the flowers in the meadow, unable to call them by their names, than the man in the pride of his nomenclature."

Of the word "slay," the present tense of *slew*, ED's dictionary says, "It is particularly applied to killing in battle, but is properly applied also the killing of an individual man or beast." Applying this rather strong word to the killing of a worm magnifies the sense of mock irony set in the first stanza. *Resurgam,* Latin for "I shall rise again," "I will live again," or "I will be resurrected from the dead," was sometimes carved into headstones or tombs. So it was for the character of Helen Burns in *Jane Eyre* by Charlotte Brontë. Most earthworms can be sliced in two and, depending on the species and where it is sliced, grow a new head or tail, a process called regeneration, and thus live again. Our *Savan passing by murmured 'Resugam'—'Centipede!'* continuing the same absurdly exaggerated tone. The centipede is a different species from the earthworm, and cannot recover from being cut in two, but our savans seems unconcerned with that distinction. Interestingly, the word centipede does not appear in ED's dictionary.

In the next verse a savan becomes a *monster with a* magnifying *glass* to examine the specimen, *computes the stamens*, the scientific name for the pollen-bearing parts of the flower, and promptly assigns it a botanical "*class.*" Dickinson disassociates herself from the word by setting it off in quotation marks, indicating that this is the monster's term, not her own. *Aforetime*,[12] she caught *the Butterfly in* her *hat,* Now, it sits erect and motionless in a scientist's *cabinet*, full, no doubt, of butterfly specimens, alas! Both the Appleton Cabinet and the Woods Cabinet and Observatory, buildings dedicated to scientific purposes, were built at Amherst College during Emily Dickinson's lifetime.

The *poles* of the Earth frisking about and standing on their heads is a carefree description of the world coming to an end, as promised in the

Bible. She's ready for *whatever prank* nature or the Deity may have in store. If it does come to pass, she hopes that *The Kingdom of Heaven* will welcome her. She seems to feel that she might appear old-fashioned to possibly *new-fashioned Children.* That the residents of heaven must be children she understands also from her Bible: "And Jesus called a little child unto him, and set him in the midst of them, And said, Verily I say unto you, Except ye be converted, and become as little children, ye shall not enter into the kingdom of heaven" (Matthew 18: 2–3). *Stile of pearl* is the poet's expression for *Heaven*'s "pearly gates," described in the Book of Revelation.[13]

Dickinson carries the theme even further in another poem, written around the same time as the one above, 1859–1860.

> If the foolish, call them "*flowers*" -
> Need the wiser, tell?
> If the Savans "Classify" them
> It is just as well!
>
> Those who read the "Revelations"
> Must not criticize
> Those who read the same Edition -
> With beclouded Eyes!
>
> Could we stand with that Old "Moses" -
> "Canaan" denied -
> Scan like him, the stately landscape
> On the other side -
>
> Doubtless, we should deem superfluous
> Many Sciences,
> Not pursued by learned Angels
> In scholastic skies!
>
> Low amid that glad Belles lettres
> Grant that we may stand,
> Stars, amid profound *Galaxies* -
> At that grand "Right hand"![14]
>
> —J168/F179/M96

Again in this poem Dickinson combines references to science with ironic humor, beginning in the first line with the word *foolish*. There are 116 occurrences of the word *flower*, plural and singular, in the poems, and the fact that she called her poems her flowers tells us that she prized the word. It's a lovely word; she doesn't really think it foolish to call a flower a flower. Let those who may consider themselves *wiser*, those *Savans* in their lofty academic posts, keep their Latin names and scientific classification numbers. Dickinson uses the Book of Revelation as a metaphor for nature's *Revelations*, which those "wiser" people *read with beclouded eyes.*

The Biblical references continue as we meet Moses again. Although he led his people out of slavery in Egypt to the Promised Land of *Canaan*, a mercurial God did not permit him to enter therein himself, an episode that Dickinson writes of with puzzlement elsewhere (See for example *It always felt to me - a wrong/To that Old Moses - done* -) (J597/F521/M255). Moses was, however, permitted to see the Promised Land from where he stood on a mountain top.[15] The scene serves as a metaphor for apotheosis. Imagining herself permitted that vision, standing there *with that Old "Moses," doubtless* she *would deem many Science*s *superfluous* from such a grand point of view.

Belles lettres, taken from the French (literally, "beautiful letters"), refers to elegant writing of essays, drama, fiction, and poetry valued for their esthetic qualities, as distinct from legal and scientific writing, rhetoric, or other forms that are valued for the information that they convey. The belle lettres that the poet hopes to stand amid, as a star, are those of God, his universe of *Galaxies.* Among some Native American peoples, stars were thought to be the spirits of the departed. The Bible expresses the idea in a simile: "And they that be wise shall shine as the brightness of the firmament; and they that turn many to righteousness as the stars for ever and ever" (Daniel 12:3). Dickinson was apparently conversant with the same idea.

> Go thy great way!
> The Stars thou meetst
> Are even as Thyself -
> For what are Stars but Asterisks
> To point a human Life?
> —J1638/F1673/M735

Two manuscripts of this poem are extant. They are identical in form and content. Each was sent with a letter. In one letter the poem served as an elegy for a departed friend. Its significance or purpose in the second letter is unknown.[16]

Dickinson's poetry celebrates the capacity of human nature to absorb all that the natural world has to show, and exalts the spiritual over the simply rational. A well-known example is "The Brain is wider than the Sky" (J632/F598/M273). Another poem on the same theme provides another look at her use of the language of science.

> I thought that nature was enough
> Till Human nature came
> But that the other did absorb
> As Parallax a Flame -
>
> Of Human nature just aware
> There added the Divine

Brief struggle for capacity
The power to contain

Is always as the contents
But give a Giant room
And you will lodge a Giant
And not a smaller man
—J1286/F1269/M565

The first stanza contrasts *nature* with a small *n*—the natural world that we can see and describe—with *Human nature*, the adjective capitalized. Human nature apprehends the natural, visible world, but much more, it can apprehend the spiritual, invisible as well. *That,* in line 3, refers to *Human nature* in line 2. Human nature absorbs nature *As Parallax* would absorb *a flame.*

PAR′AL-LAX, n.
In *astronomy*, the change of place in a heavenly body in consequence of being viewed from different points. *Diurnal parallax*, the difference between the place of a celestial body, as seen from the surface, and from the center of the earth, at the same instant. *Annual parallax*, the change of place in a heavenly body, in consequence of being viewed at opposite extremities of the earth's orbit.

And, from the EDL,

PARALLAX, n,
Apparent displacement; different angle; immense distance; disappearance by change in perspective; change in position of a celestial body due to a different point of view; difference in relative proximity.

If parallax can cause a star to seem to move or become invisible, how much more so to a mere flame!

In stanza two, having now become aware of Human nature, one experiences a *Divine/Brief struggle for capacity,* a struggle to expand Circumference and thereby one's *power to contain.* In stanza three, the speaker addresses the reader directly. *Give a Giant room* within your Circumference, *And you will lodge a* metaphorical *Giant/And not a smaller man.* By expanding your circumference, you will be greater yourself.

I would like to remind the reader here that Dickinson's poems can often allow widely different interpretations. Later chapters offer some reasons why this is might be. Some readers, for example, interpret *Human nature* in the preceding poem as meaning love.[17] The poem reads perfectly cogently that way, too, love being the ultimate expression of human nature. It sometimes comes down to which reading you find most satisfying.

In the nineteenth century scientists believed that although matter can and does change, it is not destroyed, a principal known as "conservation of matter." Dickinson speculates on extending the principal beyond the physical realm.

The Chemical conviction
That Nought be lost
Enable in Disaster
My fractured Trust -

The Faces of the Atom
If I shall see
How more the Finished Creatures
Departed me!

—J954/F1070/M480

Today, the word *Chemical* may function as a noun as well as an adjective. We may speak of magnesium sulphate, for example, as "a chemical," or we may be wary of "chemicals" in our processed food. In ED's dictionary, it was recognized only as an adjective.

CHEM′IC-AL, a.
See CHIMICAL.

CHIM′IC-AL, a. [See Chimistry.]
1. Pertaining to chimistry; as, a chimical operation.
2. Resulting from the operation of the principles of bodies by decomposition, combination, etc.; as, chimical changes.
3. According to the principles of chimistry; as, a chimical combination.

The speaker has a *conviction,* based on the science of chemistry, that nothing is ever *lost.* That conviction enables her to *Trust,* even in the face of *disaster*, even though that trust has been *fractured*, cracked or splintered. By what that trust has been fractured she does not specify, but we may infer it is that friends have *departed* from her. She says *if* she will be allowed to see *The Faces of the Atoms.* Her trust is not absolute. What atoms? To help us understand the atoms of this poem and the next, here is Ralph Waldo Emerson warning of the consequences of denying Providence, or God: "You leave him [man] alone in a universe exposed to the convulsions of disorder & the wrecks of systems [you leave him] where man is an atom unable to avert his peril or provide for his escape, you leave him destitute of friends who *are* able to control the order of nature."[18]

To the modern ear, an atom is a physical entity, comprised of protons, neutrons, and electrons. This was unknown when Emerson wrote and was also unknown to Emily Dickinson. In the 1800's an atom was a particle of matter that is irreducible to something smaller. A single atom was apart from any greater or more complex body, and so could stand figuratively to express a condition of isolation, of being apart or separated from all else. Dickinson expressed this meaning of the word in a letter: "Sunday - I haven't any paper, dear, but faith continues firm. Presume if I met with my deserts I should receive nothing. Was informed to that effect today by a dear Pastor. What a privilege it is to be so insignificant. Thought of intimating that the Atonement [See "Redemption" in Chapter 5] was not needed for such atomies."[19] If a piece of matter is smashed, we may say that it has been *atomized.* The same word can describe the human condition under certain circumstances. Laura Dassow Walls writes: "Emerson's American Scholar was a healer who would fuse the scattered and atomized individuals of the young republic into a whole, a nation.'"[20]

In the poem just considered, the atoms are separate and individual, without a negative connotation. These atoms are the individual selves around the speaker. In the next poem, a single atom is isolated by the poet herself as she selects it out from all other atoms in the universe. Here, the poet may be drawing on another aspect of the atom, as did Emerson in his essay, "The Oversoul," as a metaphor for the "divine unity" of a perfected soul.

Of all the Souls that stand create -
I have elected - One -
When Sense from Spirit - files away -
And Subterfuge - is done -
When that which is - and that which was -
Apart - intrinsic - stand -
And this brief Tragedy of flesh -
Is shifted - like a Sand -
When Figures show their royal Front -
And Mists - are carved away,
Behold the Atom - I preferred -
To all the lists of Clay!
—J664/F279/M530

Of *all the souls* in creation, from Adam and Eve down to the present day, she has *elected* a single *One*. She does not merely select, but like God choosing who are saved and who are not, she elects, conferring a most elevated station upon her One. The conventional view of death is of the spirit leaving the body and the world of the senses behind. The view from the other side of death, however, would be one of the physical senses leaving the spirit, and there the poet places us, in the third line. One by one, the senses *file away*. The word file is apt. It gives a sense of the individual senses being lost one by one, filing off as if into a vanishing distance. It is the Last Day, the end of time. *Subterfuge is done.*

SUB'TER-FUGE, n
Literally, that to which a person resorts for escape or concealment; hence, a shift; an evasion; an artifice employed to escape censure or the force of an argument, or to justify opinions or conduct

Our spirits, ourselves, are no longer concealed in a body. We are in the spirit and can no longer hide. We are revealed for who we are. At the end of time, past and present are one, and *that which is—and that which was* are all and equally present. Once more, the important word *intrinsic* appears

IN-TRIN′SIC, or IN-TRIN′SIC-AL, a.

2. Inward; internal; hence, true; genuine; real; essential; inherent; not apparent or accidental; as, the intrinsic value of gold or silver; the intrinsic merit of an action; the intrinsic worth or goodness of a person.

Everything in our past is present here on this final Day of Judgement, each showing its intrinsic value. Then, *Figures show their royal Front -/And Mists - are carved away.* These *Figures* are none other than the figures of souls, revealed at last for who they really are by the carving away of concealing mists, and now—*Behold the Atom - I preferred - To all the lists of Clay!* On this final day, the lists of the elect and of the damned, mortals made of clay (See "A single Screw of Flesh" in Chapter 1), have been compiled. The speaker presents the one, of all the souls of creation that she has singled out, and singled out by preference, not judgement. This is the Atom she *preferred.* Dr. Edward Hitchcock taught that God might preserve a single atom of the physical body to form the resurrection body: "If only a millionth part, or a ten thousand millionth part, of the matter deposited in the grave, shall be raised from thence, it justifies the representations of scripture, that there will be a resurrection of the dead."[21] One is reminded of the last lines of "One Sister have I in or house" (Chapter 6) ED's poem to her sister-in-law, Susan:

I chose this single star
From out the wide night's numbers -
Sue - forevermore!

EIGHT

The Language of Intimacy

> "If you were here - and Oh that you were, my Susie, we need not talk at all, our eyes would whisper for us, and your hand fast in mine, we would not ask for language -"—L94, 11 June 1852

In this early letter to her dear friend Susan Gilbert, the young Emily Dickinson wrote of a communion between two souls that words cannot reach. Generally, the more intimate two persons are, the fewer words they need to communicate their thoughts and feelings. A third party, overhearing such a conversation however, might easily be at a loss to understand it. It is this language of intimacy in Dickinson's poems that can draw us in so close that it seems that the poet speaks to us personally, and it is this that can at other times puzzle us completely.

When poets speak admiringly of Dickinson's poetry, one of the words that they use most frequently is "concise." They are expressing the same quality observed by her earliest editors. One of them was Thomas Wentworth Higginson, who had years earlier written a seven-quatrain (28 line) poem honoring the war dead, entitled "Decoration." (See Appendix A) Dickinson sent Higginson a poem on the same subject (Franklin version).

> Lay this Laurel on the one
> Triumphed and remained unknown -
> Laurel - fell your futile Tree -
> Such a Victor could not be -
>
> Lay this Laurel on the one
> Too intrinsic for Renown -
> Laurel - vail your deathless Tree -
> Him you chasten - that is he -
> —J1393/F1428/M600

In a letter to his co-editor Mabel Loomis Todd, Higginson wrote: "She wrote it after re-reading my 'Decoration.' It is the condensed essence of that and so far finer."[1]

It's Like She's Talking Directly to Me!

By leaving some words unwritten, the poet invites the reader to understand somewhat nonverbally. The reader recognizes a shared experience, truth, or meaning with the poet—in other words, he sees it for himself, much as one would in a conversation in which certain things are already understood between both parties. In the words of Archibald MacLeish, "No one can read these poems or any of the tens of others like them without perceiving that he is not so much reading as being spoken to."[2] We have seen poems that display this quality in preceding pages, in *So glad we are - a Stranger'd deem*, for example (Chapter 1). We did not dwell on this particular aspect of their construction. That is our purpose here. We start by reviewing some of the poems previously considered. With some poems, it's possible to reconstruct the poem simply by filling in the missing words, without having to rearrange existing words, as in this example from Chapter 4:

Four Trees - [standing] upon a solitary Acre -
Without Design
Or Order, or Apparent Action -
Maintain [themselves] -

The Sun - upon a Morning meets them -
The Wind [meets them too] -
No nearer Neighbor - have they -
But God -

The Acre gives them - [a]Place -
They [give] - Him - [the] Attention of Passer[s] by -
[and] Of Shadow[s], or of [a] Squirrel, haply -
Or [a] Boy -

What Deed is Theirs unto the General Nature -
What Plan [is Theirs, that]
They severally - retard - or further -
[is] Unknown -

—J742/F778/M382

If Dickinson had provided the words that I have supplied above, the scene that she describes would have been much easier to comprehend, and far less interesting. By grasping the unwritten words, we not so much read a description as see it for ourselves.

Next we return to the first two stanzas of "Summer begins to have the look," fulfilling a promise made in Chapter 2.

Summer begins to have the look
Peruser of enchanting Book

Reluctantly but sure perceives
A gain upon the backward leaves

Autumn begins to be inferred
By millinery of the cloud
Or deeper color in the shawl
That wraps the everlasting hill.
—J1682/F1693/M664

Except for the lone dash at the end, there is no punctuation in the first stanza. Reading from the first line to the second, the reader might feel uncertain of the meaning, as the sentences are not connected grammatically. He may have to read further in order to place the first two lines in context. Doing so, he sees that the peruser of the enchanted book is *reluctant to perceive* that she is gaining on the backward leaves—the final pages—of the book. She doesn't want it to end. Summer *is beginning to have the* same *look* to her now, which the poet describes in the second stanza. In prose, we would say "Summer begins to have the look that the peruser of an enchanting book has when she reluctantly perceives that she is gaining on the backward leaves (pages)." The leaves on the trees are beginning to change color, too, and will soon fall to the ground. The scene causes her to look *backward* over the summer now nearly passed. We feel, without being told explicitly, that the speaker is expressing her own reluctance to see the summer pass, and is projecting that feeling onto summer itself. We feel it because we can share it with her. Thus, we are drawn into an empathetic rapport with the speaker in which we feel and understand more than the words are saying.

It asks a certain involvement on the part of the reader to apprehend meaning by inferring the unspoken words, references, and thought. Margaret Freeman writes: "This practice is so characteristic of Dickinson's style that it is practically a signature. It is a cultivation of silence, of not articulating explicitly the grammatical connections, just as the sounds of departure, in their increasing intervals, paradoxically create a greater intimacy through the thoughts they leave behind."

As Accent fades to interval
With separating Friends
Till what we speculate, has been
And thoughts we will not show
More intimate with us become
Than Persons, that we know.[3]

The lines are from "The murmuring of Bees, has ceased," presented in Chapter 5.

A very concise poem, discussed in Chapter 3, offers a second example of word omission and an invitation to intimacy in the first verse.

Delight is as the flight -
Or in the Ratio of it,
As the Schools would say -
The Rainbow's way -
A Skein
Flung colored, after Rain,
Would suit as bright,
Except that flight
Were Aliment -
—J257/F317/M151

Attempting the thought in prose we might say, "Our delight in an experience is determined by *the flight* of that experience. The *ratio* of our delight to the amount of time that the experience lasts increases as the amount of time decreases. That's the *rainbow's way* of delighting us. *A colored skein flung* out after the *rain* has stopped would *suit* us as being just *as bright* as the rainbow, *except* for the fact that the rainbow's *flight* is *Aliment* (nutriment) for us."

The idea expressed in the poem, that delight is fleeting, is a familiar one, so we don't need it spelled out explicitly, as in the preceding paragraph. It is, in fact, a shared experience between reader and poet.

When Dickinson's poems were first published in the early 1890s, the editors selected a few hundred from the many hundreds available to them at that time. Others were not published until the twentieth century, and poems such as ones that we will consider in these final chapters are among them. The nineteenth century was simply not ready for them. These poems require more from the reader, and as we have already begun to realize, they tend to reward the reader proportionately. In the next poem, not published until 1945, the poet addresses a beloved "Thou." The intimacy, then, is between her and the unnamed "Thou," and her address to him (or her) is "overheard" by the reader.

Spring comes on the World -
I sight the Aprils -
Hueless to me until thou come
As, til the Bee
Blossoms stand negative,
Touched to Conditions
By a Hum.
—J1042/F999/M458

Imagine two close friends, trudging home from work on a cold winter day. One of them says, "Oh how I wish I could stretch out on a warm beach right now." The other might reply, "Yeah, well, til the summer. . . ." and leave the rest, "we will have to wait," unsaid. Spring *comes on the World,* but the bright days of April, with their myriad flowers and new green leaves, seem *Hueless*—colorless—until the person whom she is addressing comes to her. Until the Bee comes; she explains in in line four, *Blossoms stand negative.*

> NEG'A-TIVE, a.
>
> 1. Implying denial or negation; opposed to affirmative, as a negative proposition is that which denies. Matter is not spirit.
>
> 2. Implying absence; opposed to positive. There is a negative way of denying Christ, when we do not acknowledge and confess him.

In the absence of the pollinating bee, the flowers are negative in the sense of the passive absence noted in definition 2 above. When the Hum of the Bee is heard in the meadow once more, the flower is *touched,* in the sense of being deeply affected or moved, and awakens to her new *conditions.*

The approach that we've taken thus far in this section, that of filling in words that are unspoken but can be inferred, must work a little differently in a poem such as the next. What do you make of these lines, by themselves?

A Wonderful - to feel the Sun
Still toiling at the Cheek

A wonderful what? We think we get the meaning. We've all enjoyed the feeling of the warm sun on our cheek. It must go something like, "A Wonderful [thing it is] to feel the Sun." But the lines by themselves in this case are part of a single continuing thought, and we must look further into the poem for full comprehension.

A Solemn thing within the Soul
To feel itself get ripe -
And golden hang - while farther up -
The Maker's Ladders stop -
And in the Orchard far below -
You hear a Being - drop -

A Wonderful - to feel the Sun
Still toiling at the Cheek
You thought was finished -
Cool of eye, and critical of Work -
He shifts the stem - a little -
To give your Core - a look -

But solemnest - to know
Your chance in Harvest moves
A little nearer - Every Sun
The Single - to some lives.

—J483/F467/M234

The first lines of each stanza are parallel constructions, like those in a poem from Chapter 2, reproduced below:

I suppose the time will come
Aid it in the coming
When the Bird will crowd the Tree
And the Bee be booming.

I suppose the time will come
Hinder it a little
When the Corn in Silk will dress
And in Chintz the Apple

I believe the Day will be
When the Jay will giggle
At his new white House the Earth
That, too, halt a little -
—J1381/F1389/M591

The first lines of each stanza are parallel, meaning that they are similar in construction, or grammatically the same: "I suppose the time will come/I suppose the time will come/I believe the Day will be." Long before Caesar ever wrote "I came, I saw, I conquered," orators and statesmen must have used parallelism to hold their audiences. The technique is at least as effective in poetry. The ear detects the similar lines easily in *I suppose the time will come*. It is perhaps more elusive in "A Solemn thing within the Soul," because of some omitted content: "A Solemn thing within the Soul/A Wonderful [thing within the Soul] to feel the Sun/But solemnest - to know." By setting up the construction in the first line of the poem, Dickinson is able to suggest it to the reader in the first line of the second stanza without having to complete the thought, allowing her to pack more meaning into that line.

The soul, like the apple, feels itself get ripe. It is a *solemn* realization, to know that you are close to your final days, euphemistically called our "golden years." This is perhaps suggested by the golden yellow of the apples. The poem is set in a metaphorical orchard. In orchards, then as now, specialized *ladders*, wide at the base and narrow at the top, were used to reach the apples *farther up*. These particular ladders belong to no ordinary orchardist, however; they belong to *The Maker*[4]—they belong to God. Once an apple is ripe, it is harvested. If not, it will eventually *drop* from the tree. In the Maker's orchard, it is a *Being* that drops. *You hear* it. This being has not been harvested by the Maker. This being has not been elected by God. Dickinson has not only given us an almost miraculous sound/image here, as though we are hearing a soul drop into the abyss. She simultaneously places you, the reader, at the center of the poem. It is indeed about you.

She reminds you that you are undergoing, right now, the process being narrated. That is why it is Wonderful to feel the sun on your *Cheek*, which you had *thought was finished*, when feeling your soul get ripe. The *Sun* doesn't shine, or play, or warm in this orchard; he *toils*. The Sun is working for the Maker, who *shifts the stem - a little*. Emily Dickinson is describing a familiar operation quite exactly. She knew from experience, in her family's orchard in Amherst, that to examine an apple properly you hold it from beneath and lift it slightly, rather than twisting, which might well result in separating it from the tree prematurely. The Maker/orchardist is examining you to see if you are ripe and ready. *Solemnest* of all *it is* to know that someday you certainly will be. Then it will be your *chance in Harvest*, which moves a little nearer with each passing day, the last—*single*—day for some lives. In "A Solemn thing within the Soul" Dickinson establishes intimacy with the reader not only by leaving him to complete some of the thoughts himself, but also by addressing us personally, on perhaps the deepest of subjects.

A short poem, a single quatrain, also touching on the subject of death, was written about a year and a half after the death of the poet's father. She sent it with a letter to T.W. Higginson that included a note about flowers for her father's grave. It is comprised of only fifteen words in two sentences. This very concise poem has left even dedicated Dickinson readers puzzled.

To his simplicity
To die - was little Fate -
If Duty live - contented
But her Confederate.
—J1352/F1387/M714

Before trying to replace whatever has been omitted, consider the word *simplicity*. In modern usage, the word when applied to a person can be condescending at best. It often carries the meaning of the sixth definition given below.

SIM-PLIC'I-TY, n.

1. Singleness; the state of being unmixed or uncompounded; as, the simplicity of metals or of earths.
2. The state of being not complex, or of consisting of few parts; as, the simplicity of a machine.
3. Artlessness of mind; freedom from a propensity to cunning or stratagem; freedom from duplicity; sincerity. Marquis Dorset, a man for his harmless simplicity neither misliked nor much regarded.
4. Plainness; freedom from artificial ornament; as, the simplicity of a dress, of style, of language, &c. Simplicity in writing is the first of excellencies.
5. Plainness; freedom from subtilty [sic]or abstruseness; as, the simplicity of Scriptural doctrines or truth.
6. Weakness of intellect; silliness

It can hardly be inferred that Emily assigned "Weakness of intellect" or "silliness" to her father, a sober, responsible citizen whom she held in great respect. Certainly it was the more positive connotations of the word that she intended, then more current than now, as expressed by the Anglican theologian, Richard Sibbes: "You would think this to be a simple commendation, to commend himself for simplicity; but it is a Godly simplicity, whereby we are like to God, to be simple without mixture of sin and hypocrisy, without mixture of error and falsehood."[5] Indeed, in Christian theology, God Himself is simple, meaning that He has no parts. To the man of Godly simplicity of whom Dickinson writes, to die is a minor event. If such a thing as *Duty lives,* he is contented just to be *her Confederate.* He has remained on the side of duty, his conscience is clear, and so need not fear death.

In the next poem the reader must construct meaning not only by supplying what is omitted, but also by re-ordering some phrases. "The Night was wide, and furnished scant," opens on deserted streets on a cold November evening. In the last two stanzas, given below, a human figure appears:

> To feel if Blinds be fast -
> And closer to the fire -
> Her little Rocking Chair to draw -
> And shiver for the Poor -
>
> The Housewife's gentle Task -
> How pleasanter - said she
> Unto the Sofa opposite -
> The Sleet - than May, no Thee -
> —J589/F617/M503

The entire first stanza is an incomplete sentence. Who *feels* the *blinds*, *draws* the *Rocking Chair*, *and shivers*? We don't know until we reach *The Housewife.* These activities comprise her *gentle Task.* Reordering these lines yields, "It is the Housewife's gentle task to feel if the blinds are fast, draw her little Rocking Chair closer to the fire, and shiver for the poor." Remembering that there are those less fortunate, who are so poor that they can't afford a cozy hearth to sit by on this harsh evening, she shivers in sympathy. Then, she speaks to *the Sofa* situated *opposite* to where she is sitting. There is no one sitting on the sofa. Yet, she addresses it: "How much more *pleasant* is the sleet at this time, than would be the temperate month of *May* without you here." The feeling here is that, the beloved's absence must be felt more keenly when the world is waking up to new life, than it does in this raw weather, which must seem more appropriate to her loneliness. Full comprehension comes only gradually, from the uncertain empty sofa, through the piecing together the full meaning of the severely spare final line. The truth effectively dawns on the reader with a pang. Similar themes inform "I dreaded that first Robin so" (Chapter 2) and "The Morning after Woe" (Chapter 1).

Conversational Style

In investigating how it is that readers of Emily Dickinson often feel that she is addressing them directly, one finds language that sounds more like the spoken word than the written. There are expressions, figures of speech, and turns of phrase that do not usually appear in writing, but are common in daily speech. We have encountered examples in several poems already, without singling out the conversational elements. One can return to Dickinson over and over, though, through the years, and continue to find new ways of appreciating her, and with an ever-deepening admiration. Let us return to a few poems previously considered, and see if we don't find something new. In "Because I could not stop for Death" (Chapter 6), revisiting the third and fourth stanzas finds a distinctly conversational turn of phrase.

> We passed the School, where Children strove
> At Recess, in the Ring -
> We passed the Fields of Gazing Grain,
> We passed the Setting Sun -
>
> Or rather - He passed Us -
> The Dews drew quivering and chill -
> For only Gossamer my Gown -
> My Tippet - only Tulle –

In the first line of the second stanza, the narrator corrects herself. If one were writing this narrative, the practice would be to delete any reference to passing the setting sun, and to replace it with the corrected account. That is not possible in speech, and we human beings correct and edit our own speech in similar ways every day. Reading these lines, we feel that we are "not so much reading as being spoken to," as Archibald MacLeish observed.

In another poem, first presented in Chapter 2, the effect is immediate.

> These are the days when Birds come back -
> A very few - a Bird or two -
> To take a backward look.

First, the phrase *These are the days* places us in the present with the poet—or her in our presence. The second line consists of two afterthoughts, qualifying additions to what she tells us in the first line. *A Bird or two* itself is more a speech-like expression than a written one. An even more colloquial expression appears, appropriately enough, in one of the poems from our chapter on New England (Chapter 2)

I'm sorry for the Dead - Today -
It's such congenial times
Old Neighbors have at fences -
It's time o' year for Hay.

Again, this time by just the single word *Today,* we are with the speaker in the present. We hear that *It's time o' year for Hay,* a familiar expression heard from the mouths of farmers every summer in her community. Because the statement is given in the colloquial idiom, it's more as if we hear it, than that we are reading of some reported fact. In the final stanza of the same poem, she contracts a sentence slightly in a way reminiscent of the lines *A Wonderful-to feel the Sun/Still toiling at the Cheek*, read earlier in this chapter.

A Wonder if the Sepulchre
Don't feel a lonesome way -
When Men -and Boys - and Carts - and June,
Go down the Fields to "Hay" -

By saying *A Wonder* instead of I wonder, or it's a wonder, by dropping words assumed to be understood, the poet creates a certain sense of immediacy. Again, she is not so much reporting a fact, or even exclaiming for herself. Rather, she presents the wonder to us, in the present. The grammatically incorrect *Don't feel* was common usage with Dickinson and with her friends and neighbors not only in speech, but also in personal letters.

Dickinson could also create a connection with the reader by addressing him directly, as she did in "You're right - 'the way is narrow'" (Chapter 5). The final stanza contains something that would never appear in any formal writing, another qualifying afterthought.

And after *that* - there's Heaven -
The *Good* Man's - *"Dividend"* -
And Bad Men - "go to Jail" -
I guess -

By truncating the last line, she leaves a silence in place of what would otherwise be two more beats of meter. The absence of those beats persuasively renders the moment of silence that ordinarily follows a qualifying, "I guess..." at the end of a completed thought.

There are other Dickinson poems where this aspect of her writing is most prominent, poems very easy to enjoy, examples of which we turn to next.

I send Two Sunsets -
Day and I - in competition ran -
I finished Two - and several Stars -
While He - was making One -

His own was ampler - but as I
Was saying to a friend -
Mine - is the more convenient
To Carry in the Hand -
—J308/F557/M284

Emily Dickinson knew that she had a gift. She attested to it in several poems (see "It was given to me by the Gods"—J454/F455/M228, for example). She wrote poems in praise of her favorite poets, such as "All overgrown by cunning moss" discussed in Chapter 1, and poems celebrating the art of poetry itself. "I send Two Sunsets-," is just such a poem.

The *Two Sunsets* that she sends, to a friend, are two poems, each describing a sunset. At least one of them includes *several stars* in addition. While she was making them, finishing them in a single day, *Day* itself was able to complete only one sunset. His was the *ampler*, she admits, but unlike his, hers can be carried in the hand quite conveniently. She prepares us for this observation with *but as I Was saying to a friend,* as if addressing us in conversation. We feel that the poet is letting us in on her creative process with the easy familiarity of a friend.

In "Going to Him! Happy letter!," the next poem, it is the letter itself that is being addressed, rather than us readers. The address, however, is still completely conversational in form. It's as if we are there to overhear her send the letter off with breathless instructions.

Going to Him! Happy letter!
Tell Him -
Tell Him the page I didn't write -
Tell Him - I only said the Syntax -
And left the Verb and the pronoun out -
Tell Him just how the fingers hurried -
Then - how they waded - slow - slow -
And then you wished you had eyes in your pages -
So you could see what moved them so -

Tell Him - it wasn't a Practised Writer -
You guessed - from the way the sentence toiled -
You could hear the Bodice tug, behind you -
As if it held but the might of a child -

You almost pitied it - you - it worked so -
Tell Him - no - you may quibble there -
For it would split His Heart, to know it -
And then you and I, were silenter.

Tell Him - Night finished - before we finished -
And the Old Clock kept neighing "Day"!
And you - got sleepy - and begged to be ended -
What could it hinder so - to say?
Tell Him - just how she sealed you - Cautious!
But - if He ask where you are hid
Until tomorrow - Happy letter!
Gesture Coquette - and shake your Head!
—J494/F277/M529

You can almost hear the excited speaker catch her breath between the second and third line. The repetition of the instruction to *Tell Him* mimics the speech of a person whose thoughts flood tumultuously from her fervent mind to pile one atop another, and then exclaimed in successive bursts of speech. Counterbalancing the excited delivery is the deliberate considering what to tell him, and how, and what not to. Emily Dickinson was a prolific and masterly letter writer. We are granted the privilege of listening in on a creative artist at work.

She has left something out of this letter, a *page.* It is not necessarily a page of paper, but rather a page of meaning, that she *didn't write.* She has not only left it out of the letter, but she has left it out of this poem as well. We have seen how, in so many poems, that what Dickinson omits to write, and leaves for the reader to apprehend, constitutes the central import of the poem. Perhaps she is doing that here as well, in the letter, and also in the poem itself. She has left some clues for the recipient and perhaps for us too. She tells the letter that she only said the Syntax:

SYN'TAX, or SY'N-TAX'IS, n.
1. In grammar, the construction of sentences; the due arrangement of words in sentences, according to established usage.

It is from the syntax of a sentence that we derive its meaning. Poems have appeared in this book already in which Dickinson manipulates syntax to achieve her poetic ends. This is a topic explored in more detail in Chapter 9. In this poem, she has given him the syntax, and so has given him all that he should require to see her meaning. She left only *the Verb and the pronoun out.* If the verb is "love" and the pronoun is "I" or "you," she may be sending him a message that she wants him to understand without her having to write it explicitly. She wants her recipient to know how her *fingers hurried* as, at first, the words came streaming forth as fast as her pen could fly, and then how they *waded*, as she deliberated carefully about how to say what was in her heart. First, the fingers hurry until they slow down. In one sense the fingers are likened to someone hastening quickly until she comes to a body of water, which slows her down as she wades through it. This is the sense in which it is usually heard today, as one wades through a stream or wades into the surf. Emily Dickinson is using the word in a way more in keeping with her day. Definition B (EDL) below seems most appropriate for a *Happy letter!*

WADE (-ed, -s, wading), v.

A. Endure; suffer; pass laboriously through; experience the difficulty of.
B. Deliberate; luxuriate; move carefully; take the time needed to fully appreciate.
C. Persist; go on bravely.
D. Step; move; go; press forward; walk through.
E. Pilot; aviate; fly against the wind.

The speaker of this poem is not wading through anything physical. She wades purposefully and deliberately into the luxury of penning this letter. Dickinson could also use the word more in keeping with definition A, above, as wading against a force that she must struggle with. For an example, see "I can wade Grief" (J252/F312/M149). "Don't you wish *you had eyes in your pages*, she asks the letter, *so you could see* what caused my fingers to move as they do?" She poses the question rhetorically to the letter, but it is more to the recipient, and at last to us. What might it have been that has moved her so?

The second stanza begins humbly. It is the speaker presenting herself as an inexperienced writer (ED's spelling of the word "practiced" is preserved). She instructs her letter to show, by the labored (*toiled*) manner that she ascribes to her sentences (these cannot be Emily Dickinson's sentences!) how ardent is her intent. One is reminded of Bottom's dream, Shakespeare's character, Bottom, whose failed attempts to express the beauty that he has recently beheld tells more eloquently of that beauty than "practiced" letters ever could.[6] She continues to cast herself humbly, almost as a child. Tell him, she instructs s her letter, that it could hear her beating heart and labored breathing beneath her bodice as if a child were exerting herself beyond her abilities.

BOD′ICE, n.

Stays; a waistcoat, quilted with whalebone, worn by women.

Still considering carefully what to put down, she starts to give another instruction, and then checks herself. *Tell him - no - you may quibble there.* She ascribes to the letter the ability to dispute with her about what to write. What it is that she chooses not to write, because *it would split His*

Heart, she does not say. Similarly, in "I shall not murmur if at last" (Chapter 6) , a similar unspoken dread is expressed in the lines *Divulging it would rest my Heart/But it would ravage theirs.*

By the third stanza she has written all night. The sound of the clock reminds her of the neighing of an impatient horse. She asks the letter to attribute fatigue to itself, not to her—to take the blame rather than let her have to confess that she has at last grown tired. What harm could it do, she asks, *what could it hinder*, to say that? The one thing that she instructs the letter not to tell him is *where you are hid.* That would be in her bosom, no doubt. *Coquette* does not appear in Dickinson's dictionary; the EDL gives "Flirtatiously; playfully; in a teasing manner; like a flirt." The poem ends in the same happy tone with which it began.

The Omitted Center

Although I have striven to avoid the technical vocabulary of the grammarian and the language of formal literary criticism in this book, "The Omitted Center" deserves exception, because it is a term created especially for a certain feature of Emily Dickinson's poetic art. Moreover, it is a feature that plays a very significant role in involving the reader in the poem, sometimes in a deeply personal way, and is another distinctive Dickinson signature. The term was coined by Jay Leyda, in the introduction to his seminal *The Years and Hours of Emily Dickinson*: "A Major device of Emily Dickinson's writing, both in her poems and in her letters, was what might be called the 'omitted center.' The riddle, the circumstance too well known to be repeated to the initiate, the deliberate skirting of the obvious; this was the means she used to increase the privacy of her communication; it has also increased our problems in piercing that privacy."[7]

We have encountered the omitted center in several of the poems that we have already considered without identifying it as such.

- "I should have been too glad, I see -" (Chapter 5)—It was noted that "The poem leaves us with an experience of unspecified, but concentrated regret, and it does so in part by not grounding the experience in particulars." This is the work of the omitted center.
- "A Narrow Fellow in the Grass" (Chapter 1)—Most readers recognize the narrow fellow as a snake. Often children do not, yet the poem can fascinate them. This is a good poem to offer a child as a riddle.
- "I like to see it lap the Miles" (Chapter 2) It might be apparent that

"it" is a train, but even this fairly simple poem has evaded some people. At a formal poetry discussion in Amherst Massachusetts in 2008, it was agreed that "it" was a cat!

We will revisit a selection of previously discussed poems next, as well as some new ones, focusing our attention on the omitted center. Here, it will be especially interesting to learn what other readers identify as the subject of the poem. It can be fascinating as well as illuminating to learn what meaning others see in words where we see something entirely different.

We return then to "It sifts from Leaden Sieves" (Chapter 2), the first stanza of which is repeated here:

It sifts from Leaden Sieves -
It powders all the Wood.
It fills with Alabaster Wool
The Wrinkles of the Road -

The word "snow" does not appear in the poem, making this another example of an omitted center. However, to most people living in northern climes, it will be obvious that the poem describes a snowfall. But what about this next poem?

The Snow that never drifts -
The transient, fragrant snow
That comes a single time a Year
Is softly driving now -

So thorough in the Tree
At night beneath the star
That it was Febuary's Foot
Experience would swear -

Like Winter as a Face
We stern and former knew
Repaired of all but Loneliness
By Nature's Alibi -

Were every storm so spice
The Value could not be -
We buy with contrast- Pang is good
As near as memory -
—J1133/F1155/M545

After a fresh snow fall, wind may cause the snow to pile up in hilly mounds called *drifts*. What is the *Snow that never drifts*? What snow *comes a single time a Year*? The answer may not be so obvious. If you lived in Amherst or another New England town in the nineteenth century, you would be better prepared to see. Apples grew in the Dickinson orchard and all across New

England they still do. The trees blossomed a *single time a Year*, in the spring. Although, we would swear it was February, because of the snow-like petals of the apple blossoms *So thorough in the Tree*. Few people, if any today, would describe an apple tree in full bloom as *thorough*. ED applies it here more in the sense of being perfect, complete.

> THOR-OUGH, a.
> 1. Literally, passing through or to the end; hence, complete; perfect; as, a thorough reformation; thorough work; a thorough translator; a thorough poet.

And, from the EDL:

> THOROUGH (-LY), adv.
> 1. Completely; fully; perfectly; wholly.
> 2. Extensively; amply; sweeping; all encompassing.

Eventually, the blossoms fall from the tree, and may be seen blowing gently—*softly driving*—in the spring air. If you have lived in Japan, with its cherry trees and their famous blossoms, you might recognize this snow not as apple blossoms or crystallized water, but as cherry blossoms. Still another reading of "The Snow that never drifts" finds in it a description of a memory that returns annually to commemorate a certain life event.

The poet likens winter to a *stern face*—one that she *former knew*, because it's springtime, and winter is now gone. It's as if the face of winter has been repaired of its cold, its ice, and of a dormant Nature—of all but *loneliness*, which remains. *Alibi* means "Elsewhere; in another place." The *repair* is accomplished by winter's having gone to another place. We may also say that winter has *repaired* to another place.

> RE-PAIR′, v.i.
> To go to; to betake one's self; to resort; as, to repair to a sanctuary for safety.

> RE-PAIR, v.t.
> 1. To restore to a sound or good state after decay, injury, dilapidation or partial destruction; as, to repair a house, a wall or a ship; to repair roads and bridges.

By not naming the apple blossoms, the poet allows, indeed requires, readers to find their own experience in and of the poem. The general process, from the reader's point of view, was described by Charles Alphonso Smith, an American professor of English and author over 100 years ago.

> Now the life of the poet, the date of his work, the kind of meter employed, all have something to do with a poem. But they are secondary, not primary. The first thing you do is to find yourself in the poem itself. When you do this, when the poem means something to you, when you see in it a reflection or extension of yourself, when it becomes a real outlet for you, you will want to know something about the writer. Seek first, however, yourself in the poem, and all these other things will be added unto you.[8]

If you haven't read at least one biography of Emily Dickinson or read any of her letters, as you continue to read her poetry you probably will. There is a natural tendency to want to learn about the life of a favorite author. It seems to be particularly so with this very private poet.

In our treatment of "I cautious, scanned my little life" (Chapter 1), we described it as "a poem about careful husbandry," but is that all?

I cautious, scanned my little life -
I winnowed what would fade
From what would last till Heads like mine
Should be a-dreaming laid.

I put the latter in a Barn -
The former, blew away.
I went one winter morning
And lo - my priceless Hay

Was not upon the "Scaffold" -
Was not upon the "Beam" -
And from a thriving Farmer -
A Cynic, I became.

Whether a Thief did it -
Whether it was the wind -
Whether Deity's guiltless -
My business is, to find!

So I begin to ransack!
How is it Hearts, with Thee?
Art thou within the little Barn
Love provided Thee?

—J178/F175/M102

What is omitted in this poem, what she doesn't tell us we will argue, is what exactly it is that *would fade* and what it is that *would last.* She tells us that she winnowed one from the other.

WIN'NOW, v.t.
1. To separate and drive off the chaff from grain by means of wind. Grain is winnowed by a fan, or by a machine, or by pouring it out of a vessel in a current of air.
2. To fan; to beat as with wings.
3. To examine; to sift for the purpose of separating falsehood from truth.
4. To separate, as the bad from the good

Is the speaker, then, a disappointed farmer, whose valued harvest has vanished from the barn? That would be the literal reading, but this is *priceless hay.* Dickinson's art was priceless to her (and to us), and some have interpreted the poem with that in mind, the grain being a metaphor for poetry. Literary critic Henry W. Wells took this view: "Poetry comprises the form or spiritual body preserving the divine heart of man long after his physical heart within his mortal body has disintegrated into dust."[9]

Wells draws parallels between the physical body and dust (which blows *away*), and between poetry and the immortal spiritual body (which will *last*). (Recall the biblical distinction between the physical body and the spiritual body from Chapter 5). In the poem however, the opposite occurs. The narrator stores *what would last* in the barn, and it is this *precious Hay* that is lost. What has been lost, then, may be something of value other than poetry, a faith in principles or belief, perhaps. The hay was stored in what appeared to be a place of safety, only to vanish later, causing her to abandon formerly cherished values and become a cynic. Author and Dickinson editor Theodora Ward took this view: "In a mood of retrospection the poet takes stock in the values stored up in her past, only to find they have vanished."[10] If values have been lost or beliefs abandoned, they are not named. Need they be? That, too, depends on the reader. For some, the poem is one of profound, disorienting loss as an aspect of the human condition, not tied to some specific loss. Reading the poem this way, most of us can "find ourselves in the poem." For others, it may indeed concern something specific to Dickinson's personal experience and philosophy, the poem reflecting a loss of faith in the tenets of religion or in the Christian God. In this view the poem "...appears to be exceedingly valuable in ascertaining some measure of her philosophy."[11] Whether the cause of her loss is man-made (*a Thief*), a chance of nature (*the wind*), or God himself (*Deity*), her *business is to find* out. God is not always to be trusted, a sentiment entirely congruent with the larger body of Dickinson's work. For other examples of theological doubt, see "It always felt to me - a wrong" (J597/F521/M255) or "Those - dying then" (J1551/F1581/M638).

By not specifying what, exactly, "it" might be, the poet invites the reader to "bring something to the table." This is a primary way in which she forms such strong bonds with some of her readers. Perhaps no Dickinson poem better exemplifies this than the following one.

It was not Death, for I stood up,
And all the Dead, lie down -
It was not Night, for all the Bells
Put out their Tongues, for Noon.

It was not Frost, for on my Flesh
I felt Siroccos - crawl -
Nor Fire - for just my Marble feet
Could keep a Chancel, cool -

And yet, it tasted, like them all,
The Figures I have seen
Set orderly, for Burial,
Reminded me, of mine -

As if my life were shaven,
And fitted to a frame,
And could not breathe without a key,
And 'twas like Midnight, some -

When everything that ticked - has stopped -
And Space stares all around -
Or Grisly frosts - first Autumn morns,
Repeal the Beating Ground -

But, most, like Chaos - Stopless - cool -
Without a Chance, or Spar -
Or even a Report of Land -
To justify - Despair.

—J510/F355/M187

In this poem, the narrator fails to name or in any way identify "it," not out of choice, but rather because she is unable. She proceeds through a series of negations, listing several things that it is not—*And yet, it tasted, like them all.* What she observes contradicts her own senses, potentially a disorienting and even frightening experience.

It was not Death, but she knew that only because she was stranding up. The tone is perhaps one of surprised wonder. A *tongue* may be not only the muscle that we use to speak with, it may also be the thin length of metal that hangs inside the bell, causing it to ring, also called the "clapper" or simply the "ringer." Some readers have found a possible pun on "Belles"—young ladies—chatting in the noonday sun, which indicates that it is day, not *Night*. It was somewhat like *Frost,* too, but her very flesh persuaded her otherwise.

SI-ROC′CO, n.

A pernicious wind that blows from the south-east in Italy, called the Syrian wind. It is said to resemble the steam from the mouth of an oven.

The sirocco didn't waft gently over her; it *crawled,* like an insect or a scorpion. In contrast to that sensation, her *Marble feet/Could keep a Chancel, cool.* Recall that marble is among the words that Dickinson would use to imply "white" (Chapter 5). Additionally, a slang expression for fear is "cold feet." The church would get hot and stuffy during summer, crowded with parishioners. Just her feet would keep it cool, she tells us, so cold were they.

CHAN′CEL, n.

That part of the choir of a church, between the altar or communion table, and the balustrade or railing that incloses it, or that part where the altar is placed; formerly inclosed with lattices or cross bars, as now with rails

Dickinson would have known that in the ancient cathedrals of Europe, the bodies of especially prominent people were interred beneath the floor of the chancel. In the past, she has seen *Figures Set orderly, for Burial* right at home in Amherst. There were no funeral homes or other very formal establishments for treatment of the dead. The body was placed in a parlor or other room of the house for viewing before burial. "Am I alive or dead?"—seems to be the underlying question. It's as if her own *life were shaven and fitted to a frame..*

> SHAVE, v.t.
> 1. To cut or pare off something from the surface of a body by a razor or other edged instrument, by rubbing, scraping or drawing the instrument along the surface; as, to shave the chin and cheeks; to shave the head of its hair.
> 2. To shave off, to cut off.
> 3. To pare close.
> 4. To cut off thin slices; or to cut in thin slices

When a person died, a coffin was made to fit the body, but here the opposite occurs. It is her life that is being cut off and pared in order to fit into this particular confining space where she *could not breathe* under her own agency. The word "some" at the end of line 20 would be common in speech, but not in writing. In writing, it would be "somewhat like midnight." Here then is another conversational touch that helps create the feeling that we are being spoken to. The tone of this manner of speaking is offhand, casual. While the poem describes a descent into chaos, the tone has become cool and objective.

It's *like midnight*, she reports, when time has *stopped and space stares* like a living thing. Or, it's like that time of year when *Grisly frosts* fall on the land and still the life *Beating* in the *Ground.* And finally, *Chaos.* It is *stopless,* no power can prevail against it. There is no predictable cause and effect. Anything could happen without a discernable reason, making hope impossible. If there were any chance of relief, a ship's spar from the wreck that she might cling to (or the spar of a rescue ship in the distance), *Or even a Report of Land*—land not even visible over the horizon, none of these existed to inspire hope, and so there was nothing to despair of. For another example of a poem that associates despair with cool objectivity, see "The difference between Despair" (J305/F576/M263). She does not tell what event or crisis may have precipitated this state of absolute nihilistic oblivion, but a tertiary definition of despair in Emily Dickinson's dictionary is "Loss of faith in the mercy of God." Such would be the meaning from the point of a reprobate (one not elected by God for salvation after the resurrection of the dead, one who might well observe that, *It was not Death, for I stood up*.

In the following poem, the poet describes a spectral, almost other-worldly scene, but a scene of what, exactly, she does not tell. She intends her readers to see it for themselves.

A chilly Peace infests the Grass
The Sun respectful lies -
Not any Trance of industry
These shadows scrutinize -

Whose Allies go no more astray
For service or for Glee -
But all mankind deliver here
From whatsoever sea -
—J1443/F1469/M612

There are perhaps some unanticipated words in this poem, beginning with the first line, where one might expect "infects the Grass" rather than *infests.* "Infests" suggests bugs or vermin invading a house to modern ears. A more general definition was recognized in Dickinson's time:

IN-FEST′, v.t.
To trouble greatly; to disturb; to annoy; to harass.

The *Peace* in the scene is not a comfortable one. It disturbs the very grass. *Chilly Peace,* in fact, is an example of Dickinson's putting two somewhat contradictory or contrasting words together to achieve her poetic purpose. (We examine this literary technique, which Dickinson made her own, in Chapter 9.) It suggests the cold of the grave where souls "rest in peace," and at the same time the chill that the thought of the grave suggests.

Another unanticipated word in this stanza is *Trance.* Not uncommonly, it will be read aloud as "Trace" instead of *Trance.* "Not any Trace of Industry" would be a definite way of describing a lack of activity. "There is no trace of activity here," in other words.

TRANCE, n
1. An ecstacy; a state in which the soul seems to have passed out of the body into celestial regions, or to be rapt into visions. When they made ready, he fell into a trance, and saw heaven opened. Acts 10:10.
2. In medicine, catalepsy, i.e. total suspension of mental power, and voluntary motion; pulsation and breathing continuing; muscles flexible; body yielding to, and retaining any given position, not incompatible with the laws of gravitation.

The unconscious aspect of a trance enforces the peace and the stillness of the scene. It derives from the Latin *transitus,* "a passing over," suggesting the passing of the soul "out of the body into celestial regions." *The Sun* is properly respectful of this ground. That it *lies* tells us that this is not high noon, and, considering the cool stillness, probably sunset rather than sunrise.

At that time of day, it would cast long *Shadows,* or are these shadows perhaps of a different nature?

> SHAD′OW, n.
> 6. A spirit; a ghost. [Obs.] [In this sense, shade is now used.]

Dickinson used the word shadow in this older sense in another poem, "Like Men and Women Shadows walk" (J1105/F964/M447), and in that sense the word lends a gothic feeling to the poem under consideration. If souls are in transit, if the sun looks respectfully on the scene, if spirits remain nearby, we are perhaps in a cemetery. Other readers have perceived a battlefield in the aftermath of battle; if so the second stanza should bear it out.

The shadows have *Allies,* those united with them in the bond of death, perhaps. They're not going anywhere, but why *no more astray*? Why not more directly with "no more away?"

> AS-TRAY′, adv.
> Out of the right way or proper place, both in a literal and a figurative sense. In morals and religion, it signifies wandering from the path of rectitude, from duty and happiness.

To say that someone has "gone astray" is to express something like the above, not merely a wandering away like an errant child, but something very much more serious. It was a familiar understanding from the Bible: "All we like sheep have gone astray; we have turned every one to his own way; and the LORD hath laid on him the iniquity of us all" (Isaiah 53:6). It was a familiar understanding from the sermons and hymns heard in church every Sabbath day, such as this from Psalm 14 Part 1 by Isaac Watts:

> By nature all are gone astray,
> Their practice all the same;
> There's none that fears his Maker's hand;
> There's none that loves his name.
>
> Their tongues are used to speak deceit,
> Their slanders never cease;
> How swift to mischief are their feet,
> Nor know the paths of peace!
>
> Such seeds of sin (that bitter root)
> In every heart are found;
> Nor can they bear diviner fruit,
> Till grace refine the ground

Note the promise of a redemptive saving grace in the final line of the hymn. Nevertheless, the allies will go no more astray physically, nor will they do so spiritually, whether or not they are among the saved.

Dickinson's final two lines proclaim that everyone winds up here, no matter where they came from. The words *deliver here* can be puzzling. Deliver what? Deliver to whom? These questions are resolved by reading "deliver here" without a direct object, with it being understood that they deliver themselves to this place. Similarly, the word *maintain* used in this way, was noted in Chapter 4:

> Four Trees - upon a solitary Acre -
> Without Design
> Or Order, or Apparent Action -
> Maintain –

The four trees maintain themselves, maintain their own lives. Dickinson will use as few words as possible. Among several alternate word choices that she recorded in her manuscript was "All mankind do anchor here/From whatsoever sea."[12] There are 136 instances of the word *sea* in the poems. Dickinson employed it metaphorically in a wide variety of ways too numerous to survey here. In this case, it is not literal seas or oceans that she means, but rather *whatsoever* sources or points of origin (EDL).

Another favorite metaphor of Dickinson's is that of a house. She uses the language of architecture in the next poem to convey something more abstract, an idea beyond the reach of ordinary language.

> I dwell in Possibility -
> A fairer House than Prose -
> More numerous of Windows -
> Superior - for Doors -
>
> Of Chambers as the Cedars -
> Impregnable of Eye -
> And for an Everlasting Roof
> The Gambrels of the Sky -
>
> Of Visitors - the fairest -
> For Occupation - This -
> The spreading wide my narrow Hands
> To gather Paradise -
>
> —J657/F466/M233

The language of architecture is used metaphorically to describe the world of possibility in which the poet dwells, as one might say, "It opened doors for me," or, "It gave me new windows on the world—new ways of seeing." Something has done that for her, but she doesn't say what. The poet works to create a recognizable feeling, an emotional response in the reader, apart from any reference to the fostering experience. Those responses vary among readers of this poem. Some will read it as a response to nature. The Transcendentalist notion of direct experience of the divine, through the natural world, was a generally familiar one. Others will perceive a description of an awareness of heaven, or a spiritual awakening, as when the scales fall from one's eyes and the world expands into infinite possibility. Whatever these readers find in this poem, they have to respond to it in a personal way that is not simply intellectual or analytical. In doing so, each draws from his own experience and associations to find something of himself there. By not tying the experience described here to a particular, the poet gives us a more universal poem. We all dwell in possibility.

Still other readers will observe that the poet contrasts *Possibility* with *Prose*, suggesting poetry itself, or artistic imagination more generally. This appears to be the consensus reading among Dickinson scholars.[13] If, however, she had actually written "I dwell in poetry, not prose," she would have been saying much less. The more abstract word, possibility, now stands in for all the power of language and artistic imagination, as the word prose strands for ordinary, hum-drum, matter-of-fact experience. Indeed, ED did use the word prose in this figurative way, as we might use the word prosaic: "[…] but for our sakes dear Susie, who please ourselves with the fancy that we are the only poets — and every one else is prose […]"[14]

Among the many splendors of her house of possibility are *Chambers as the Cedars*. There is a biblical allusion here. The Cedar wood of Lebanon was important in Biblical times and even earlier. In the Epic of Gilgamesh (circa 2100 BCE) the cedar groves of Lebanon were the dwelling-place of the Gods, and the wood was used all over the Mediterranean world for religious and civil constructs, the most famous of which are King Solomon's Temple in Jerusalem and David's and Solomon's Palaces. Cedar is fragrant, durable, and very long lived. As such it stood for stability and permanence. These chambers, moreover, are *Impregnable of Eye.* One cannot peer into them from outside. A clue to the meaning of this aspect of the dwelling may be found in another poem.

> Best Things dwell out of Sight
> The Pearl - the Just - Our Thought.
> —J998/F1012/M461

Only *the fairest* of *Visitors* are received here. Emily's sister, Lavinia, once observed that Emily "was always on the lookout for the rewarding person." The poet welcomes those with an ear not too dull, who can dwell in her domain naturally. The spre*ading wide* her *narrow hands* and gathering *paradise* has been interpreted as the very act of writing, and more generally as bringing the abstraction of possibility into the physical world. Writing was her *Occupation*, and poetry was the house of possibility that she occupied.

The final example of an omitted center for this chapter is another of Dickinson's better-known poems.

A Route of Evanescence
With a revolving Wheel -
A Resonance of Emerald -
A Rush of Cochineal -
And every Blossom on the Bush
Adjusts its tumbled Head -
The mail from Tunis, probably,
An easy Morning's Ride -
—J1463/F1489/M618

This poem is all activity, the speaker describing a series of quick impressions. We don't know who or what is travelling the route, but it quickly vanishes. In the third line, Dickinson combines sound and colors—a reverberating, intensifying of *emerald* green and *cochineal*—a deep red made from the crushed bodies of the insect of that name. Next, she notices *every Blossom on the Bush* vibrating in the aftermath of some passing thing. It was *probably the mail from Tunis*, she muses, presumably with an inner smile. Dickinson used distant geographic place names to stand, in a general way, for any far-off spot on the globe or to some half-imagined exotic realm. Tunis in this instance may allude to Shakespeare (EDL):

TUNIS, PROPER N.
Capital of Tunisia; city in northern Africa; [allusion] kingdom of Queen Claribel in Shakespeare's *The Tempest* (2.1.246-248): "She that is the queen of Tunis; she that dwells/Ten leagues beyond man's life; she that from Naples/Can have no note, unless the sun were post."

ED evidently was satisfied with this poem. She sent it to at least six recipients[15] and identified it as a hummingbird in each case. This explains the *revolving Wheel*. The wings of the hummingbird do not flap as do those of other birds. The wing can rotate backwards in its socket allowing it to describe a figue-8 pattern.

The concision of this poem is often compared with a longer and much earlier hummingbird poem, "Within my Garden, rides a Bird" (J500/F370/M197). In both poems, the narrator is alerted to a vanished presence by vibrating blossom, but there the similarity ends.

As we have explored in this section and encountered in previous chapters, Dickinson regularly leaves unspoken the object of the poem's attention. Over and over again, she describes an experience, the aftermath of an experience, something she sees or is thinking about, without naming or identifying the underlying cause. This was a conscious choice in order to make the reader a participant in the poem. She confessed it quite plainly herself.

Good to hide, and hear 'em hunt!
Better, to be found,
If one care to, that is,
The Fox fits the Hound -

Good to know, and not tell,
Best, to know and tell,
Can one find the rare Ear
Not too dull -
—J842/F945/M441

Words Beyond Words

At the beginning of Chapter 1, in the poem "The sun in reining to the West," a Whiffletree of Amethyst appeared, two words combined for a poetical purpose, not a literal one. To envision an actual bar made of amethyst would be to miss Dickinson's poetics entirely. In "I'm sorry for the Dead - Today," in Chapter 2, the neighbors' laughter made the "Fences smile." Close your eyes and try to see, in your mind's eye, the actual fences literally smiling. You can't do it; a fence has no mouth with which to smile. Nevertheless, the words say something that ordinary language cannot. Such constructs have been called, among other terms, "imageless images." We have also seen cups of chrysolite, By-Thyme, A Goblin on the Bloom, and a panting *Ancle*. In this section, we examine five poems we have not yet discussed, with special attention to this particular feature, beginning with a deservedly well-known seasonal poem.

A Light exists in Spring
Not present on the Year
At any other period -
When March is scarcely here

A Color stands abroad
On Solitary Fields
That Science cannot overtake
But Human Nature feels.

It waits upon the Lawn,
It shows the furthest Tree
Upon the furthest Slope you know
It almost speaks to you.

Then as Horizons step
Or Noons report away
Without the Formula of sound
It passes and we stay -

A quality of loss
Affecting our Content

As Trade had suddenly encroached
Upon a Sacrament.
—J812/F962/M446

The poem ends on a disturbing note. It is as if something as sacred as a sacrament has been trespassed upon by something profane. A nineteenth-century reader would be reminded of a story from the Bible:

> And the Jews' passover was at hand, and Jesus went up to Jerusalem And found in the temple those that sold oxen and sheep and doves, and the changers of money sitting: And when he had made a scourge of small cords, he drove them all out of the temple, and the sheep, and the oxen; and poured out the changers' money, and overthrew the tables; And to those selling doves He said, "Take these things from here! Do not make My Father's house a house of trade [John 2:13–15].

How is a changing light like such a thing? It's as if a very fact of nature, a natural phenomenon, were somehow not right, as if the natural light were to remove and be supplanted by some usurper light. It feels wrong, and it is a feeling, rather than a rational simile or an objective assessment of the scene. The second stanza expresses the related thought more directly. In Emily Dickinson's lifetime, Science was indeed overtaking the mysteries of nature and explaining them as natural phenomena. This light, she tells us, is, to borrow one of her own words, overtakeless. Science cannot explain it, but *Human Nature feels* it. Light doesn't actually *wait*, but at a certain time of day, and the observer in perhaps a meditative state of mind, time will seem suspended, and the light may seem to linger on the grass. With the words *It waits upon the Lawn,* the poet captures such a moment of reverie. In the last line of the stanza, a personal pronoun appears for the first time, and it is *you.* She has been bringing you in slowly from the beginning. The first stanza is an impersonal observation of a natural scene. In the second stanza, *Human Nature* appears by name, inviting your human nature to *feel* the *Color* standing abroad on the field. The responsive reader may feel something of the "overtakelessness" of that ineffable light.

Whether the "It" in the last line of stanza three refers to the Light of the first stanza, to the Color of the second, or to the combined effect of both, *it almost speaks to you*, but it doesn't, repudiating the natural theologians. All her life Emily Dickinson heard instruction on how to find evidence of God's divine plan in nature but she does not read a typological sign in what she beholds. Nature has not spoken of God's promise to her, and the vanishing light reflects the faith that has been lost.

It is remarkable that in so evocative a poem, no adjectives appear. The *Light exists*, *A Color stands, Science cannot overtake, Human Nature feels, It waits, It shows, It almost speaks.* The action continues in the fourth stanza. *Steps* and *reports* are military terms. The soldier reports to the commanding officer, or the barracks, or for a drill or ceremony. *Horizons* step like marching soldiers. A military band would play ceremonial music at these times as part of the *formula*. Formula is something of a special word which Dickinson found useful in four other poems: "I got so I could take his name" (J293/F292/M137), "I watched the Moon around the House" (J629/F593/M270), "Somehow myself survived the Night" (J1194/F1209/M501), and "'Tis Seasons since the Dimpled War" (J1529/F1551/M631).

FORM′U-LA, or FORM′ULE, n. [L.]
1. A prescribed form; a rule or model

The final two stanzas bring the narrator into the experience with us. It is *our Content* that is affected. The light passes *Without the Formula of sound*, and *we stay.* We can't quite picture horizons stepping or noons reporting, but we recognize that something almost sacred has passed, and done so in an orderly, pre-ordained way that is indifferent to our apprehension that we have lost something. It is an apprehension not unique to ourselves, but rather is seated in our shared *human nature.*

In a poem less well known than the previous one, and light-hearted in comparison, Dickinson gives us an imageless image in one of the stanzas, and figures of speech in the others that are not quite the same thing. It will be instructive to note the distinctions.

A Drop fell on the Apple Tree -
Another - on the Roof -
A Half a Dozen kissed the Eaves -
And made the Gables laugh -

A few went out to help the Brook
That went to help the Sea -
Myself Conjectured were they Pearls -
What Necklaces could be -

The Dust replaced, in Hoisted Roads -
The Birds jocoser sung -
The Sunshine threw his Hat away -
The Bushes - spangles flung -

The Breezes brought dejected Lutes -
And bathed them in the Glee -
Then Orient showed a single Flag,
And signed the Fete away -
—J794/F846//M389

At first, a single drop falls. Since this is the first line of the poem, we are not prepared for this sudden event, and thus the line reproduces, in its unanticipated notice, the little surprise that one often experiences on hearing that first splash of water in the street, even though the gathering clouds and gusts of wind have foretold it. Shortly, the rain has *kissed the Eaves* and *made the Gables laugh*. Gables don't laugh, but this is not really an imageless image. It's not an image at all, in fact. It is a poetic way of referring to the sound of the rain as it falls on (kisses) the house, just as we might speak of the merry sound of sleigh bells when in fact bells are not merry nor is sound in itself merry. Rather, the narrator's pleasant disposition is projected onto the inanimate matter around her.

There were two different kinds of *Hoisted Roads* in the Dickinson's America. She refers here to neither, but rather borrows the term for her own purposes. One kind of hoisted road was a drawbridge, which was raised mechanically to let a boat pass beneath. The other was a wooden walkway built out over a swampy or marshy area. Dickinson uses the term to describe the dust of the road that has been *hoisted* (lifted) into the air by gusts of wind that preceded the rain. By agency of the rain, it has been *replaced* in the road again. The birds are singing *jocoser* (coined word for "more jocosely"), the shower is abating. *The Sunshine threw his Hat away,* and here is our imageless image. Throwing one's hat into the air is a gesture of jubilance and celebration. In this imageless image, the poet assigns this same spirit to the newly emerging sun. With his hat off, he is suddenly fully visible. The sunlight gives to the drops on the still wet bushes the appearance of *Spangles*, sparkling brilliantly.

The Breezes brought dejected Lutes is, like the raindrops in the eaves and upon the gables, a poetic way of describing a phenomenon of sound, rather than an image that we might try to visualize. The sounds of the storm, which has now passed, are transformed in the storm's aftermath. *Orient* is a word Dickinson sometimes chose to represent the east. In the manuscript, she recorded two alternate lines, *The East put out a single flag,* and *Nature put out a Single flag.* It is morning, and the sun is rising in the east. The flag is a metaphor for the first ribbon of light that appears on the horizon. For another appearance of this same metaphor, see "A something in a summer's Day" (J122/F104/M75).

Chapter 1 included a section on "The Language of Home," which showed how Dickinson employed domestic imagery in daring ways. In the next poem, the household broom takes on new power.

Like Brooms of Steel
The Snow and Wind
Had swept the Winter Street -
The House was hooked

The Sun sent out
Faint Deputies of Heat -
Where rode the Bird
The Silence tied
His ample - plodding Steed
The Apple in the Cellar snug
Was all the one that played.
—J1252/F1241/M708

The scouring icy wind of a passing storm is described persuasively as being *Like Brooms of Steel.* In such weather, the windows of New England houses were shuttered. The shutters were fastened with *hooks* for protection. Thus, *The House was hooked.* Now, Nature's work has been done, and the sun's rays, appearing here as his deputies, begin a *faint* effort to provide some relief from the cold.

DEP′U-TY, n.
1. A person appointed or elected to act for another, especially a person sent with a special commission to act in the place of another; a lieutenant; a viceroy. A prince sends a deputy to a diet or council, to represent him and his dominions. A sherif appoints a deputy to execute the duties of his office. The towns in New England send deputies to the legislature. In the latter sense, a deputy has general powers, and it is more common to use the word representative.
2. In law, one that exercises an office in another's right, and the forfeiture or misdemeanor of such deputy shall cause the person he represents to lose his office.

Again Dickinson draws on the vocabulary of the law and of politics. The mighty sun, the real power, does not present himself in person. He sends deputies in his stead, who provide only a faint measure of his power. However original, *Deputies of Heat* is a simple metaphor for the faint rays of the sun. The imageless image is in the next three lines. *Where rode the Bird* refers to the air above. Dickinson lived in the days of horse and carriage. When a traveler arrived at his destination, he dismounted and tied his steed to a hitching post or fence. We cannot actually picture silence performing these actions, but we understand that he has arrived with the stillness following the storm.

To the modern ear, to *play* connotes activity of some kind. Apples stored properly in New England basements would last all winter. In what manner might they play? The EDL suggests an answer with its third definition, or meaning:

PLAY v.i.
3. Rest; relax; enjoy leisure; take a break from labor.

There would have been more than one apple in the cellar, yet it is *The Apple,* singular. We would say usually say "the apples were *all the ones that played,"* apples being plural. By means of the singular, the poet draws attention not to the collective apples, but, but to the apple representative of their singular leisure. We understand that the worst of the storm is over, but only just, and no one has yet ventured outside.

In another poem capturing the moment following a storm, a pair of imageless images, possibly even more ineffable, appear.

Like Rain it sounded till it curved
And then I knew 'twas Wind -
It walked as wet as any Wave
But swept as dry as sand -
When it had pushed itself away
To some remotest Plain
A coming as of Hosts was heard
That was indeed the Rain -
It filled the Wells, it pleased the Pools
It warbled in the Road -
It pulled the spigot from the Hills
And let the Floods abroad -
It loosened acres, lifted seas
The sites of Centres stirred
Then like Elijah rode away
Upon a Wheel of Cloud.
—J1235/F1245/M558

When conditions are right, wind in the trees can sound like rain a short distance off. As the wind *curved,* the narrator realizes that she *knew 'twas Wind.* We wouldn't use the word *curved* in this way in normal speech; we would say "it changed direction" or something similar. The EDL concurs.

CURVE (-ed), v.
Bend; turn; change course.

Saying that the wind curved gives the wind more definite agency, as if it were acting on its own volition, as she described the frost as *The Blonde Assassin* who *passes on*, after beheading a flower (Chapter 2). The dual nature of the sound is emphasized in lines three and four. Note how the repeated W's in line three create a liquid sound, as the S's in the fourth create a dry sound. Next, the narrator recognizes the sound of rain, still in the distance—*A coming as of Hosts* was heard.

HOST, n.
1. An army; a number of men embodied for war.
2. Any great number of multitude.

The sound reminds her of the thundering hoofs and chariots that constituted such hosts before the twentieth century. The welcome rain arrives to *fill the wells* and *please the pools;* it sounds like music in the road. Next it pulls imaginary *spigots* from the heavens to release more rain. There follows a series of imageless images—*It loosened acres - lifted seas.* The poem has advanced from a literal, if figurative description of the wind that precedes a rainstorm, moved into simple metaphor, and then beyond that into language that challenges the imagination. The loosening of acres may reflect the beneficial impact of the rain over a wide area, and the lifting of seas the great power of this natural phenomenon. A rainstorm in central Massachusetts is not going to literally lift seas, and it would take a powerful storm to do so anywhere else. *The sites of Centres stirred* is a sentence that has no literal correlation to the physical world. What sites? What Centres (alternate spelling of Centers)? Stirring, however, is an activity. The centres are not being stirred; they are themselves stirring in response to the rain, as life everywhere does. The poet has expressed all of this in a very few words. A rainstorm is a common and familiar event, but with vital consequences in nature every time one occurs. A narrative of so wondrous an event must have a suitably glorious finale, and for that Emily Dickinson resorts to her Bible: "And it came to pass, as they still went on, and talked, that, behold, *there appeared* a chariot of fire, and horses of fire, and parted them both asunder; and Elijah went up by a whirlwind into heaven" (II Kings 2:11). A chariot of fire would not suit the rain, water being the contrary element, and so it rides away to glory rather on a *Wheel of Cloud.*

The final imageless image to ponder in this section appears in another of Dickinson's best-known poems. This poem has been read as a pious recognition of the promise of immortality and it has been read as exactly the opposite. We take the latter view here. Several different versions of this poem exist, as the poet re-worked the second stanza. The version below is the one that appears in most modern editions.

> Safe in their Alabaster Chambers -
> Untouched by Morning -
> And untouched by Noon -
> Lie the meek members of the Resurrection -
> Rafter of Satin - and Roof of Stone -
>
> Grand go the Years-in the Crescent-above them-
> Worlds scoop their Arcs-
> And Firmaments-row-
> Diadems - drop - and Doges-surrender -
> Soundless as dots - on a Disc of Snow -
>
> —J216/F124/M83, 122

As noted in Chapter 5, *Alabaster* was one of Dickinson's words for indicating the color white. The poet paints the image of sepulchers of fine white stone. She may have read of actual sepulchers of alabaster that held the remains of prominent people in Europe. Sepulchers in America were of plainer stuff. In a different version of this poem, Dickinson wrote *sleep* instead of *lie* in the first line. From the beginning, Christians have spoken of the dead as being asleep and waiting for the day of resurrection, as noted in Chapter 5. Those whom God saves then dwell with Him in Paradise. The belief comes from the Bible: "And if Christ be not raised, your faith *is* vain; ye are yet in your sins. Then they also which are fallen asleep in Christ are perished. If in this life only we have hope in Christ, we are of all men most miserable. But now is Christ risen from the dead, *and* become the first fruits of them that slept. For since by man *came* death, by man *came* also the resurrection of the dead" (I Corinthians 15:17–21). Why are the *members of the Resurrection* called *meek?* There, too, the Bible holds the key: "Blessed *are* the meek: for they shall inherit the earth" (Matthew 5:5). Those elect who lie within are *Safe,* because they are among the "saved." Both words, along with "salvation," come from the Latin *salvus*, "uninjured." They are also safe from worldly temptations. The word carries a hint of irony, suggesting a retreat or avoidance rather than anything sacred.

Rafter of Satin describes the lining of a coffin or perhaps a sepulcher. *Roof of Stone* can apply to a headstone, as would be the case in Emily Dickinson's America, or the solid roof of a splendid alabaster sepulcher in old Venice. The meek members have been lying there for a long time. *Grand go the Years* implies momentous sweeps of history, a longer history than nineteenth-century America could boast, stretching back to a time when ornate alabaster sepulchers were carved by skilled artists.

The hope for immortality has long gone unfulfilled. David Porter sees "Promise and denial, forever inseparable … symbolized by the bright satin beneath the impenetrable stone."[16] The stillness in the tomb is contrasted with the grand activity outside. *Worlds scoop their Arcs* makes active agents of the very planets. *Firmament* is a word Dickinson chose for twenty-three poems. It is normally a singular noun—there is only one firmament—but she pluralized it in six of the twenty-three.

FIRM´A-MENT, a.

The region of the air; the sky or heavens. In Scripture, the word denotes an expanse, a wide extent; for such is the signification of the Hebrew word, coinciding with *regio*, region, and reach. The original therefore does not convey the sense of solidity, but of stretching, extension; the great arch or expanse over our heads, in which are placed the atmosphere and the clouds, and in which the stars appear to be placed, and are really seen. And God said, Let there be a firmament in the midst of the waters, and let it divide the waters from the waters [Gen. 1:6].

And God said, Let there be lights in the firmament [Gen. 1:1].

It is not possible actually to visualize firmaments rowing; but with these two words the poet creates an infinity of churning heavens. Rowing was a favorite Dickinson way of indicating motion or physical activity. *Diadems - drop* from the crowned heads of the mighty, who have joined the meek members. Doge was the title of the chief magistrate of Venice and Genoa, a very powerful man. The poet adopts the term to represent all those with great earthly power, all of whom must come to the same silent end. The final line brings the reader abruptly back from the riotous activity outside to the cold silence of the tomb and leaves him there. The imageless image, *dots - on Disc of Snow*, is one of cold inert finality. The *dots* are small and insignificant, we understand without being told.

A final caution; it is possible to mistake a poetic description of something perfectly concrete for an imageless image. For example, as noted in Chapter 2, some readers have taken the expression *Not all Pianos in the Woods* in the poem "I dreaded that first Robin so," to be a surrealistic abstraction, when surely it is a poetic way of referring to the music of birds and other creatures which Emily Dickinson found so dear. Again, as noted in Chapter 6, a stanza in the poem "Because I could not stop for Death" is a quite accurate description of the Amherst Town Tomb:

> We paused before a House that seemed
> A Swelling of the Ground -
> The Roof was scarcely visible -
> The Cornice - in the Ground -

Never having seen or known of such a structure, many have interpreted these words variously as a bizarre image of coffin being lowered into the ground, or as a coffin emerging from a burial mound, as can happen after a great flood. It is by placing poems in context, whenever and to whatever extent that is possible, that we can uncover the intended meaning.

NINE

The Poet's Toolbox

"All men say 'What' to me, but I thought it a fashion."—L271 August 1862

In the previous chapter, we examined literary techniques of Emily Dickinson that establish a sense of intimacy between poet and reader. In this final chapter, we will take a further look into literary devices that the poet employed to achieve other ends. These writing practices are very effective in creating the rich multi-faceted poems for which Dickinson is renowned, and they are also what make those poems challenging to interpretation no matter how much one knows about her life and times. It is often the very structure of the poems, the arrangement of the phrases, the novel word combinations, and the absence of standard punctuation that pose the challenges. Learning to recognize these literary practices and becoming familiar and comfortable with them can reward the reader with bountiful insight into great poetry.

"If no mistake you have made, losing you are"

The above words, from the character Yoda in the movie *Star Wars*, is somewhat disordered. It is understandable, but normally we would say "If you have made no mistake, you are losing." Emily Dickinson reverses the order of words and phrases often in the same way. Many examples have appeared in the preceding chapters. The very first poem in Chapter 1, "There is no Frigate like a Book" includes the line, "This traverse may the poorest take," whereas in normal speech we would say "The poorest may take this traverse." The former order is necessary to preserve the iambic meter. Similarly, "Besides the Autumn Poets sing" (Chapter 2) includes the lines "Perhaps a squirrel may remain/My sentiments to share," rather than

"Perhaps a squirrel may remain to share my sentiments" When Dickinson combines such a reversal of word order with other techniques, she moves even further away from the forms of spoken language. In "I suppose the time will come" (Chapters 2 and 8), for example, word order is reversed and words that Dickinson considered unnecessary are dropped.

I suppose the time will come
Hinder it a little
When the Corn in Silk will dress
And in Chintz the Apple

In prose, one would write, "I suppose the time will come - Hinder it a little—when the corn will dress in silk and the apple will dress in chintz." In Chapter 1 we re-cast lines into prose in a similar way for "So glad we are - a Stranger'd deem." This aspect of Dickinson's poetry once caused your author to misread the following first stanza of a longer poem:

I had been hungry, all the Years -
My Noon had Come - to dine -
I trembling drew the Table near -
And touched the Curious Wine -
—J579/F439/M176

Grammatically, line 3 says that the speaker reached out to the table and drew it near to her. That is not what the poet intends. A word is omitted and among those remaining some are reversed. Re-casting into prose, we have, "Trembling, I drew near to the table." This is an example of a case where the meaning is simply not recoverable from the words on the page alone. The reader is required to see past the words to what the poet must mean. If a reader were to argue that the speaker took the table in hand and pulled it toward her, one could not prove otherwise based solely on what is written in the lone verse.

To say that one can never really know another person would not be to utter an original idea, and would not likely inspire further thought. With the tools of her craft that are under consideration here, the poet allows the reader to form the idea almost independently:

His mind of man, a secret makes
I meet him with a start
He carries a circumference
In which I have no part

Or even if I deem I do
He otherwise may know
Impregnable to inquest
However neighborly -
—J1663/F1730/M674

Recasting…

Man makes a secret of his mind.
I meet him with a start.
He carries a circumference
In which I have no part.
Or even if I deem [that] I do [have a part in it]
He may know otherwise.
[He is] Impregnable to inquest
However neighborly [he is].

In these spare and concise eight lines, Dickinson makes a plumbless mystery of the familiar neighbor, the single word *circumference* serving to suggest the vast unknowable that is *The mind of man.*

That the boundary between pleasure and pain can blur, that joy and sorrow can exist in a single experience, are also familiar thoughts, thoughts that poets have dwelt on throughout the centuries. Emily Dickinson is among them, as in "So glad we are - a Stranger'd deem" (Chapter 1), to cite one example. The poet explores the subject from a slightly different angle in the following poem:

One Joy of so much anguish
Sweet nature has for me
I shun it as I do Despair
Or dear iniquity -
Why Birds, a Summer morning
Before the Quick of Day
Should stab my ravished spirit
With Dirks of Melody
Is part of an inquiry
That will receive reply
When Flesh and Spirit sunder
In Death's Immediately -
—J1420/F1450/M607

This twelve-line poem consists of just two sentences. "Why birds" begins the second sentence. The lines and one additional word could be rearranged this way to recast the poem into prose.

Sweet nature has
One Joy of so much anguish for me [that]
I shun it as I do Despair
Or dear iniquity. *Dear in the sense of "at high cost."*
Part of an inquiry
That will receive reply
When Flesh and Spirit sunder
In Death's Immediately is,
why Birds a Summer morning,

Before the Quick of Day,
Should stab my ravished spirit
With Dirks of Melody.

Sweet nature is something for the narrator in which *Joy* and *anguish* coexist. That something is the beautiful singing of the birds before dawn. *Why* that music should *stab* her *ravished spirit* is part of a larger question that will receive its reply in the afterlife, *When Flesh and Spirit sunder*. What that larger question might be is left unsaid. The word *ravished*, with its various meanings, is well-chosen.

RAV'ISH, v.t.

1. To seize and carry away by violence.
2. To have carnal knowledge of a woman by force and against her consent.
3. To bear away with joy or delight; to delight to ecstasy; to transport.

Emily Dickinson is probably the only one ever to say or write "In Death's immediately." One expects "In Death's immediacy," perhaps, but immediacy is a noun. Immediately is an adverb. Immediately means "right now" or "instantly," and that is perhaps what the poet intends the reader to feel.

"Further in Summer than the Birds," covered in Chapter 4, now bears a second look. We treated this poem fairly extensively, but omissions and word- reversals present were not pointed out explicitly. It may clarify the poem more to do that here, now that we've studied other examples of this aspect of the poet's work.

Further in Summer than the Birds -
Pathetic from the Grass
A minor Nation celebrates
Its unobtrusive Mass.

No Ordinance be seen
So gradual the Grace
A pensive Custom it becomes
Enlarging Loneliness.

Antiquest felt at Noon
When August burning low
Arise this spectral Canticle
Repose to typify

Remit as yet no Grace
No Furrow on the Glow
Yet a Druidic Difference
Enhances Nature now

—J1068/F895/M534

Except for the absence of standard punctuation, the first stanza comprises a grammatically correct and unambiguous sentence. The punctuation, or lack thereof, renders the reading of the second stanza uncertain. Is it *No*

Ordinance be seen/So gradual the Grace, or *So gradual the Grace/A pensive Custom it becomes*? In Chapter 4, the former reading was assumed, but there is in fact nothing in the structure or grammar of this poem to establish it as the one only reading. This feature is found in many Dickinson poems, where a line or group of lines can be read as going with either of two different parts of the poem, and is the subject of the next section of this chapter. The same situation arises in stanza three. Is it felt most antique at noon when August is burning low, or is it when August is burning low that this spectral canticle arises, or both? In Chapter four both were assumed, but again the structure and punctuation don't force a single way of reading it. And again, the reader must find meaning on her own.

The first line of stanza four is without a definite subject. Who or what remits? Some have suggested that it might be the *Canticle* of the crickets. In our earlier review of this poem, it was taken to be more in the perception of someone present at the magic hour described. Reading or reciting, one could imagine oneself there, observing that there is as yet *No Furrow on the Glow,* and perceiving for oneself that *no Grace* has been remitted, without needing to ask, "By whom?" The possibilities engage our interest and draw us into the poem as an experience.

Double Duty Words

Making a group of words serve more than one purpose is, like the Omitted Center discussed earlier, practically a Dickinson signature, and like the Omitted Center, it has vexed generations of her readers. We have encountered examples of this literary device already, and touched on it with "The Hollows round His eager Eyes" (Chapter 3) and "'Faithful to the end' Amended" (Chapter 5). A telling example of how this device can result in a misreading occurred when one of Dickinson's poems was published (without her permission) in *The Springfield Republican* newspaper, 14 February 1866. We saw one version of that poem in Chapter 1. In another version, the poet chose *instant* instead of *sudden* in the fourth line. The first stanza is:

A narrow Fellow in the Grass
Occasionally rides -
You may have met Him - Did you not
His notice instant is –

The newspaper printed this[1]:

A narrow fellow in the grass
Occasionally rides;
You may have met Him - did you not?
His notice instant is,

When Emily Dickinson discovered that the newspaper had placed a question mark after the third line she was quite indignant. She explained in a letter to a friend that the poem was robbed of her, and that it was "...defeated too of the third line by the punctuation. The third and the fourth were one."[2] She had intended "You may have met him. Did you not, his notice instant is." As the newspaper has it, it reads, "You may have met him, did you not? His notice instant is." Later editors propagated the error by including the question mark. The edited versions obviously change the literal meaning. Yes, a Dickinson poem can often be read in multiple ways, but it is also possible to read it wrong.

We endeavor to make no such mistakes here, but with Dickinson a confident certainty remains ever elusive. In this next poem, for example, one interpretation was offered in Chapter 2.

Conjecturing a Climate
Of unsuspended Suns -
Adds poignancy to Winter -
The Shivering Fancy turns

To a fictitious Country
To palliate a Cold -
Not obviated of Degree -
Nor eased - of Latitude -
—J562/F551/M281

Is it the *Cold* that is not *obviated of degree nor eased of latitude*, or the *fictitious Country*? As read in Chapter 2, it is the *fictitious Country,* but it reads just as well the other way. In general, critics are in agreement that writing in such a way that a line or group of words cannot be assigned one specific meaning is an intentional practice of Dickinson's that, although often challenging for the reader, yields a richer poem by concentrating meaning.

In "Forever—is composed of Nows," discussed in Chapter 3, your author artfully dodged a two-word phrase, "to These," in the second stanza, to which we now turn our attention.

From this - experienced Here -
Remove the Dates - to These -
Let Months dissolve in further Months -
And Years - exhale in Years–

One way of reading it: "From this experienced here, remove the dates. To these [experiences], let months dissolve in further months and [let] years exhale in years." And another way: "From this experienced here, remove the dates to these [experiences]. Let months dissolve in further months and [let] years exhale in years."

In the rest of this section, we'll take on double-duty words in poems not yet presented, beginning with another very well-known one in which the dual-purpose element has been observed by more than one critic.[3]

A Bird came down the Walk -
He did not know I saw -
He bit an Angleworm in halves
And ate the fellow, raw,

And then he drank a Dew
From a convenient Grass -
And then hopped sidewise to the Wall
To let a Beetle pass -

He glanced with rapid eyes
That hurried all around -
They looked like frightened Beads, I thought -
He stirred his Velvet Head

Like one in danger, Cautious,
I offered him a Crumb
And he unrolled his feathers
And rowed him softer home -

Than Oars divide the Ocean,
Too silver for a seam -
Or Butterflies, off Banks of Noon
Leap, plashless as they swim.

—J328/F359/M189

As already noted, Emily Dickinson shared with others of her time, including the Transcendentalists, a love of nature that could cause her to "transcend" the daily world and approach the divine. In "A Bird came down the Walk," the poet performs that very transcendence within a narrative, beginning very simply with an observation of some minor natural activity on a walkway. This is a poem that can mesmerize a young child. It is a minutely observant, somehow humorous account of a bird not knowing at first that he is observed. Referring to a worm as a *Fellow* brings a smile. The bird's act of stepping aside *to let a Beetle pass* assigns a polite decorum on the creature that must bring another. By noting that he *drank a Dew/From a convenient grass* instead of the grammatically correct "he drank some Dew/From the convenient grass," the poet narrates from the bird's point of view. To us humans, the dewdrops on the grass are a collective entity. We do not recognize, usually, individual drops of dew or blades of grass, but a bird might. A blade of grass might be as tall as or taller than he, and a drop of dew to him a full flagon.

The jaunty easiness of the first two stanzas begins to give way in the third, as the bird now begins to glance about rapidly. Does he begin now to sense the presence of an observer? The eyes of many species of birds are bead-like, and rapid glances suggest apprehension. Dickinson captures it with her *frightened beads*. Beads do not feel anything, but anyone who has ever watched a small bird on the ground recognizes exactly what the poet is describing. As the bird stirs his *velvet head*, he is becoming aware that he is not alone, and here a dual reading is possible, which itself reflects this moment of uncertainty in the narrative. Who is *Like one in danger*, the bird or the narrator? Who is *cautious*? Line 12 is without punctuation, which would tend to indicate that it should read "He stirred his velvet head like one in danger, cautious." The bird, being out of his element and always wary of predators on the ground, would naturally be cautious. In the one other surviving manuscript of this poem however, a period ends line 12, making "*He stirred his velvet head*" a completed sentence. In that version, it is the narrator who is like one in danger and cautious as she offers her crumb.

One can easily read through the above poem one way or another without much puzzlement. When the poet combines ambiguous lines with word omissions, however, the reader is more likely confounded, at least initially. The following poem, concise to the point of indecipherability, will take some work to try and unpack:

> We miss Her, not because We see -
> The Absence of an Eye -
> Except its Mind accompany
> Abridge Society
>
> As slightly as the Routes of Stars -
> Ourselves - asleep below -
> We know that their superior Eyes
> Include Us - as they go -
>
> —J993/F771/M358

The second stanza presents little difficulty Dickinson offers her familiar notion of those departed watching over us benevolently from above. It is in the first stanza that we are stopped. Lines 3 and 4 seem almost independent of the rest of the poem. What does *its* refer to, and what or who is it that would *Abridge Society?* (Dickinson wrote three other word choices for "abridge" on her manuscript—impair, debar, and deprive.)

A-BRIDGE´, v.t.
1. To make shorter; to epitomize; to contract by using fewer words, yet retaining the sense in substance-used of writings;
2. To lessen; to diminish; as, to abridge labor; to abridge power or rights.
3. To deprive; to cut off from; followed by of; as, to abridge one of his rights, or enjoyments. To abridge from, is now obsolete or improper.

Part of the difficulty lies in the lack of punctuation to indicate completed thoughts. The reader may try to place a mental period at the end of line 3. Reading the first three lines as a sentence, however, leaves line 4 hanging. A second difficulty is the peculiar phrase *see the absence of an eye.* A third is the phrase *Except its Mind accompany*. Below is a suggested breakdown and recasting of lines 1 through 3:

The Absence of an Eye—"We don't see each other" or, "We don't see her."
We see/the absence of an Eye—"We perceive that we don't see each other"
Except its Mind accompany—Except if her mind were to accompany her physical absence and also be unavailable to us.

We interpret *its* as referring to *Her*, because only people have minds. However, one may speak figuratively of "the mind's eye," and, this being Dickinson, one could argue that *its* refers to the eye that belongs to the mind. or both together. Lines 1 through 4 may then be read, "We miss her not because we perceive that we don't see each other. Except if her mind were to accompany her in her absence and also be unavailable to us, it [her physical absence] would abridge our society as slightly as the routes of stars do to us while we're asleep." But, how can someone be absent while her mind is not absent? Emily Dickinson kept in contact with people—other minds—through prolific letter-writing. In one of those letters she wrote: "A Letter always feels to me like immortality because it is the mind alone without corporeal friend."[4]

Stars, like asterisks, can represent the souls of the departed. The final two lines ostensibly suggest that the *Routes of Stars* abridge society very slightly indeed, but Dickinson may be turning the tables on us with her conclusion. Along with the suggestion of stars' indifferent effect on our lives, she offers the cherished belief that those above, the souls of the departed whom the stars represent, are benignly watching over us.

A Poet's License

The second stanza of "A Spider sewed at Night," discussed in Chapter 3, is repeated below.

If Ruff it was of Dame
Or Shroud of Gnome
Himself himself inform.

Conventional grammar would have it "He informs himself." The reader will have probably noticed that several of the poems throughout this book use words such as "ourself," "itself," "herself" etc., known as collective pronouns, in ways not commonly heard today. Why the poet chose *Himself* instead of *He* must be open to conjecture. (We assume that had she chosen *He* that she would have adjusted the rest of the line for meter). I will offer the suggestion that *Himself* orients the reader more closely to the spider, but perhaps she just preferred the sound of the words. In any case, Emily Dickinson did not invent this form of usage. She encountered it in the Bible, and in some of her favorite authors:

> Himself took our infirmities, and bare our sicknesses—Matthew 8:17
>
> For me, I wrote False poems, like the rest, and thought them true Because myself was true in writing them—Elizabeth Barrett Browning[5]
>
> Myself could show a catalogue of doubts never yet imagined or questioned by any [...]—Sir Thomas Browne[6]

In the stanza above the meaning is clear. The idiosyncratic language does not impede understanding. In other instances, such as with the poem below, the reader must see the meaning despite the grammatical irregularities by seeing what it *must* mean. Here again, Dickinson insinuates, "Oh *you* know what I mean. I needn't spell it out - not for *you*."

Exultation is the going
Of an inland soul to sea,
Past the houses - past the headlands -
Into deep Eternity -

Bred as we, among the mountains,
Can the sailor understand
The divine intoxication
Of the first league out from land?
—J76/F143/M81

What manner of sea is this, that takes us out into *deep Eternity?* Emily Dickinson lived in a valley within sight of hills and mountains, far from the sea by nineteenth-century measures. She probably never saw the ocean, although she may well have seen Boston Harbor when visiting that city. For her then, the sea could represent the unknown, and by association, the possibility of danger and even death. Recall from Chapter 4 part of a letter that she wrote when still in her teens: "The shore is safer Abiah, but I love to buffet the sea - I count the bitter wrecks here in these pleasant waters, and hear the murmuring winds, but oh, I love the danger."

Into deep Eternity. Not only out of the hill country, but out of time and out of this life, and that, she proclaims, *is Exultation!* An exhilarating first stanza! We want to buffet the sea with her. The difficulty arises in the next stanza, comprised of a single sentence. Grammatically, it is the sailor who is *bred among the mountains.* But that can't be what the poet intends. First, not all sailors are bred among the mountains, and it hardly seems likely that she writes of one particular sailor who did. Secondly, a single sailor bred among the mountains would remember his first voyage and *understand the Divine Intoxication* that he felt then. In this situation we need to see what must be the meaning. "As we are bred among the mountains, I ask, can the sailor understand the divine intoxication that we feel on our first league out from land?" Dickinson has expressed this thought in as few words as could possibly be done without losing the meaning beyond recovery. The reader arrives at this meaning not by thinking so much as by feeling.

A similar example of a poem's meaning not being evident strictly from the arrangement of the words is one expressing the poet's dismissive attitude toward fame.

Fame is a fickle food
Upon a shifting plate
Whose table once a
Guest but not
The second time is set
Whose crumbs the crows inspect
And with ironic caw
Flap past it to the
Farmer's Corn
Men eat of it and die
—J1659/F1702/M666

Fame is pictured as an untrustworthy *food.* The implication is that people seek sustenance from fame, but as they try to partake of it, the *plate shifts* to another place. The first two lines form a complete, even prosaic sentence. Starting on the third line, however, questions arise. Whose *table* is it? Let us presume this is the table that the food of fame is on. Even so, lines 3 through 5 are not clear, seem broken somehow, and have left many a reader frowning at the page. The notion that fame is fleeting is a familiar one, however, and we sense that observation animating this poem. The table is set once for the hungry guest, but not a second time. The *crows,* an intelligent species, are too smart to partake of it. It is fatal to our species alone.

If you were to try to describe in words the sound that a crow makes to someone who had never heard one, what would you say? The words the poet chose are another wonderful an example of her unrivaled originality in the use of common vocabulary. *Caw* is the familiar name of the sound. In describing the caw as *ironic* Dickinson chose a word not in her dictionary, and that she used in this poem only. The EDL gives this:

IRONIC, adj.
Dissembled; derisive; cunning; guileful.

Sweet Torment and Sumptuous Despair

Some words are so incompatible that, in prose writing, it would be an error to pair them. In poetry however, two normally incompatible words can come together to create new meaning, as Dickinson did in "Her losses make our Gains ashamed," discussed in Chapter 3.

Her Losses make our Gains ashamed -
She bore Life's empty Pack
As gallantly as if the East
Were swinging at her Back.
Life's empty Pack is heaviest,
As every Porter knows -
In vain to punish Honey -
It only sweeter grows.
—J1562/F1602/M727

One cannot literally *punish Honey*. To punish is to chastise or inflict pain or deprivation, and honey does not feel pain nor can it experience deprivation. With these two words the poet conveys the notion of the sweet nature of the woman who is the subject of the poem enduring deprivation—the punishment of *Life's empty Pack*—as if it were a blessing. Once again, Dickinson expresses her theme of purification, or refinement, through adversity.

The following poem had a central place in the 1982 film *Sophie's Choice,* which sounded its depth brilliantly. Yet, perhaps because of the metaphors employed, it has at other times been completely misread.

Ample make this Bed -
Make this Bed with Awe -
In it wait till Judgment break
Excellent and Fair.

Be its Mattress straight -
Be its Pillow round -
Let no Sunrise' yellow noise
Interrupt this Ground -
—J829/F804/M499

Every year around May 15th, the date of Emily Dickinson's death, a "Poetry Walk" takes place in Amherst, organized by the Emily Dickinson Museum. At this casual, free event, participants walk through town in a group, stopping at various spots to hear a host tell of the significance of that spot in the poet's life, and to read a few poems. At one such event, after hearing the poem above recited at Dickinson's gravesite, a man in his thirties, accompanied by his young son, allowed that this was a fine bedtime poem for a child. This *bed*, however, is of another kind. Nor is Emily thinking of the flower beds in her garden, as some have inferred. In this bed, the occupant must wait until the day of *Judgement*. The last line tells us that this bed is in the ground, which may be what has suggested flower beds to some readers. But flowers also need the sun, and no bright sunshine nor any sounds of life from the wakening world above—all captured in Dickinson's *yellow noise*—will find their way here. There is something poignant in beginning the final lines as an invocation, or a prayer, with the words *Let no*, as if the speaker were commanding that it be so, as if we mortals had the power to will otherwise.

Other pairs of strikingly incompatible and contradictory words are paired in "I would not paint - a picture." Because it contains other surprises as well, it carries us nicely into the next and final section of this final chapter.

A Turn at the End

In another poem, "Tell all the Truth but tell it slant" (J1129/F1263/M563), Dickinson's speaker advises the reader to stick to the truth, but also to "tell it slant." It is evident from the poems that we've examined so far that she followed her own advice. A private vocabulary, images that have no literal referent in the physical world, parts of thoughts left unspoken and mysterious metaphors, all combine to communicate indirectly. To these techniques, add another, called the turn. The turn, also called the volta, is a trope that was first developed in the sonnet form by Petrarch in the 14th century. Just as the word sonnet comes from the Italian "sonnetto" meaning "little song," "volta" is the Italian word for "turn." A turn is a change in direction. In a poem, it is a change in the direction, usually toward the end, that the poem has been heading, shifting focus, subject, or meaning. In Dickinson, the turn can be a sudden surprise that reverses the initially understood meaning of the entire poem.

I would not paint - a picture -
I'd rather be the One
It's bright impossibility
To dwell - delicious - on
And wonder how the fingers feel
Whose rare - celestial - stir -
Evokes so sweet a Torment -
Such sumptuous - Despair -

I would not talk, like Cornets -
I'd rather be the One
Raised softly to the Ceilings-
And out, and easy on -
Through villages of Ether -
Myself endued Balloon
By but a lip of Metal -
The pier to my Pontoon-

Nor would I be a Poet -
It's finer - own the Ear -
Enamored - impotent - content -
The License to revere,
A privilege so awful
What would the Dower be,
Had I the Art to stun myself
With Bolts of Melody!
—J505/F348/M184

The speaker expresses the notion that she prefers the exquisite pleasure of looking at a picture to the imagined experience of actually painting one herself. To convey the intensity of that pleasure, she offers a series of word pairs; *bright impossibility* being one, and it might be tempting to try to read it literally, as some impossible thing in the picture, such as a bright sunrise that never ends, or a winged spirit glowing radiantly. If so, she would simply be reporting a fact. The painting's bright impossibility is not a literal thing or physical part of the picture, but rather a quality. It's as if the painter has accomplished the *impossible* by capturing some incorporeal *brightness*. We cannot point to some physical thing depicted and say, "There it is!" We must try to locate it within ourselves. Any reader who has ever been inspired by a work of art to yearn for a bright impossibility will understand.

Although she *would not paint a picture,* still, she wonders what the painter does experience in executing it, *how the fingers feel* that can *evoke sweet Torment* and *sumptuous Despair.* The words in each of these pairs are so discordant, the reader may feel a mild shock at first. Of course, torment is never sweet to one who is enduring it, but a painting such as one on a religious subject, portraying the suffering of a saint perhaps, may evoke an exalted response in the viewer that may be very sweet indeed. Likewise, a state of despair would not be experienced as sumptuous by the despairing. A scene of despair however, such a Thomas Cole's *Expulsion from the Garden of Eden,* may be painted sumptuously.

SUMPTUOUS, adj.
1. Delicate; delicious; luscious; lavish.
2. Blissful; peaceful; grand.

The second stanza moves from the visual realm to the aural. With the image of being physically lifted into the air and carried away by the music, the poet conveys the elevating and transporting effect of fine music on the soul. which she claims to prefer to playing music herself. The sound carries her *Through villages of Ether*, perhaps because the cliché "castles in the air" was already familiar, and she would "never consciously touch a paint mixed by another person."[7] She likens herself in this state to a balloon, granted her *By but a lip of Metal*, the mouthpiece of the *Cornet* or of any brass wind instrument generally. Her dictionary redirects from the word endue to its alternate spelling.

IN-DUE′, v.t. (This word coincides nearly in signification with endow, that is, to put on, to furnish.)
1. To put on something; to invest; to clothe; as, to indue matter with forms, or man with intelligence.
2. To furnish; to supply with; to endow.

This spelling is now out of date. "Endow" is the form in current use. The relationship to *endow,* a favorite word of the Poet's, and which also appears, in its noun form, in the third stanza of this poem, is noted.

EN-DOW′, v.t.
3. To enrich or furnish with any gift, quality or faculty; to indue; man is *endowed by his Maker with reason.*

The speaker tells in three words—*Myself endued Balloon*—how she feels the uplifting music as a gift—endowing her with a buoyant feeling and freedom like a balloon aloft. She maintains contact with the material world *By but a lip of Metal,* which she likens to a pier for her *Pontoon.* She is afloat.

PONTOON, n.
Ferry; skiff; small, flat-bottomed boat; buoyant structure used to support a floating bridge.

The third stanza opens with a surprising claim. The writer of the sixteen preceding lines of fine poetry *would not be a Poet*! It's better to *own the Ear* that hears the poetry, she asserts. Revering the poetic *license* that that enables the poet to turn words into art she asks, what would such a gift entail? *What would the Dower be?*

DOW'ER, n.

1. That portion of the lands or tenements of a man which his widow enjoys during her life, after the death of her husband.
2. The property which a woman brings to her husband in marriage.
3. The gift of a husband for a wife.
4. Endowment; gift.

Some readers find this a beautiful poem written from the point of view of someone who is deeply moved by art—painting, music, and poetry—to the extent that she desires no more—that the joy that she experiences as a listener, viewer, or reader is preferable to whatever the artist experiences in its creation. The final two lines hold the kernel of a deeper reading however. In stanza one she wonders what the artist feels when painting; she does not know. In stanza two she doesn't even wonder what the musician experiences; she speaks entirely from the point of view the listener. But in those final lines, she reveals that she does indeed know what the poet experiences when inspiration strikes, and who but a great poet would be able to describe it as she has done?

Even a seemingly simple child-like poem may be saying more than a too-cursory reading reveals.

Could I but ride indefinite
As doth the Meadow Bee
And visit only where I liked
And No one visit me

And flirt all Day with Buttercups
And marry whom I may
And dwell a little everywhere
Or better, run away

With no Police to follow
Or chase Him if He do
Till He should jump Peninsulas
To get away from me -

I said "But just to be a Bee"
Upon a Raft of Air
And row in Nowhere all Day long
And anchor "off the Bar"

What Liberty! So Captives deem
Who tight in Dungeons are.
—J661/F1056/M474

As previously noted, Dickinson often creates a humorous tone, as she does here, by employing Latinate or other high-sounding words in slightly incongruous ways. In this case the word *doth*, familiar from such great and venerable sources as the Bible and Shakespeare, was by Dickinson's time archaic. Applied to the carefree roving *Meadow Bee* it brings a smile. She very probably also is playing on a familiar hymn of Isaac Watts, a sermon-like set of verses that offer the industrious bee as a role model for avoiding idleness, and thereby foiling Satan. The first verse is:

How doth the little busy bee
Improve each shining hour,
And gather honey all the day
From every opening flower!

Dickinson's bee departs from this model of virtue by riding *indefinite.* The EDL gives us:

INDEFINITE, adv.
1. Freely; browsing; ranging; anywhere; imprecisely; randomly seeking; without limitations; in any direction; in a wandering manner.

The speaker expresses a longing for a carefree life of idle pleasure diametrically opposed to that of Watts' bee, and one that Watts explicitly warns against in subsequent stanzas of his hymn. Moreover, she may choose to escape even from that carefree flight and *run away.* She offers the humorous notion that if *Police* should *follow,* she would turn around and chase him *Till He should jump Peninsulas* to evade her. Although we have not encountered the word "peninsula" before, it is another one that Dickinson made poetically her own, to imply distance or remoteness, in a total of nine poems. The fleeing officer would skedaddle far away, she declares.

Stanza four relies on a recurring metaphor in Dickinson, the air as a sea. A raft may travel on air. The bee may *row in Nowhere* and finally *anchor "off the Bar."* Among several definitions for "bar" her dictionary offers:

BAR, n.
3. The shore of the sea, which restrains its waters.

"*What Liberty!*" she exclaims, but is this the real sentiment of the speaker after all? The wistful longing given voice in this poem is that of those who are not already free, those *Who in tight in Dungeons are.* The reader becomes aware that to the extent that he has been carried away by the thought of the carefree life of a Meadow Bee, he too may be a *Captive.* The humorous tone of the poem suggests that the speaker is not thus confined.

Even though the next poem addresses the needs of the dying, it adopts a deceptively easy, straightforward style and a conversational *Dear* in the first line. The reader is unprepared for the turn at the end.

The Dying need but little, Dear,
A Glass of Water's all,

A Flower's unobtrusive Face
To punctuate the Wall,

A Fan, perhaps, a Friend's Regret
And Certainty that one
No color in the Rainbow
Perceive, when you are gone.
—J1026/F1037/M468

For the first verse and the start of the second, *The dying need* only a few simple amenities for a peaceful passing. This is a portrayal of what was called "the good death," in which the dying person, assured of salvation, does not fear to die, but rather is willing. During the death watch, those close to the dying person would search her expression and hang on any words she might utter, in the earnest hope of seeing some sign that she was willing to die. It was believed that in passing from this life into the next, one might even have a glimpse of the afterlife, and that evidence of that glimpse might be discernible on the person's features.

After the simple fan, however, the poem ventures into more serious concerns with *a Friend's Regret.* We want to be remembered, a deeper need than for *a Glass of Water* or a *fan.* One even greater and deeper hope remains—moving from third person plural to second person singular—that someone loves you so much that she will *Perceive No color of the rainbow when you are gone.* The dying—*you*—need, perhaps, a little more than *but little.*

The final poem we will consider is a rarely heard one, and also a fitting one with which to end this book. The turn at the end provides an essential key to reading Emily Dickinson's poetry.

As if some little Arctic flower
Upon the polar hem -
Went wandering down the Latitudes
Until it puzzled came
To continents of summer -
To firmaments of sun -
To strange, bright crowds of flowers -
And birds, of foreign tongue!
I say, As if this little flower
To Eden, wandered in -
What then? Why nothing,
Only, your inference therefrom!
—J180/F177/M103

The poet imagines a *flower wandering down* from the gray *Arctic* cold into a warm dazzling world of sun and color. Her arctic region exists above a latitude that she names *the polar hem,* likening it to the hemline of a woman's dress, and invoking the associations with the north covered in Chapter 3. There the newly arrived flower beholds blooms that it has never before beheld, and hears bird songs it has never before heard. It's as if it had *wandered in to Eden.* "What do you make of that, Dear Reader?" the poet asks. Make of it what you will, she advises. This is the one place where Dickinson explicitly instructs us that the poem is a template for us to make something of, just as the script of a play of Shakespeare is for the actors. Find yourself in the poem.

Afterword

"Once she grabs you, she doesn't let go." So says Dickinson biographer and historian Polly Longsworth. If Emily Dickinson has enthralled you as she has so many, then you may "get grabbed" and want to continue on with her. The chapters of this book can be no more than a small part of such a journey. Outlined here are some suggestions on how to expand and deepen an existing appreciation of this great American poet, based in part on the three strategies identified in the introduction.

First, examine the language practices that were available to her in her time and place.

The easiest and best resource for this is the online Emily Dickinson Lexicon (EDL) on which this book has constantly relied. If that option is not available, then an American Dictionary of the English language from the mid–nineteenth century would be valuable.

Second, identify distinctly personal, biographical, and local references, along with historical context.

This is the most wide-ranging and essentially unlimited scope of activity to pursue. The more that you enjoy reading history and exploring other cultures, the more that you will want to do in this direction. Below are some suggestions, including several resources that have proven especially worthwhile to your author. Among them are books now out of print, but that are still available from online sources such as abebooks.com.

Biographies

Richard B. Sewall, *The Life of Emily Dickinson*
Alfred Habegger, *The Life of Emily Dickinson, My Wars Are Laid Away In Books*

Thomas H. Johnson, *Emily Dickinson, an Interpretive Biography*
George Frisbee Whicher, *Emily Dickinson, This was a Poet*

History

Barry Hankins, *The Second Great Awakening and the Transcendentalists*
R. Todd Falton, *A Journey into the Transcendentalists' New England*
Robert D. Richardson, *Emerson, The Mind on Fire*
John T. McNeill, *The History and Character of Calvinism*
Michael McGiffert editor, *Puritanism and the American Experience*
James M. McPherson, *Battle Cry of Freedom: The Civil War Era*
Drew Gilpin Faust, *This Republic of Suffering: Death and the American Civil War*

Third, consider her vocabulary and literary tropes in the context of the entire body of her work

The more familiar that you are with the poems and letters, the more you will read in this way. It's like becoming familiar with the speech of a close friend or family member. Your sources are the Johnson, Franklin, and Miller editions of the poems and the Johnson edition of the letters identified in the introduction. You can also sample some of the numerous books of analysis that are referenced in this book and identified in the endnotes.

In my experience, however, there is no better way to dig into this poetry than in conversation with others. Form your own Emily Dickinson discussion group. One way to start would be in conjunction with your local library, as is the case with the monthly Emily Dickinson Poetry Conversation in Amherst. A sign posted in the library and a notice in the library newsletter invites people to participate. The conversation takes place in a comfortable conference room, where, at the end of the meeting, those present choose three or four poems for the next month's consideration. We may choose a poem because it's difficult, or because it's a favorite, or in order to explore a certain theme or idea, such as Circumference The group leader distributes an email notice, listing the poems to be discussed, to one and all so people can look at them ahead of time if they wish.

You may also host a group in your own home, of course, if you are so inclined and have the space to do so. This allows for a selective company. Such is the case with the Emily Dickinson Reading Circle, held monthly in western Massachusetts, now in its eleventh year with many long-term members at the time of this writing. This particular discussion is organized more regularly around a theme. For instance, a recent discussion focused on a particular group of poems that Dickinson sewed into one of her homemade books, fascicle number 40. Sometimes we will have a discussion leader. Recently, composer Alice Parker lead a discussion of poems that she had set to music, explaining their musical aspects and the use of pauses indicated by Dickinson's dashes.

A third possibility would be to involve a local cultural institution that might have an interest in poetry or cultural history. The Emily Dickinson Museum is owned by Amherst College, and is thus able to hold its monthly Emily Dickinson Museum Poetry Discussion on campus. In this particular group, a facilitator is chosen who prepares a presentation in advance, with which to initiate the discussion. Recent discussions have included "Emily Dickinson and Emerson," and "Don't tell!, Emily's Strategies of Secrecy in Poems and Letters."

It can sometimes feel like some kind of divine grace is at work when a group of people, initially uncertain about what a poem is saying, come together in discussion and, somehow, clarity emerges. Very important to this success is that no one tries to establish their view as the pre-eminent one. We don't argue. If someone decides that *Ample make this Bed* is a child's bedtime poem, it is duly noted, and then others express their own thoughts

Beginning in July of 2015, I began posting transcripts from the these discussions at http://justemilydickinson.blogspot.com/. For most readers, hearing someone else read a poem can be illuminating, revealing alternate interpretations, tones, or emphasis. Recordings of these poems, read mostly by myself, but by others when I can record a fine recital, are at my YouTube channel, Just Emily Dickinson, https://www.youtube.com/channel/UCnwRLPiq53ZEQMGzUTsTUAg

Membership in the Emily Dickinson International Society (EDIS) will keep you informed of new and recent books, conferences, and academic papers on Dickinson. A scholarly journal and an informative bulletin are sponsored twice each per year. A discussion group may be formed as a local chapter of EDIS. Guidelines for doing so may be found at the EDIS website, under "Local Chapters," http://www.emilydickinsoninternationalsociety.org/node/265.

Appendix A

"The Death of Flowers" by William Cullen Bryant (1794–1878)

The melancholy days are come, the saddest of the year,
Of wailing winds, and naked woods, and meadows brown and sere.
Heaped in the hollows of the grove, the autumn leaves lie dead;
They rustle to the eddying gust, and to the rabbit's tread;
The robin and the wren are flown, and from the shrubs the jay,
And from the wood-top calls the crow through all the gloomy day.

Where are the flowers, the fair young flowers, that lately sprang and stood
In brighter light and softer airs, a beauteous sisterhood?
Alas! they all are in their graves, the gentle race of flowers
Are lying in their lowly beds, with the fair and good of ours.
The rain is falling where they lie, but the cold November rain
Calls not from out the gloomy earth the lovely ones again.

The wind-flower and the violet, they perished long ago,
And the brier-rose and the orchis died amid the summer glow;
But on the hills the golden-rod, and the aster in the wood,
And the yellow sun-flower by the brook in autumn beauty stood,
Till fell the frost from the clear cold heaven, as falls the plague on men,
And the brightness of their smile was gone, from upland, glade, and glen.

And now, when comes the calm mild day, as still such days will come,
To call the squirrel and the bee from out their winter home;
When the sound of dropping nuts is heard, though all the trees are still,
And twinkle in the smoky light the waters of the rill,
The south wind searches for the flowers whose fragrance late he bore,
And sighs to find them in the wood and by the stream no more.

"Autumn" (fragment) by James Thompson (1700–1748)

Crowned with the sickle and the wheaten shief
While Autumn, nodding oe'r the yellow plain,
Comes jovial on; the Doric Reed once more,
Well pleased, I tune. Whate'er the wintry Frost
Nitrous prepared; the various blossomed Spring
Put in white promise forth; and Summer-Suns
Concocted strong, rush boundless now to view'
Full, perfect all, and swell my glorious theme.

"The Snow-Storm" by Ralph Waldo Emerson (1803–1882)

Announced by all the trumpets of the sky,
Arrives the snow, and, driving o'er the fields,
Seems nowhere to alight: the whited air
Hides hills and woods, the river, and the heaven,
And veils the farm-house at the garden's end.
The sled and traveller stopped, the courier's feet
Delayed, all friends shut out, the housemates sit
Around the radiant fireplace, enclosed
In a tumultuous privacy of storm.

Come see the north wind's masonry.
Out of an unseen quarry evermore
Furnished with tile, the fierce artificer
Curves his white bastions with projected roof
Round every windward stake, or tree, or door.
Speeding, the myriad-handed, his wild work
So fanciful, so savage, nought cares he
For number or proportion. Mockingly,
On coop or kennel he hangs Parian wreaths;
A swan-like form invests the hidden thorn;
Fills up the farmer's lane from wall to wall,
Maugre the farmer's sighs; and, at the gate,
A tapering turret overtops the work.
And when his hours are numbered, and the world
Is all his own, retiring, as he were not,
Leaves, when the sun appears, astonished Art
To mimic in slow structures, stone by stone,
Built in an age, the mad wind's night-work,
The frolic architecture of the snow.

"There Is a Land of Pure Delight" by Isaac Watts (1674–1748)

There is a land of pure delight
Where saints immortal reign;
Infinite day excludes the night,
And pleasures banish pain.

There everlasting spring abides,
And never-withering flowers:
Death like a narrow sea divides
This heavenly land from ours.

Sweet fields beyond the swelling flood
Stand dressed in living green:
So to the Jews old Canaan stood,
While Jordan rolled between.

But timorous mortals start and shrink
To cross this narrow sea,
And linger shivering on the brink
And fear to launch away.

O could we make our doubts remove,
These gloomy doubts that rise,
And see the Canaan that we love
With unbeclouded eyes,

Could we but climb where Moses stood,
And view the landscape o'er,
Not Jordan's stream, nor Death's cold flood,
Should fright us from the shore.

A Passage from Aurora Leigh *by Elizabeth Barrett Browning (1806–1861)*

'The worthiest poets have remained uncrowned
Till death has bleached their foreheads to the bone,
And so with me it must be, unless I prove
Unworthy of the grand adversity, -
And certainly I would not fail so much.
What, therefore, if I crown myself to-day
In sport, not pride, to learn the feel of it,
Before my brows be numb as Dante's own
To all the tender pricking of such leaves?
Such leaves? what leaves?'
I pulled the branches down,
To choose from.
'Not the bay! I choose no bay;
The fates deny us if we are overbold:

Nor myrtle - which means chiefly love; and love
Is something awful which one dare not touch
So early o' mornings. This verbena strains
The point of passionate fragrance; and hard by,
This guelder rose, at far too slight a beck
Of the wind, will toss about her flower-apples.
Ah - there's my choice,–that ivy on the wall,
That headlong ivy! not a leaf will grow
But thinking of a wreath. Large leaves, smooth leaves,
Serrated like my vines, and half as green.
I like such ivy; bold to leap a height
'Twas strong to climb! as good to grow on graves
As twist about a thyrsus; pretty too,
(And that's not ill) when twisted round a comb.'
Thus speaking to myself, half singing it,
Because some thoughts are fashioned like a bell
To ring with once being touched, I drew a wreath
Drenched, blinding me with dew, across my brow,
And fastening it behind so, . . turning faced
…My public!

—Chapter 2, lines 28–59

"Decoration" by Thomas Wentworth Higginson (1823–1911)

MID the flower-wreathed tombs I stand
Bearing lilies in my hand.
Comrades! in what soldier-grave
Sleeps the bravest of the brave?

Is is he who sank to rest
With his colors round his breast?
Friendship makes his tomb a shrine;
Garlands veil it: ask not mine.

One low grave, yon trees beneath,
Bears no roses, wears no wreath;
Yet no heart more high and warm
Ever dared the battle-storm.

Never gleamed a prouder eye
In the front of victory,
Never foot had firmer tread
On the field where hope lay dead,

Than are hid within this tomb,
Where the untended grasses bloom,
And no stone, with feigned distress,
Mocks the sacred loneliness.

Youth and beauty, dauntless will,
Dreams that life could ne'er fulfill,
Here lie buried; here in peace
Wrongs and woes have found release.

Turning from my comrades' eyes,
Kneeling where a woman lies,
I strew lilies on the grave
Of the bravest of the brave.

Appendix B

The Online Emily Dickinson Lexicon (EDL): A Tutorial

At the time of this writing there are valuable sources at the EDL website that offer insight into Dickinson's vocabulary, which in turn clarifies much of her poetry. This is a brief lesson that explains how to use two of the resources that the website provides.

1. The Emily Dickinson Lexicon itself (Hallen, Cynthia, ed. Renovated Online Edition of Noah Webster's 1844 American Dictionary of the English Language. Provo, Utah: Brigham Young University, http://edl.byu.edu/index.php, 2009), and
2. A renovated edition of Noah Webster's 1844 Dictionary, *An American Dictionary of the English Language,* the dictionary that Emily Dickinson used at home (Hallen, Cynthia, ed. Emily Dickinson Lexicon. Provo, Utah: Brigham Young University, http://edl.byu.edu/index.php, 2007).

Words can change in meaning and in common usage. Discovering how a word was commonly used in mid–nineteenth-century America can throw sudden and clear light on a poem. The steps below show how to access each of the two resources and tell what each has to offer. Additional help is available on the website. To access all that EDL has to offer, you must register with a (Free) username and password.

1. Go to http://edl.byu.edu/, or type "Emily Dickinson Lexicon" into your web browser.
2. Click the Register tab and fill in the brief form. You are now ready to use the EDL.

The Welcome Page from the Emily Dickinson Lexicon (used by permission).

First, we will find a single word in the EDL, and then we'll find the same word in Webster's.

1. Click the "ED Lexicon" tab (or remain on the Home tab; both give the same results).
2. In the "Searches" box, enter the word "candid."
3. The following screen appears.

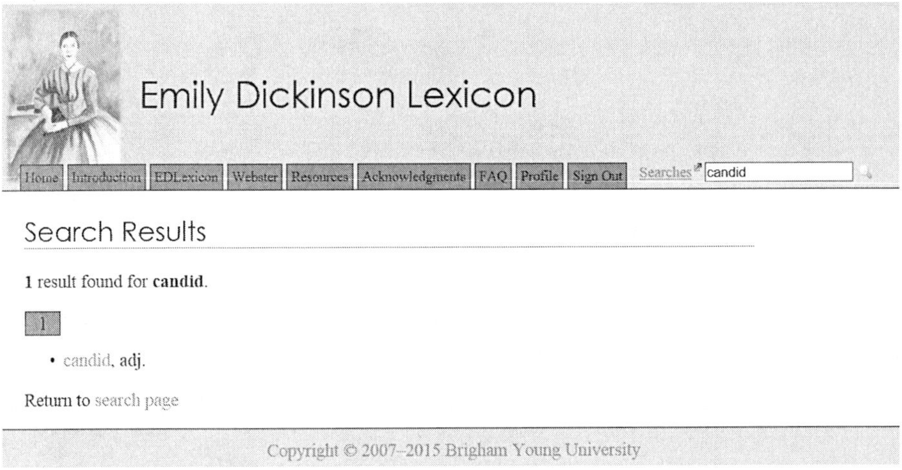

Searches for "candid" in the Emily Dickinson Lexicon (used by permission).

Click on the "candid" hyperlink. The resulting screen, shown below, displays a literal definition of the word, followed by figurative definitions, that is, poetic ways in which the poet used that word. Below that is a line from a Dickinson poem containing that word. Lastly there is a Reference List of the line (or lines) in every poem in which Dickinson used that word. The EDL shows that she used the word “candid” in a total of two poems. Without having entered a username and password, you won’t get the reference list of poems.

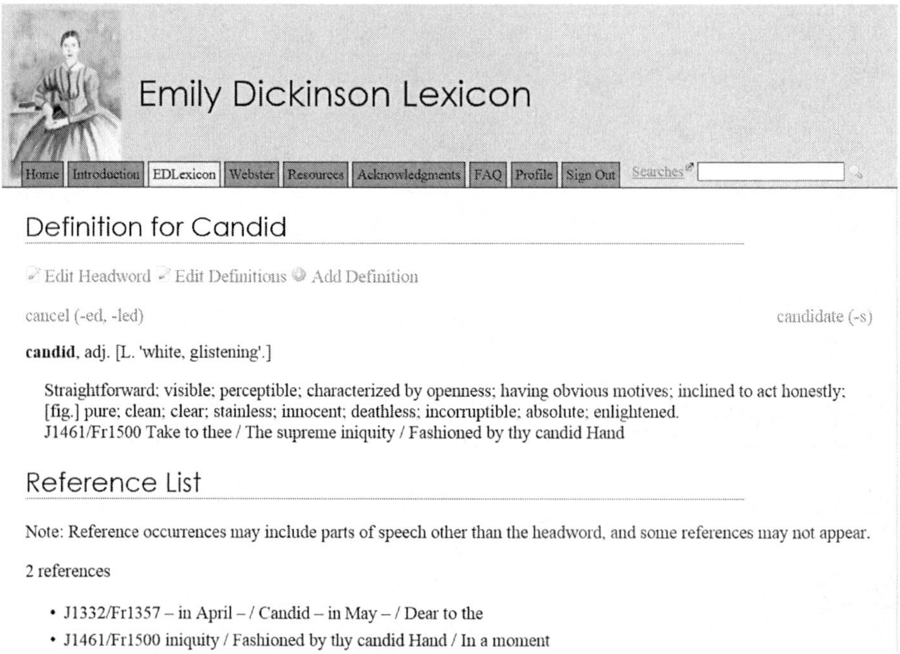
Emily Dickinson Lexicon

Home | Introduction | EDLexicon | Webster | Resources | Acknowledgments | FAQ | Profile | Sign Out | Searches

Definition for Candid

Edit Headword Edit Definitions Add Definition

cancel (-ed, -led) candidate (-s)

candid, adj. [L. 'white, glistening'.]

Straightforward; visible; perceptible; characterized by openness; having obvious motives; inclined to act honestly; [fig.] pure; clean; clear; stainless; innocent; deathless; incorruptible; absolute; enlightened.
J1461/Fr1500 Take to thee / The supreme iniquity / Fashioned by thy candid Hand

Reference List

Note: Reference occurrences may include parts of speech other than the headword, and some references may not appear.

2 references

- J1332/Fr1357 – in April – / Candid – in May – / Dear to the
- J1461/Fr1500 iniquity / Fashioned by thy candid Hand / In a moment

The display results page for “candid” in the Emily Dickinson Lexicon (used by permission).

Next, we’ll find the same word in ED’s Webster’s dictionary.

4. Click on the “Webster’s” tab.
5. In the “Searches” box, enter the word “candid.” The screen at the top of the next page appears.
6. Click on the “candid” hyperlink. The following screen appears.

From the Webster tab, you are reading the definition from the dictionary that Emily herself owned and used, a gift from her father, Edward. Here, as noted in the preface to this book, is an example of a word that has changed its meaning since the time that the poet used it. The first definition for candid listed, “white” is no longer common in today’s usage. Knowing that can dispel the puzzlement a reader might otherwise feel when reading either of the two poems listed by the EDL in this example.

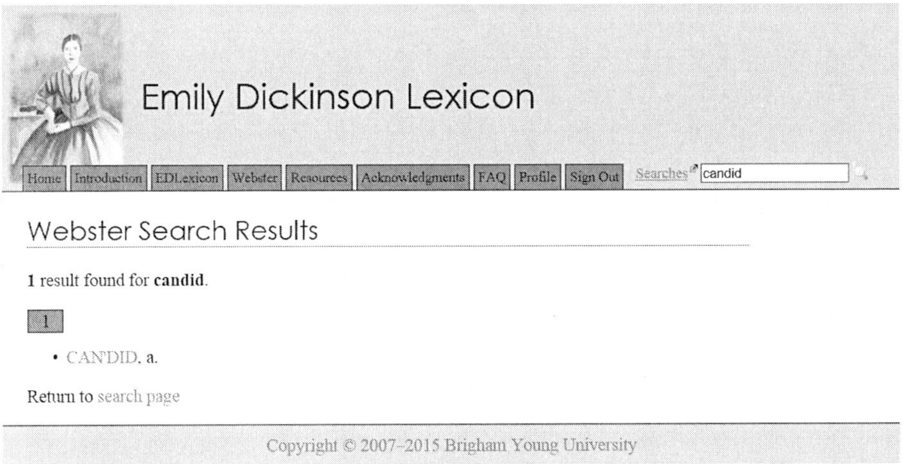
Emily Dickinson Lexicon

Home | Introduction | EDLexicon | Webster | Resources | Acknowledgments | FAQ | Profile | Sign Out | Searches candid

Webster Search Results

1 result found for **candid**.

1

- CAN'DID, a.

Return to search page

Copyright © 2007–2015 Brigham Young University

Webster's Dictionary searches for "candid" as shown in the Emily Dickinson Lexicon (used by permission).

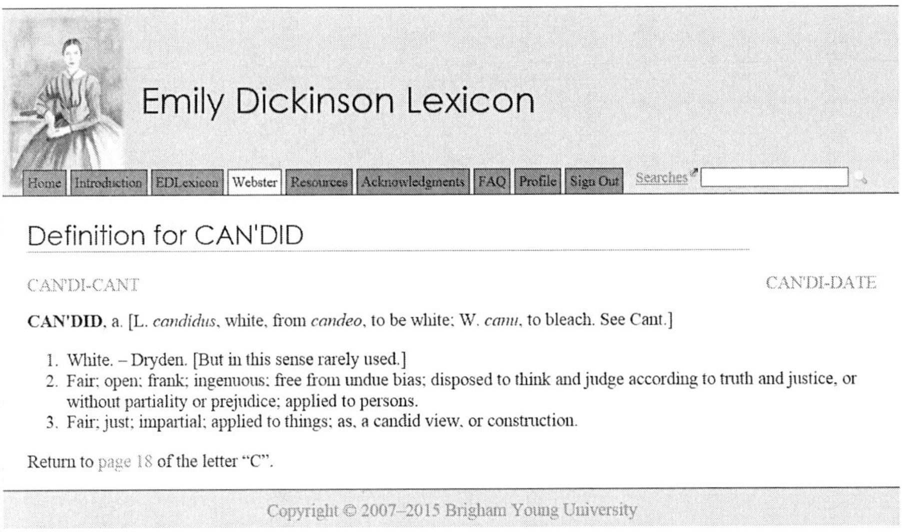
Emily Dickinson Lexicon

Home | Introduction | EDLexicon | Webster | Resources | Acknowledgments | FAQ | Profile | Sign Out | Searches

Definition for CAN'DID

CAN'DI-CANT CAN'DI-DATE

CAN'DID, a. [L. *candidus*, white, from *candeo*, to be white; W. *canu*, to bleach. See Cant.]

1. White. – Dryden. [But in this sense rarely used.]
2. Fair; open; frank; ingenuous; free from undue bias; disposed to think and judge according to truth and justice, or without partiality or prejudice; applied to persons.
3. Fair; just; impartial; applied to things; as, a candid view, or construction.

Return to page 18 of the letter "C".

Copyright © 2007–2015 Brigham Young University

Webster's Dictionary display results for its definitions for "candid" as shown in the Emily Dickinson Lexicon (used by permission).

There are other valuable resources at the online Emily Dickinson Website which anyone interested in Dickinson will find worthwhile to explore.

Chapter Notes

Preface

1. Hallen, Cynthia, ed. Emily Dickinson Lexicon. Provo, Utah: Brigham Young University, http://edl.byu.edu/index.php, 2007.

2. *A Poet's Grammar*, by Cristanne Miller (Cambridge, MA: Harvard University Press, 1987), 1.

Chapter One

1. Richard B. Sewall, *The Lyman Letters: New Light on Emily Dickinson and her Family* (Amherst: The University of Massachusetts Press, 1965), 78.

2. Hallen, Cynthia, ed. Renovated Online Edition of Noah Webster's 1844 American Dictionary of the English Language. Provo, Utah: Brigham Young University, http://edl.byu.edu/index.php, 2009.

3. L536,to Ms. Samuel Bowles, Early 1878, *The Letters of Emily Dickinson,* Volume 1, Ed. Thomas H. Johnson and Theodora Ward (Cambridge, MA: The Belknap Press of Harvard University Press, 1958).

4. Richard B. Sewall, *The Life of Emily Dickinson, Volume 2* (New York: Farrar, Straus and Giroux, 1974), 349 footnote.

5. Richard Green Parker, *Aids to English Composition* (New York: Harper and Brothers, 1845), 26, 30.

6. Gerda Lerner (1920–2013) was an historian, author and teacher. She has been described as "the single most influential figure in the development of women's and gender history since the 1960s."—.

7. Gerda Lerner, *The Creation of Feminist Consciousness: From the Middle Ages to Eighteen-Seventy* (New York: Oxford University Press, 1993), 181.

8. See Karen Lystra, *Searching the Heart: Women, Men, and Romantic Love in Nineteenth-Century America* (New York: Oxford University Press, 1989).

9. Hans Kurath, *World Geography*, 64, as referenced by Brita Lindberg-Seyersted, *The Voice of the Poet: Aspects of Style in the Poetry of Emily Dickinson* (Cambridge: Harvard University Press, 1968), 64.

10. L316, to Thomas Wentworth Higginson, early 1866.

11. Thirteenth Annual Report of the State Board of Agriculture made to the General Assembly at its January Session, 1898 (Rhode Island).

12. Ralph W. Franklin, *The Poems of Emily Dickinson, Variorum Edition,* Volume 2 (Cambridge, MA: The Belknap Press of Harevard University Press, 1998), 951–955.

13. Alfred Habeggar, "*My Wars are laid away in books*": *The Life of Emily Dickinson* (New York: Random House, 2001) 36

14. L9, to Abiah Root, 12 January 1846.

15. William Howard, "Emily Dickinson's Poetic Vocabulary," *PMLA*, Vol. 72, No. 1 (1957), 238.

16. Charles Dickens, *All the Year Round*, Vol. 24 (1883).

17. William Schurr, *The Marriage of Emily Dickinson* (Lexington: University of Kentucky Press, 1983), 177.

18. Dickinson sewed over 800 of her poems into 40 little books. See "My Wars are laid away in books" (J1549/F1579/M637) The books are known today as "fascicles," meaning bunch or

bundle, or, in botany, a cluster of flowers or leaves. Fascicle is not a term that Dickinson used.

19. Attributed to Sigmund Freud, but very possibly apocryphal.

20. William Thomas Fernie *Herbal Simples Approved for Modern Uses of Cure* (Bristol, England: John Wright and Company, 1897).

21. Brita Lindberg-Seyersted, *The Voice of the Poet: Aspects of Style in the Poetry of Emily Dickinson* , 111, referring to "So glad we are - a Stranger'd deem" (J329/F608/M278).

22. John Milton, *Paradise Lost, Fourth Edition, Book V* (London: Private Printing, 1757).

23. Reformed Protestantism, or The Church Reformed According to the Word of God, is the name given to that branch of Christianity which arose from the work of John Calvin (1509–1564). It is sometimes confused with the Protestant Reformation (or simply, "the Reformation"), the schism within Western Christianity, of which it was a major part among various others.

24. L271, To Thomas Wentworth Higginson, August 1862.

Chapter Two

1. Jay Leyda, *The Years and Hours of Emily Dickinson, Volume 1* (New Haven, CT: Yale University Press, 1960), 367.

2. David T. Porter, *The Art of Emily Dickinson's Early Poetry* (Cambridge MA: Harvard University Press, 1966), 142.

3. L100, about February, 1853.

4. Dickinson uses the term "Indian Summer" in only one poem, "Except the smaller size" (J1067/F606/277), in the fourth stanza. It is in the three-volume Franklin Variorum and in the three-volume Johnson Edition. The single-volume Readers Editions from both editors print the first two stanzas only.

5. Genevieve Taggard, *The Life and Mind of Emily* Dickinson (New York: Alfred A. Knopf, 1930) 107–110; Carol Damon Andrews, "Thinking Musically, Writing Expectantly: New Biographical Information about Emily Dickinson," *The New England Quarterly* Vol. LXXXI, No. 2 (June 2008), 333.

6. For this and more on connections between Dickinson manuscripts and the poet's personal life, see Mike Kelly, Carolyn Vega, Mara Verner, Susan Howe, Richard Wilbur, *The Networked Recluse: The Connected World of Emily Dickinson* (New York: The Morgan Library and Museum, 2017), 37.

7. "Report by Dr. Elliotson," *The Zoist: A Journal of Cerebral Psychology and Mesmerism and Applications to Human Welfare, Vol. VI, No 21, April 1848* (London: Hyppolite, Bailliere Publisher),7.

8. L644, to Mrs. Samuel Bowles.

9. L813, To publisher Thomas Niles, mid–March, 1883.

10. L127, June 13, 1853.

Chapter Three

1. L97, to Susan Gilbert (Dickinson), Early December 1852.

2. Exodus 20:17 KJV.

3. A topos is any traditional theme or formula in literature.

4. Barton Levy St. Armand, "Emily Dickinson and the Occult," *Prairie Schooner*, Vol. 51, No. 4 (Winter 1977/1978), 356.

5. L235, to Mrs. Samuel Bowles.

6. Cynthia Griffin Wolff, *Emily Dickinson* (New York: Alfred Knopf, 1986), 248.

7. For perhaps the most thorough treatment of this topic, see Rebecca Patterson, *Emily Dickinson's Imagery,* Chapter 7, "The Cardinal Points" (Amherst: The University of Massachusetts Press, 1979).

8. L368, Early 1871.

9. Perry Miller, *Error into the Wilderness,* From the title of a sermon given by Samuel Danforth (1626–1674) in 1670, *A Brief Recognition of New-England's Errand into the Wilderness* (New York: Harper Row, 1956), 1.

10. Anais Nin, *The Diary of Anais Nin, volume 3, 1939–1944*, ed. Gunther Tuhlman (San Diego: Swallow Press/Harcourt Brace Jovanovich, 1969).

11. The others are "On my volcano grows the Grass" (J1677/F1743/M679), "Volcanoes be in Sicily" (J1705/F1691/M663) and "The reticent volcano keeps" (J1748/F1776/M687).

12. L203, March, 1859

13. "I cant tell you - but you feel it" (J65/F164/M93).

14. Each degree divides into sixty "minutes," but since that kind of minute does not appear in Dickinson's poetry, it need not concern us here.

15. Richard B. Sewall, *The Life of Emily Dickinson, Volume 1*, 204.

16. L868, Early October, 1883.
17. "Snow," Outdoor Papers; (Cambridge MA: The Riverside Press, 1889 and 1900) p166; Also, *Atlantic Monthly*, Jan. 1862.
18. L235 to Mrs. Samuel Bowles, about August 1861.
19. *Twelfth Night*: Act 3, Scene 1.
20. "You inquire my books. For poets, I have Keats, and Mr. and Mrs. Browning. For prose, Mr. Ruskin, Sir Thomas Browne, and the Revelations."—L261, to T.W. Higginson, 25 April 1862.
21. Sir Thomas Browne, *Religio Medici Part 2* (Cambridge UK: The University Press, 1963), 73–74.
22. Martha Dickinson Bianchi, *Emily Dickinson Face to Face* (Boston: Houghton Mifflin Company, 1932), 127.

Chapter Four

1. "I Dwell in Possibility" (J657/F466/233).
2. "… for we must consider that we shall be as a City upon a Hill, the eyes of all people are upon us; so that if we shall deal falsely with our god in this work we have undertaken and so cause him to withdraw his present help from us, we shall be made a story and a by-word through the world."—Winthrop speaking to the pilgrims aboard the *Arbella* (spelling modernized).
3. For an excellent treatment of this topic, see Perry Miller, *Errand into the Wilderness* (New York: Harper & Row, 1956).
4. Dickinson names Whitfield jokingly in a hilarious letter to her brother, Austin, L79, March 2, 1852.
5. Abby Wood, another school friend.
6. "Then shall the King say unto them on his right hand, Come, ye blessed of my Father, inherit the kingdom prepared for you from the foundation of the world"—Matthew 25:34.

"Then he will say to those on his left, 'Depart from me, you who are cursed, into the eternal fire prepared for the devil and his angels."—Matthew 25:41.

7. Or ever the silver cord be loosed, or the golden bowl be broken, or the pitcher be broken at the fountain, or the wheel broken at the cistern.—Ecclesiastes 12:6.
8. L11 28 March 1846.
9. L23, 16 May 1848.
10. Cynthia Griffin Wolff, *Emily Dickinson*, 100.
11. William S. Tyler, *A History of Amherst College* (New York: Frederick H. Hitchcock, 1895), 277.
12. "And he said, Go forth, and stand upon the mount before the Lord. And, behold, the Lord passed by, and a great and strong wind rent the mountains, and brake in pieces the rocks before the Lord; but the Lord was not in the wind: and after the wind an earthquake; but the Lord was not in the earthquake:

And after the earthquake a fire; but the Lord was not in the fire: and after the fire a still small voice.

And it was so, when Elijah heard it, that he wrapped his face in his mantle, and went out, and stood in the entering in of the cave. And, behold, there came a voice unto him, and said, What doest thou here, Elijah?"—1 Kings 19:11–13, KJV.

13. L39. Late 1850.
14. L936 to Mrs. J G Holland.
15. *The Articles of Faith and Government of the First Church in Amherst, MA, Adopted February 13, 1834.*
16. "For by grace are ye saved through faith; and that not of yourselves: *it is* the gift of God."—Ephesians 2:8.
17. Beginning in the Middle Ages, theologians believed that nature could be read much like a book along with scripture to reveal God's truth to man.
18. "Natural Theology" is the technical term for knowledge about God which is supported by human reason acting upon observable phenomena, or what is today popularly called "Science." It is contrasted with "Revealed Theology" which attempts to consider only the authority of scripture.

- Reverend T. Robert Ingram, *Natural Theology and Creation Science, 1. In* William Paley, *Paley's Theology* (Houston, TX: St. Thomas Press, 1972).

19. Edward Hitchcock, *Religious Lectures on Peculiar Phenomena in the Four Seasons […], Delivered to the Students in Amherst College, in 1845, 1847, 1848 and 1849; also delivered at Mount Holyoke Female Seminary* (Amherst, MA: J.S. and C. Adams, 1851), 11, 27, 33.
20. L319 to T.W. Higginson, 9 June 1866.
21. Thought to be Benjamin F. Newton,

who studied in her father's law office, 1847–49. Newton died of tuberculosis in 1853 at age 32.

22. L265 to T.W. Higginson, 7 June 1862.

23. Matthew 14:22–33, KJV.

24. Karen Lystra, *Searching the Heart, Women, Men, and Romantic Love in Nineteenth-Century America,* 248, 249.

25. Polly Longsworth, *Austin and Mabel* (New York: Farrar Straus Giroux, 1984), 284.

26. In his Readers Edition, Thomas Johnson amended Savans to Savants.

27. At the time Dr. Hitchcock was speaking and writing, *euthanasia* meant simply "Good Death." It appears to have acquired its present meaning, "Mercy Killing," later, in the 1860s.

28. Judith Farr, "Dickinson and the Visual Arts," *The Emily Dickinson Handbook* (Amherst: University of Massachusetts Press, 1998), 75–76.

29. Edward Hitchcock, *The Religion of Geology and Its Connected Sciences,* Lecture VI, "Geological Proofs of the Divine Benevolence" (Boston: Phillips, Sampson and Company, 1854), 180.

30. William Paley, *Natural Theology, or, Evidence of the Existence and Attributes of the Deity Collected from the Appearances of Nature* (Houston, TX: St. Thomas Press, 1972), 1.

31. L471, To Louise and Francis Norcross, August 1876.

Chapter Five

1. "Even so faith, if it hath not works, is dead, being alone."—James 2:17.

2. Carroll Smith-Rosenberg, "Puberty to Menopause: The Cycle of Femininity in Nineteenth-Century America," *Feminist Studies,* Vol. 1 No. 3/4 (Winter-Spring 1973) 65.

3. *Ibid.*, 63–64.

4. Accomplished by fitting a semi-sphere with a grated surface under the eyelid.

5. This line occurs also in Luke, 12:7. Dickinson references Matthew more often than the other three Gospels..

6. L477, to Thomas Wentworth Higginson, late October 1876.

7. L330, to Thomas Wentworth Higginson, June 1869.

8. The language is Aramaic.

9. Calvary was a small hill outside the walls of Jerusalem, also called Golgotha, meaning, "the place of the skull" for its resemblance to a skull cap.

10. L912, to Susan Dickinson, about 1884.

11. The cubit is an ancient measure of length, equal to the average length of a man's forearm. It was typically about 18 inches, or 44 cm.

12. There can be some confusion. Sometimes a writer will refer to the hanging in the fabric outer wall as a vail. That would make the second vail to which we refer the third vail, but it is technically incorrect. Two different words are used in the original Hebrew of the Old Testament, *masak,* for the outer hanging and *paroket* for the two inner vails.

13. Not the same John as the one who authored the gospel.

14. "For in the resurrection they neither marry, nor are given in marriage, but are as the angels of God in heaven."—Matthew 22:30.

15. "And they clothed him with purple, and platted a crown of thorns, and put it about his *head.*"—Mark 15:17.

16. L171 to Henry Vaughn Emmons, 18 August 1854.

17. Charles R. Anderson, *Emily Dickinson's Poetry: Stairway of Surprise* (New York: Holt, Rinehart, and Winston, 1960), 185.

18. Anderson refers to "Those who have been in the Grave the longest" (J922/F938/M439) and "Publication - is the Auction -" (J709/F788//M386.)

19. Acts 3:7 and Ezekiel 47:3. Some modern editions of the King James Bible have converted to the more familiar "Ankle."

20. Judith Farr, *The Passion of Emily Dickinson* (Cambridge, MA: Harvard University Press, 1992), 33.

21. In order to maximize the impression of spirituality, celebrated singer Jenny Lind wore white during her concerts. Dickinson and her family heard Lind in concert. "Herself, and not her music, is what we seemed to love." (L46).

22. Domhnall Mitchell, "Northern Lights: Class, Color, Culture, and Emily Dickinson," *The Emily Dickinson Journal* Vol. 9, No. 2 (Johns Hopkins University Press for The Emily Dickinson International Society, Fall 2000).

23. Calvin's Commentaries, Vol. 42: Philippians, Colossians, and Thessalonians.
24. L133, to Mr. and Mrs. J.G. Holland, Early 1853.
25. Jack Capps, *Emily Dickinson's Reading* (Cambridge, MA: Harvard University Press 1960, 30.
26. Calvinists are Trinitarians; that is, they believe in one God existing in three divine persons, Father, Son (Jesus), and Holy Spirit..
27. Thahy-uh-tahy'-ruh. The ancient name of the modern Turkish city of Akhisar.

Chapter Six

1. Correct spelling would be "didn't." Dickinson regularly wrote contractions her own way.
2. L248, early 1862? Dickinson left three draft letters to "Master," known collectively as "The Master Letters." to a person unknown, the subject of much scholarly speculation.
3. Martha Dickinson Bianchi, *The Complete Poems of Emily Dickinson* (Boston: Little, Brown and Company, 1924), 129.
4. L222, To Catherine Scott Turner (Anthon), summer 1860?
5. L735, To Thomas Wentworth Higginson, about 1881.
6. *Amherst Record*, April 19, 1876, As cited in Jay Leyda, *The Years and Hours of Emily Dickinson Volume 2*, 249.
7. Testimony of J.L. Jenkins, in the Republican, April 18, 1879, As cited in Jay Leyda, *The Years and Hours of Emily Dickinson Volume 2*, 246.
8. *Massachusetts Reports*, Volume 133, by Massachusetts. Supreme Judicial Court.
9. Jay Leyda, *The Years and Hours of Emily Dickinson, Volume 2*, 248.
10. Mason A. Green, "Another Shocking Clerical Scandal," *Springfield Republican*, as cited in Jay Leyda, *The Years and Hours of Emily Dickinson Volume 2*, 248
11. This quote is also provided in George Mamunes' *"So has a Daisy vanished": Emily Dickinson and Tuberculosis* (Jefferson, NC: McFarland, 2008), 9–10; an excellent, thorough treatment of this topic.
12. Several eminent authors believed that the floating particles in the air in flour mills could be beneficial to tubercular lungs.
13. L401, To cousins Louise and Francis Norcross,
14. L752a
15. "And Moses lifted up his hand, and with his rod he smote the rock twice: and the water came out abundantly, and the congregation drank, and their beasts also."—Numbers 20:11, KJV; Exodus 17:6.
16. L298, To cousins Louise and Francis Norcross, 1864?
17. *Emily Dickinson Second Series*, eds. Mable Loomis Todd and Thomas Wentworth Higginson (Boston: Roberts Brothers, 1892), 190.
18. Geoffrey C. Ward, Ken Burns, Ric Burns, *The Civil War* (New York: Vintage Books, 1990), 218.
19. *The Dial: A Magazine for Literature, Philosophy, and Religion*, Vol. 1, 1840.
20. L6, 7 May 1845.
21. See for examples, Helen Vendler, *Dickinson: Selected Poems and Commentaries* (Cambridge, MA: The Belknap Press of Harvard University Press, 2010), 225–230; David Porter, *The Modern Idiom* (Cambridge, MA: Harvard University Press, 1981) 61; Charles R. Anderson, *Emily Dickinson's Poetry: Stairway of Surprise*, 241–244; Ken Hiltner, "Because I, Persephone, Could Not Stop for Death: Emily Dickinson and the Goddess," *The Emily Dickinson Journal*, Volume 10, Number 2, 2001, 22–42; Daneen Wardrop, *Emily Dickinson's Gothic: Goblin with a Gauge* (Iowa City: University of Iowa Press, 1996), 88–94.
22. Isaac Watts, *The psalms, hymns, and spiritual songs*; *Watts Psalms carefully suited to the Christian Worship in the United States of America.*

Samuel Worcester, *Christian Psalmody, in four parts: comprising Dr. Watts's Psalms abridged; Dr. Watts's hymns abridged; select hymns from other authors; and select harmony; together with directions for musical expression.*

23. Thomas H. Johnson, *The Poems of Emily Dickinson:* (Cambridge, MA: Belknap Press of Harvard University Press, 1974), 83.

Chapter Seven

1. Robert Weisbuch, "Prisming Emily Dickinson; or, Gathering Paradise by Letting Go," *The Emily Dickinson Handbook*, 197.

2. "One of the maxims of equity is 'Equity aids the vigilant, not those who slumber on their rights,' and the narrator of this poem has 'slumbered' on her rights as property owner. Considered in a broader legal context, the inaction may be construed as *laches:* 'Unreasonable delay in pursuing a right or claim—almost always an equitable one—in a way that prejudices the party against whom relief is sought.—Also termed *sleeping on rights*' (Black's 891).—James R. Guthrie, *A Kiss from Thermopylae: Emily Dickinson and the Law* (Amherst: University of Massachusetts Press, 2015), 62.

3. For a thorough treatment of this poem, including an explanation of equity law vs. common law, as in definition 4, see James R. Guthrie, *A Kiss from Thermopylae,* 58–70.

4. Ps and Is are the biblical books of Psalms and Isiah, respectively, given with chapter numbers.

5. James Guthrie, "Law, Property, and Provincialism in Dickinson's Poems and Letters to Judge Otis Phillips Lord," *The Emily Dickinson Journal* Vol. 5, No. 1, 1996.

6. A short walk from her home, Emily Dickinson attended Amherst Academy, located on Amity Street.

7. Richard B. Sewall, *The Life of Emily Dickinson,* 627.

8. Thomas H. Johnson, *The Poems of Emily Dickinson* 85. Johnson attributes this information to a note from Dickinson's early editor, Mabel Loomis Todd.

9. Charles Anderson, *Emily Dickinson's Poetry: Stairway of Surprise,* 134.

10. See, for example, Revelation, Chapter 4.

11. See Barry Hankins, *The Second Great Awakening and the Transcendentalists, Chapter 2, Transcendentalism as a New Religious Movement* (Westport, CT: Greenwood Press, 2004), for an insightful and cogent treatment of this topic.

12. Meaning "at a time in the past." Seldom heard today, it is found occasionally in the Bible, e.g., "They brought to the Pharisees him that aforetime was blind."—John. 9:13.

13. "And the twelve gates *were* twelve pearls; every several gate was of one pearl: and the street of the city *was* pure gold, as it were transparent glass."—Revelation 21:21.

14. "If ye then be risen with Christ, seek those things which are above, where Christ sitteth on the right hand of God."—Colossians 3:1.

15. "And Moses went up from the plains of Moab unto the mountain of Nebo, to the top of Pisgah, that is over against Jericho. And the LORD shewed him all the land of Gilead, unto Dan."—Deuteronomy 24:1.

16. L67, February 1885 to Benjamin Kimball and L970, early 1885, to Mrs. James S. Cooper respectively.

17. See Helen Vendler, *Dickinson: Selected Poems and Commentaries,* 18.

18. *Journals and Miscellaneous Notebooks of Ralph Waldo Emerson, Volume II 18212–1826,* eds. William H. Gilman, Alfred R. Ferguson, and Merrel R. Davis (Cambridge, MA: Belknap Press of Harvard University Press, 1961), 252.

19. L194 to Susan Gilbert Dickinson, 26 September 1858.

20. Laura Dassow Walls, *Emerson's Life in Science: The Culture of Truth* (Ithaca, NY: Cornell University Press, 2003), 33.

21. Edward Hitchcock, *Religious Lectures on Peculiar Phenomena in the Four Seasons,* 17.

Chapter Eight

1. Thomas H. Johnson, *The Poems of Emily Dickinson,* 961.

2. Archibald MacLeish, "The Private Poet," *Emily Dickinson: Three Views* (Amherst: Amherst College Press, 1959), 19.

3. Margaret Freeman, *Emily Dickinson and the Discourse of Intimacy,* in Gudrun M. Grabher and Ulrike Jessner, eds. *Semantics of Silences in Linguistics and Literature* (Heidelberg: Carl Winter, 1996).

4. "Thus saith the LORD, thy redeemer, and he that formed thee from the womb, I *am* the LORD that maketh all *things*; that stretcheth forth the heavens alone; that spreadeth abroad the earth by myself."—Isaiah 44:24.

5. *The Complete Works of Richard Sibbes, Volume III* (Edinburgh: James Nichol; London: James Nisbet and Co.; Dublin: W. Robertson, 1862).

6. William Shakespeare, *A Midsummer Night's Dream,* Act IV, Scene I.

7. Jay Leyda, *The Years and Hours of Emily Dickinson Volume 1,* xxi.

8. C. Alphonso Smith, *What Can Literature Do for Me?* (Garden City, NY: Doubleday, Page, and Company, 1913).

9. Henry W. Wells, *Introduction to Emily Dickinson* (Chicago: Hendricks House, Packard and Co., 1947).

10.Theodora Ward, *Capsules of the Mind: Chapters in the Life of Emily Dickinson* (Cambridge, MA: the Belknap Press of Harvard University Press, 1961), 46.

11. Gary D. Elliott, "A Note on Dickinson's 'I cautious scanned my little life,'" *Markham Review* Vol. 2 No. 4 (October 1970),78–79.

12. Thomas H. Johnson, *The Poems of Emily Dickinson*, 1000.

13. See, for example, David T. Porter, *The Art of Emily Dickinson's Early Poetry,* 97; Helen Vendler, *Dickinson: Selected Poems and Commentaries*, 222–224.

14. L56 to Susan Gilbert (Dickinson), 10 October 1851.

15. L602 to Helen Hunt Jackson, 1879; L627 to Mrs. Edward Tuckerman, early 1880; Lg75 to Thomas Wentworth Higginson, November 1880; L774 to Mabel Loomis Todd, Autumn 1882; L 814 to April 1883. A sixth manuscript, sent to Dickinson's Norcross cousins, is now lost.

16. David T. Porter, *The Art of Emily Dickinson's Early Poetry,* 168.

Chapter Nine

1. Cristanne Miller, *Reading in Time: Emily Dickinson in the Nineteenth Century* (Amherst: University of Massachusetts Press, 2012) 179. A photograph of the poem in the Springfield Republican appears on this page.

2. L316, To Thomas Wentworth Higginson, 17 March1866.

3. See, for example, Cristanne Miller, *Emily Dickinson, A Poet's Grammar,* 38.

4. L330 To Thomas Wentworth Higginson, June 1869.

5. Elizabeth Barrett Browning, *Aurora Leigh* (New York: Dodd, Mead and Company, 1856), 38.

6. Sir Thomas Browne, *Religio Medici*, in *Sir Thomas Browne's Works Including his Life and Correspondence,* William Pickering, ed. (London: Josiah Fletcher, 1835), 30.

7. L271 to Thomas Wentworth Higginson, August 1862.

Bibliography

Anderson, Charles R., *Emily Dickinson's Poetry: Stairway of Surprise,* New York: Holt, Rinehart, and Winston, 1960.

Andrews, Carol Damon, "Thinking Musically, Writing Expectantly: New Biographical Information about Emily Dickinson," *The New England Quarterly*, Vol. LXXXI, No. 2, June 2008.

Bianchi, Martha Dickinson, *Emily Dickinson Face to Face,* Boston and New York: Houghton Mifflin Company, 1932. *The Complete Poems of Emily Dickinson,* Boston: Little, Brown and Company, 1924.

Browne, Sir Thomas, *Religio Medici Part 2,* Cambridge, England: The University Press, 1963.

Browning, Elizabeth Barrett, *Aurora Leigh,* New York: Dodd, Mead and Company, 1901.

Capps, Jack L., *Emily Dickinson's Reading, 1836–1886,* Cambridge, MA: Harvard University Press, 1966.

Dickens, Charles, *All the Year Round,* Vol. 24, 1883.

Dickinson, Emily, ed., Mable Loomis Todd, Thomas Wentworth Higginson, *Emily Dickinson Second Series,* Boston: Roberts Brothers, 1892.

Elliotson, Dr., *The Zoist: A Journal of Cerebral Psychology and Mesmerism and Applications to Human Welfare,* Vol. VI, No 21, April 1848, London: Hyppolite, Bailliere.

Elliott, Gary D., "A Note on Dickinson's 'I cautious scanned my little life,'" *Markham Review,* Vol. 2, No. 4, October 1970.

Emerson, Ralph Waldo, "New Poetry," *The Dial: A Magazine for Literature, Philosophy, and Religion,* Vol. 1, 1840. Journals and Miscellaneous Notebooks of Ralph Waldo Emerson, Vol. II, 1821–1826, Cambridge, MA, London, England: Belknap Press of Harvard University Press, 1961.

Farr, Judith, *The Passion of Emily Dickinson,* Cambridge, MA: Harvard University Press, 1992. "Dickinson and the Visual Arts," *The Emily Dickinson Handbook,* Amherst: University of Massachusetts Press, 1998.

Fernie, William Thomas, *Herbal Simples Approved for Modern Uses of Cure,* Bristol, England: John Wright and Company, 1897.

Franklin, Ralph W., *The Poems of Emily Dickinson, Variorum Edition,* Vol. 2, Cambridge, MA, London, England: Belknap Press of Harvard University Press, 1998.

Freeman, Margaret H., Emily Dickinson and the Discourse of Intimacy (1996). SEMANTICS OF SILENCE IN LINGUISTICS AND LITERATURE, Gudrun M. Grabher, Ulrike Jessner, eds., pp. 191–210, Universitätsverlag, winter, 1996. Available at SSRN: https://ssrn.com/abstract=1428430.

Guthrie, James R., *A Kiss from Thermopylae: Emily Dickinson and the Law,* Amherst and

Boston: University of Massachusetts Press, 2015. "Law, Property, and Provincialism in Dickinson's Poems and Letters to Judge Otis Phillips Lord," *The Emily Dickinson Journal*, Vol. 5, No. 1, 1996.

Habegger, Alfred, *My Wars are Laid Away in Books: The Life of Emily Dickinson*, New York: Random House, 2001.

Hankins, Barry, *The Second Great Awakening and the Transcendentalists,* Westport, CT, London: Greenwood Press, 2004.

Higginson, Thomas Wentworth, "Snow," *Outdoor Papers,* Cambridge, MA: Riverside Press, 1889 and 1900.

Hiltner, Ken, "Because I, Persephone, Could Not Stop for Death: Emily Dickinson and the Goddess," *The Emily Dickinson Journal,* Vol. 10, No. 2, 2001.

Hitchcock, Edward, *Religious Lectures on Peculiar Phenomena in the Four Seasons,* Amherst MA: J.S. and C. Adams 1851. *The Religion of Geology and Its Connected Sciences,* Lecture VI, *"GEOLOGICAL PROOFS OF THE DIVINE BENEVOLENCE,"* Boston: Phillips, Sampson and Company, 1854.

Holmes, William, *Religious Emblems and Allegories,* London: William Tegg, 1868.

Howard, William, "Emily Dickinson's Poetic Vocabulary," *PMLA,* Vol. 72, No. 1, 1957.

Humphrey, Heman, *Revival Sketches and Manual,* New York: The American Tract Society.

Johnson, Thomas H. (ed.), *The Letters of Emily Dickinson,* Belknap Press of Harvard University Press, 1958 (three volume edition).

Kelly, Mike; Vega, Carolyn; Verner, Marta; Howe, Susan; Wilbur, Richard, *The Networked Recluse: The Connected World of Emily Dickinson,* New York: Morgan Library and Museum, 2017.

Kirby, Mandy, *A Victorian Flower Dictionary: The Language of Flowers Companion,* New York: Ballantine Books, 2011.

Lerner, Gerda, *The Creation of Feminist Consciousness: From the Middle Ages to Eighteen-seventy,* New York: Oxford: Oxford University Press, 1993.

Leyda, Jay, *The Years and Hours of Emily Dickinson*, Volumes 1 and 2, New Haven: Yale University Press, 1960.

Lindberg-Seyersted, Brita, *The Voice of the Poet: Aspects of Style in the Poetry of Emily Dickinson,* Cambridge, MA: Harvard University Press, 1968.

Longsworth, Polly, *Austin and Mabel,* New York: Farrar Straus Giroux 1984. *The World of Emily Dickinson,* New York, London: W. W. Norton & Company, 1990.

Lystra, Karen, *Searching the Heart: Women, Men, and Romantic Love in Nineteenth-Century America,* New York, Oxford: Oxford University Press, 1989.

MacLeish, Archibald, "The Private Poet," *Emily Dickinson: Three Views,* Amherst: Amherst College Press, 1959.

Mamunes, George, *So has a Daisy vanished: Emily Dickinson and Tuberculosis,* Jefferson, NC, and London: McFarland, 2008.

McNeill, John T., *The History and Character of Calvinism,* London, Oxford, New York: Oxford University Press, 1954.

Miller, Cristanne, *A Poet's Grammar,* Cambridge, MA, London, England: Harvard University Press, 1987. *Reading in Time: Emily Dickinson in the Nineteenth Century,* Amherst: University of Massachusetts Press, 2012.

Miller, Perry, *Error into the Wilderness,* New York, Evanston, London: Harper & Row, 1956.

Milton, John, *Paradise Lost*, Fourth Edition, Book V, London: Private Printing, 1757.

Mitchell, Domhnall, "Northern Lights: Class, Color, Culture, and Emily Dickinson," *The Emily Dickinson Journal*, Vol. 9, No. 2, Johns Hopkins University Press for the Emily Dickinson International Society, fall, 2000.

Nin, Anaïs, *The Diary of Anaïs Nin*, volume 3, 1939–1944, San Diego, New York, London: Swallow Press/Harcourt Brace, 1969.

Paley, William, *Paley's Theology,* Houston, Texas: St. Thomas Press, 1972. *Natural Theology, or, Evidence of the Existence and Attributes of the Deity Collected from the Appearances of Nature,* Houston: St. Thomas Press, 1972.
Parker, Richard Green, *Aids to English Composition*, New York: Harper and Brothers, 1845.
Patterson, Rebecca, *Emily Dickinson's Imagery,* Amherst: University of Massachusetts Press, 1979.
Porter, David T., *The Art of Emily Dickinson's Early Poetry,* Cambridge, MA: Harvard University Press, 1966. *The Modern Idiom,* Cambridge, MA: Harvard University Press, 1981.
Rhode Island State Board of Agriculture, Thirteenth Annual Report, January 1898.
St. Armand, Barton Levi, *Emily Dickinson and Her Culture,* New York: Cambridge University Press, 1984. "Emily Dickinson and the Occult," *Prairie Schooner,* Vol. 51, No. 4, winter, 1977/1978.
Schurr, William, *The Marriage of Emily Dickinson,* Lexington: University of Kentucky Press, 1983.
Sewall, Richard B., *The Life of Emily Dickinson,* New York: Farrar, Straus, and Giroux, 1974. *The Lyman Letters: New Light on Emily Dickinson and Her Family,* Amherst: University of Massachusetts Press, 1965.
Shakespeare, William, *Twelfth Night,* New Haven: Yale University Press, London: Oxford University Press, 1917. *Hamlet,* New Haven: Yale University Press, London: Geoffrey Cumberlege, Oxford University Press, 1917. *A Midsummer Night's Dream,* New Haven: Yale University Press, London: Oxford University Press, 1917.
Sibbes, Richard, *The Complete Works of Richard Sibbes,* Vol. III, Edinburgh: James Nichol; London, James Nisbet and Co.; Dublin, W. Robertson, 1862.
Smith, C. Alphonso, *What Can Literature Do for Me?* Garden City, NY: Doubleday, Page, and Company, 1913.
Smith-Rosenberg, Carroll, "Puberty to Menopause: The Cycle of Femininity in Nineteenth-Century America," *Feminist Studies,* Vol. 1, No. 3/4, winter-spring, 1973.
Taggard, Genevieve, *The Life and Mind of Emily Dickinson,* New York, London: Alfred A. Knopf, 1930.
Tyler, William S., *A History of Amherst College,* New York: Frederick H. Hitchcock, 1895.
Vendler, Helen, *Dickinson: Selected Poems and Commentaries,* Cambridge, MA, London, England: Belknap Press of Harvard University Press, 2010.
Vowell, Sarah, *The Wordy Shipmates,* New York: Riverside Books, 2008.
Walls, Laura Dassow, *Emerson's Life in Science: The Culture of Truth,* Ithaca, NY, London: Cornell University Press, 2003.
Ward, Geoffrey C.; Burns, Ken; Burns, Ric, *The Civil War,* New York: Vintage Books, a Division of Random House, 1990.
Ward, Theodora, *Capsules of the Mind: Chapters in the Life of Emily Dickinson,* Cambridge, MA: Belknap Press of Harvard University Press, 1961.
Wardrop, Daneen, *Emily Dickinson's Gothic: Goblin with a Gauge,* Iowa City: University of Iowa Press, 1996.
Watts, Isaac, *Psalms, Hymns, and Spiritual Songs,* Boston: Crocker and Brewster, 1859.
Weisbuch, Robert, "Prisming Emily Dickinson; or, Gathering Paradise by Letting Go," *The Emily Dickinson Handbook,* Amherst: University of Massachusetts Press, 1989.
Wells, Henry W., *Introduction to Emily Dickinson*, Chicago: Hendricks House, Packard and Co., 1947.
Wolff, Cynthia Griffin, *Emily Dickinson,* New York: Alfred Knopf, 1986.

Index of First Lines

An asterisk indicates that the first line only appears on the page.
A partial reproduction of poems is also noted.

General Index